FEMALE AUTHORSHIP AND THE DOCUMENTARY IMAGE

FEMALE AUTHORSHIP AND THE DOCUMENTARY IMAGE
Theory, Practice and Aesthetics

Edited by Boel Ulfsdotter and
Anna Backman Rogers

EDINBURGH
University Press

Edinburgh University Press is one of the leading university presses in the UK. We publish academic books and journals in our selected subject areas across the humanities and social sciences, combining cutting-edge scholarship with high editorial and production values to produce academic works of lasting importance. For more information visit our website: edinburghuniversitypress.com

© editorial matter and organisation Boel Ulfsdotter and Anna Backman Rogers, 2018
© the chapters their several authors, 2018

Edinburgh University Press Ltd
The Tun – Holyrood Road
12 (2f) Jackson's Entry
Edinburgh EH8 8PJ

Typeset in 10/12.5 pt Sabon by
Servis Filmsetting Ltd, Stockport, Cheshire

A CIP record for this book is available from the British Library

ISBN 978 1 4744 1944 4 (hardback)
ISBN 978 1 4744 1945 1 (webready PDF)
ISBN 978 1 4744 1946 8 (epub)

The right of the contributors to be identified as authors of this work has been asserted in accordance with the Copyright, Designs and Patents Act 1988 and the Copyright and Related Rights Regulations 2003 (SI no. 2498).

CONTENTS

List of Illustrations — vii
Notes on the Contributors — ix

Foreword — xiii
Belinda Smaill

    Introduction — 1
    Boel Ulfsdotter and Anna Backman Rogers

PART ONE   DOCUMENTARY PRACTICES

1. Women in the Director's Chair: The 'Female Gaze' in Documentary Film — 9
Lisa French

2. New Day Films: Collective Aesthetics and the Collection — 22
Elizabeth Coffman and Erica Stein

3. More Than One — 40
Sharon Daniel

    Interview: 'The Final Projects of Hannah Wilke and Jo Spence' – A Dialogue between Elena Crippa and Anna Backman Rogers — 66

PART TWO DOCUMENTARY THEORIES

4. The Feminist Voice: Improvisation in Women's Autobiographical Filmmaking 75
   Gabrielle McNally

5. Speaking About or Speaking Nearby? Documentary Practice and Female Authorship in the films of Kim Longinotto 90
   Rona Murray

6. A Politics of Nearness: Uses of Montage and Haptics in Documenting Cultural Experiences of Communities of India 107
   Aparna Sharma

PART THREE FEMALE AUTHORSHIP AND GLOBAL IDENTITIES

7. The Other, The Same: Towards a Metamodern Poetics with Heddy Honigmann 127
   Annelies van Noortwijk

8. The Memories of *Belleville Baby*: Autofiction as Evidence 144
   Boel Ulfsdotter

9. To::For::By::About::With::From:: Towards Solid Women: On (not) Being Addressed by Tracey Moffatt's *Moodeijt Yorgas* 159
   Sophie Mayer

10. Constructing an Intimate Sphere through her Own Female Body: Naomi Kawase's Documentary Films 171
    Wakae Nakane

11. Celebrity/Activist/Photographer: Mia Farrow 186
    Catherine Summerhayes

    'Being a Woman Documentary Maker in Taiwan' – An interview with Singing Chen and Wuna Wu, by Chris Berry 205

Select Bibliography 214
Index 217

ILLUSTRATIONS

Figure 1	New Day Films poster, 1973. Courtesy of Liane Brandon.	23
Figure 2	New Day founders Liane Brandon, Jim Klein, Julia Reichert and Amalie Rothschild, 1976.	25
Figure 3	*Betty Tells Her Story* (New Day Films, 1972).	27
Figure 4	Director Pamela Yates in the Guatemalan Highlands with the crew filming *Granito: How to Nail a Dictator*. Photo: Dana Lixenberg.	36
Figure 5	'Can't you take me with you?' Rekha in *Pink Saris* (Ginger Productions/Vixen Films, 2010).	95
Figure 6	Brenda sings to her girls in *Dreamcatcher* (Green Acres Films/Vixen Films, 2015).	98
Figure 7	Gujarati women pray at the Swaminarayan Temple, Cardiff.	112
Figure 8	A wooden model of the Kamakhya shrine, by Suban Das, 2010.	116
Figure 9	*O Amor Natural* (Heddy Honigmann, 1996). Courtesy Pieter van Huystee Film & TV.	136
Figure 10	*O Amor Natural* (Heddy Honigmann, 1996). Courtesy Pieter van Huystee Film & TV.	137
Figure 11	*Belleville Baby* (2013). Photo: Mia Engberg.	150
Figure 12	*Belleville Baby* (2013). Photo: Mia Engberg.	152
Figure 13	*Katatsumori*. © Kumie Inc.	177
Figure 14	*Genpin*. © Kumie Inc.	182

Figure 15	UNICEF Goodwill Ambassador Mia Farrow holds a baby at a warehouse in the city of Gonaïves, Haiti (20 September 2008). Roger LeMoyne for UNICEF. © Roger leMoyne/UNICEF.	191
Figure 16	*The Dream Never Sets* (Wuna Wu, 2010).	207
Figure 17	Poster for *The Walkers* (Singing Chen, 2014).	208

NOTES ON THE CONTRIBUTORS

Anna Backman Rogers is a Senior Lecturer in Film Studies at the University of Gothenburg, Sweden. She is the author of *American Independent Cinema: Rites of Passage and the Crisis Image* (Edinburgh University Press, 2015) and the co-editor, with Laura Mulvey, of *Feminisms* (2015). Her monograph entitled 'Sofia Coppola: The Politics of Visual Pleasure' is forthcoming in 2017/2018.

Chris Berry is Professor of Film Studies at King's College, London, UK. In the 1980s, he worked for China Film Import and Export Corporation in Beijing, and his academic research is grounded in work on Chinese-language cinemas and other Chinese-language screen-based media, as well as neighboring countries. Primary publications include *China on Screen* (with Mary Farquhar, 2006), *Postsocialist Cinema in Post-Mao China* (2008), *Public Space, Media Space* (edited with Janet Harbord and Rachel Moore, 2013) and *The New Chinese Documentary Film Movement* (edited with Lu Xinyu and Lisa Rofel, 2010).

Elizabeth Coffman is a documentary filmmaker and Associate Professor of Film and Digital Media at Loyola University Chicago. She writes about avant-garde film, video history, and documentary media, and serves on the editorial board for the *Journal of Film and Video*. Coffman has co-produced documentary films and experimental installations on nation building, climate change, creative writing, and the Jewish ghetto in Venice, Italy, with Ted Hardin and their company Long Distance Productions. She is currently completing a National Endowment for the Humanities-supported documentary on US author Flannery O'Connor.

Sharon Daniel is a Professor in the Film and Digital Media Department and the Digital Arts and New Media MFA program at the University of California, Santa Cruz where she teaches Digital Media Art and expanded forms of documentary practice. Daniel's essays have been published in books, academic and online journals. She is also a media artist who produces interactive and participatory documentaries focused on issues of social, economic, environmental and criminal justice. Her work has been exhibited internationally in festivals and museums as well as on the Internet.

Lisa French is Professor and Dean, School of Media and Communication, RMIT University, Australia. She co-authored the book *Shining a Light: 50 Years of the Australian Film Institute* (2009, 2014), and co-wrote/edited the anthology *Womenvision: Women and the Moving Image in Australia* (2003). She produced the film *Birth of a Film Festival* (2003), a documentary about the first Melbourne International Film Festival. She is co-chair of a UNESCO global research network on Media, Gender and ICTs, and is the author of the forthcoming (2018) book *The Female Gaze in Documentary Film – An International Perspective*.

Gabrielle McNally is Assistant Professor of Digital Cinema in the School of Art and Design at Northern Michigan University, USA. She received an MFA in Film/Video Production from the University of Iowa in 2014, where she also explored Gender, Women, and Sexuality Studies. Her scholarly work currently examines the notions of voice, improvisation, memory, performance, autobiography and gender as they relate to nonfiction filmmaking. As a practising artist and filmmaker, McNally works in experimental autobiographical and essayistic nonfiction. Her videos have been screened internationally in several film festivals and galleries.

Sophie Mayer is the author of *Political Animals: The New Feminist Cinema* (2015) and *The Cinema of Sally Potter: The Politics of Love* (2009). She co-edited *Lo personal es politico: feminismo y documental* (with Elena Oroz, 2011) and *There She Goes: Feminist Filmmaking and Beyond* (with Corinn Columpar, 2010). She is a regular contributor to *Sight & Sound*, *The F-Word* and *Literal* magazines, and works with queer feminist film curation collective Club des Femmes, and with Raising Films, a community and campaign for parents and carers in the UK film and TV industry.

Rona Murray is finalising her PhD, a comparative study of women's film authorship across institutional and cultural contexts, at Lancaster University, UK. Previous writing on film subjects includes a published chapter on Agnès Varda and she is currently working on Lena Dunham and *Girls*. She is a member of the Steering Committee for the Women's Film and Television History Network (UK and Ireland).

Wakae Nakane is an MA candidate at Nagoya University, Japan. She specialises in cinema studies, focusing on personal documentary films made by female filmmakers. Her publications include 'Female Performers as Authors: Documentary Film *Extreme Private Eros: Love Song 1974* and the Women's Liberation Movement [Sakusha to shite no Shutsuenjosei: Dokyumenri-eiga *Kyokushiteki Erosu: Renka 1974* to Uman Ribu]' in *JunCture* 7 (2016).

Annelies van Noortwijk is a Senior Lecturer at the department of Arts, Culture and Media studies at the University of Groningen, the Netherlands. She teaches film studies, literature, and art history and theory. Her research focuses on contemporary documentary, literature and journalism with a specific interest in questions of engagement, resistance and ethics and the penetration of the artistic discourse into nontraditional forms of art. She is the author of *Triunfo: De revista ilustrada a revista de las luces. Historia y significado de Triunfo, 1946–1982* (2004) and co-editor of *Periodismo y Literatura* (1997). She is currently preparing a monograph on the films of Heddy Honigmann.

Aparna Sharma is a documentary filmmaker and theorist. Her films document experiences and narratives that are overlooked in the mainstream imagination of the Indian nation. She works in India's northeastern region, documenting cultural practices of indigenous communities. As a film theorist she is committed to writing about non-normative subjects in Indian cinema with an emphasis on documentary films. In *Documentary Films in India: Critical Aesthetics at Work* (2015) she explores non-canonical documentary practices from India. She has previously written on Indo-Pak ties through documentary and the representation of gender in Indian cinema. She is Associate Professor at the Department of World Arts and Cultures/Dance, UCLA.

Belinda Smaill is Associate Professor of Film and Screen Studies at Monash University, Australia. Her research interests encompass women and cinema, Australian film and television and documentary film. Most recently she has been researching nonfiction screen media and animals and the environment. She is the author of *The Documentary: Politics, Emotion, Culture* (2010) and *Regarding Life: Animals and the Documentary Moving Image* (2016) and co-author of *Transnational Australian Cinema: Ethics in the Asian Diasporas* (2013).

THE CONTRIBUTORS

Erica Stein is Assistant Professor of Film at Vassar College, USA. Her work focuses on the intersection of narratology and urban studies and has appeared in the *Journal of Film and Video* and *Studies in the Humanities*. She is the co-founder and managing editor of *Mediapolis: A Journal of Cities and Culture* and is currently completing a manuscript about city symphonies, urban planning and utopias.

Catherine Summerhayes is an Adjunct Fellow in the School of Literature, Languages and Linguistics at the Australian National University (ANU). Her research areas are in documentary studies, visual media, new media studies and performance. Her monograph *Google Earth: Outreach and Activism* was published in 2015 and her monograph *The Moving Images of Tracy Moffatt* in 2007. She has published in major international journals and contributed chapters to several anthologies. She taught documentary and new media studies for thirteen years at the ANU and currently supervises postgraduate students.

Boel Ulfsdotter, formerly a Senior Lecturer at the Documentary Media Production programme at Skövde University College, is an independent media scholar specialising in screen studies, and currently affiliated with the Department of Cultural Sciences at the University of Gothenburg, Sweden. Her areas of research include narrative and aesthetic perspectives in documentary and popular cinema; visual studies related to *mise en scène* and screen costuming; and visual culture in general. Her recent work has been published in the *Journal of Scandinavian Cinema*, the *Journal of European Popular Culture* and the *Journal of Film, Fashion and Consumption*. Ulfsdotter is also a freelancing visual arts critic at Sweden's second largest newspaper, *Göteborgs-Posten*.

FOREWORD

The relationship between feminist approaches and documentary film has never been adequately addressed in film studies. The important history of the female documentarian, moreover, has never been told. While a handful of key texts address this area, their number is dwarfed when compared to feminist film criticism's attention to fiction. As a result, feminist analytical paradigms for documentary have not been established with any significant force. This omission has occurred, perhaps, because the stakes have been misjudged – documentary has been relegated to the realm of education, considered to lack the expressivity or influence of arthouse cinema or popular cinema respectively. Such assumptions, however, do not adequately account for the documentary form, its diversity and its potential for affective charge. They also fail to acknowledge the clear importance of the nonfiction mode for feminism and female filmmakers.

As has been a rich topic of debate in the popular press in recent years, female creative practitioners have been denied significant or equal access to the Hollywood industrial machine and the markers of prestige that accompany it. This is despite the growing number of female executives. Documentary is frequently produced on a lower budget, with projects more plentiful, often tied to television and allowed more capacity for exploring themes that address a female audience. These are some of reasons why women have access to documentary production when they are greatly under-represented in fiction. As Kathleen McHugh writes, an alternative history of women filmmakers 'emerges when we follow the (production) money'.[1] A full appreciation of the diverse pathways women take through film and television industries requires an investigation into what enables the representation of women on screen, supports the styles of production often favoured by women or intervenes in the dominant models that perpetuate all-male crews. Such an investigation would find that documentary (in all its different modalities) is frequently integral to the careers of female filmmakers. It is critical to women's representation in the industry in many parts of the world. Thinking more in terms of documentary pedagogy, nonfiction is also the preferred genre for activists and grass-roots organisers working at the forefront of feminist politics.

This book brings together a cluster of scholars, focusing attention on the intellectual work being done in this field. It also effectively raises the profile of the female documentarian. These are both crucial projects. More than this, however, the approach the editors of this volume have taken, perceiving documentary through the optic of female authorship, is inspired because it addresses key questions in documentary studies. While director studies in fiction film abound, they are less common in documentary. Nevertheless, authorship in documentary is tied to verisimilitude and documentary realism – as viewers we are asked to have faith in the moral and social compass of the director and others behind the camera. We are asked to acknowledge and, to some degree, be complicit with their version of the real, whether it is conveyed on the terms of subject matter or form and style. This volume of essays recognises an additional layer, focusing on the biographical and gendered subjectivity of the author. Such an enterprise is necessarily complex. It requires that we attend to questions of voice and subjectivity, both within the frame and in relation to the historical world outside the frame. This must be done in a way that observes the tensions between acknowledging this world and resisting simple equations with biological determinism or authorial power. These tensions position the study of female authorship and the documentary image as a very important project.

If the history of the female documentarian has not yet been written, this volume takes a leap that brings us closer. It contributes to the colossal task of producing knowledge about this diverse and under-theorised aspect of film culture and it does so with insight and care. *Female Authorship and the Documentary Image* is also timely. The book comes on the heels of the release of a number of high profile films directed by women. These include Sarah Polley's Oscar nominated *Stories We Tell* (2012), Laura Poitras's Academy Award winning *Citizenfour* (2014) and Chantal Akerman's landmark *No Home Movie* (2015). Each, in very different ways, provides a rich study for understanding the efficacy and position of the author, both within and beyond the frame, while also furthering our understanding of film art and film politics. In fact, in these instances the author is intricately entangled with the filmic endeavour and its appeal to the audience. These examples are, however, just the tip of the iceberg – I would suggest that we are experiencing an era when the range of women working in documentary has resulted in a film culture with a complexity and profile that we have not seen for thirty years. As this volume demonstrates, however, feminist scholarship is best served by approaches that encompass more than just the illustrious high points of the documentary landscape. Approaches must avoid following the temptation to explore the genre via only a handful of exceptional women filmmakers that have achieved success and notoriety, erasing the systemic effects and cultural histories that shape, for example, cross-border and intergenerational film practices. This book shows what can be gained by looking at a range of examples and enabling contexts, a diversity of theoretical and cultural perspectives, to illuminate our understanding of women and the documentary image.

Belinda Smaill

Note

1. Kathleen McHugh, 'The world and the soup: historicizing media feminisms in transnational contexts', *Camera Obscura*, 72, 2009, p. 131.

INTRODUCTION

Boel Ulfsdotter and Anna Backman Rogers

The topic of this book, as well as its companion volume, *Female Agency and Documentary Strategies: Subjectivities, Identity and Activism*, is an internationally focused study of female authorship in relation to the documentary image. Addressed by a group of scholars and practitioners at the forefront of contemporary views on this issue, these two volumes are defined by a collaborative effort to map and report on authorship from a global perspective. Given the widespread interest, and indeed nearly obsessional need, to document ourselves and the world around us in the contemporary moment, this two-volume monograph addresses issues as varied as: How do theory and praxis coalesce (if at all) for female practitioners within documentary image making practices? How do technology and contemporary media shape the strategies that inform female authorship and subjectivity? Has the digital turn brought about any major shifts in terms of female subject formation and activism? Which is the central mode of address currently in the field? Which are the key issues being dealt with? How is female authorship made manifest within a global context? Why is the notion of authorship of sustained relevance and importance to female documentary practitioners? Is female authorship always implicitly or explicitly imbricate with feminist theory?

   It is commonly agreed that women's increasing claims to equal societal rights and vocalisation on a global scale have had a decisive impact on female agency in relation to the documentation of contemporary issues. Of course, this is not a new phenomenon per se; in terms of culture and scholarship, women have been seeking to establish myriad voices and perspectives on issues of gender, politics, history and selfhood throughout the various waves of social emancipation and emerging feminist agendas. Female documentary filmmakers have taken a particularly progressive stance in this practice since the arrival of lightweight equipment in the late 1950s. The 1960s women's movement further encouraged the documentation of women's lives and female agency in particular. The current impetus of an increasing globalisation, consciously reframed socio-political discourses, new technologies, not to mention developing education and job opportunities in countries outside of Western Europe and the USA, have, however, once again had a decisive impact on the way women experience and document their own lives. In these volumes we therefore seek to explore what female authorship is from the perspective of multiplicity and cultural diversity, without paying any special heed to already well researched filmmakers such as Agnès Varda and Chantal Akerman. Instead, our interest lies in mapping out the theoretical, political and aesthetic discourses that contribute to female documentary practices. Is it possible to discern a political agenda that goes beyond problematic essentialism?

Given the dominant position of documentary filmmaking in this volume, it seems crucial to focus in this introduction on the issue of female authorship in relation to this particular medium. This issue was never addressed in the early days of documentary filmmaking, simply because the person behind the camera was excluded from delineating what a documentary image does beyond its function of documenting, and how it should function prescriptively (especially in relation to Direct Cinema). Those who claim that the question of authorship is of little relevance base this claim on the fact that the documentary practice supposedly centres on the close and neutral observation of the subject before the camera. This belief, by extension, also gave us Bill Nichols's basic 'modes' of documentary practice, according to which documentary filmmaking has mostly been verified, certified and taught until very recently. It is our contention that the overall pivotal turn of documentary image production towards a more widespread and prolific field of work has already been reflected in works by scholars who are seemingly interested in identifying a more finely tuned discourse in relation to new documentary cinema, such as Stella Bruzzi.[1] It has also prompted the need for a study engaging with the relationship between female authorship and the documentary image, which is driven by a scholarly interest without aiming for – indeed, wishing to avoid – political essentialism.

Is the term 'female authorship' of taxonomic importance or value for the documenting community? Michael Renov admitted the central importance of the subject of documentary more than ten years ago when he discussed the new subjectivities that had emerged within the realm of self-representation in the Post-verité Age between 1970 and 1995.[2] The emerging subjectivity he is referring to, was one that urged making the self's hybrid nature visible to others, knowing that such a multivocal personage was hardly unique, but still exists all over the world. This fluidity resulted not only in citizens being portrayed as more deeply social selves, but reflected the multifaceted nature of society in a more truthful and inclusive documentary discourse. Self-inscription no longer had to stand back from the neutrality of the apparatus. More to the point, observational cinema could no longer take the lead because of the protean and fluid social contracts that were under way. Alisa Lebow confirms this necessity to acknowledge the personal viewpoints that come to the fore in contemporary documentary cinema, when she writes: 'The designation "first person film" is foremost about a mode of address: these films "speak" from the articulated point of view of the filmmaker who readily acknowledges her subjective position.'[3]

From Laura Rascaroli's perspective, Renov's discussion of modern documentary practice was more finely tuned not only to intervene with the post-millennium discourse of a markedly hybrid notion of documentary's authorial voice, but also to recognise a new film form: namely, the essay film. It would seem that according to Rascaroli's historiography, the format secures the existence of documentaries with a 'well-defined, extra-textual authorial figure as their point of origin', who is also of 'constant reference' in the film.[4] It would thus seem that in confirming the essay film as a self-sufficient documentary format, Rascaroli indirectly presumes a strong, individual authorship as the predicate of the image. Given that it was never our intention to limit the study of female authorship in relation to the documentary image to essay films only, it is interesting to note that the collected chapters in these books indicate that no matter which documentary form is being analysed, the style of authorship that emerges is strongly connected to the tradition of the 'director-auteur', looking to exert, in Rascaroli's words, 'a strong influence and control over the creative process and its final product'.[5] Laura Rascaroli's contention is also the central tenet of our understanding of female authorship in relation to the documentary image as evinced in terms of its voice and gaze, by the international contributions to this two-volume book project.

In order to render visible the major paradigm shifts in women's uses of documentary image production this collection of essays, like its sister volume, has a thematical layout that serves to preclude a focus on historical chronology or choice of technical medium. The themes have been formed in response to the proposed chapters we received after our call for contributions and, in this book, centre on the documentary image directly within the more traditional arenas of theory and practice (especially within the context of gaze and author theory), with the last part opening out onto more philosophical questions of aesthetics, identity, the female body and globalisation. We would, however, like to emphasise the fact that the essays are of a hybrid nature, and thus may also fit into parts other than their allotted one. Both volumes also contain a number of interviews, albeit each with a different scope, that abide with issues of female authorship and the documentary image. The first interview in this volume addresses Hannah Wilke and Jo Spence's use of documentary photography as autobiographical practice. The second interview concerns local conditions of production for female documentarists in Taiwan today, and has been placed in the book's final part.

In terms of the collected chapters, the first part is concerned with documentary practices, and opens with Lisa French's chapter on women in the director's chair. She examines the concept of a 'female gaze' in documentary film alongside a specific consideration of the work and viewpoints of women directors. The central questions posited are whether film as a creative artefact and employment opportunities within the film industry are affected by the fact that the person making the film is biologically female.

Elizabeth Coffman and Erica Stein's essay on the collective aesthetics championed by New Day Films in New York from the 1970s is an extremely important contribution to the historiography of female agency within the community of documentarists, regardless of its time period. Learning to operate the new lightweight film cameras on their own, through trial and error, the female founding members of New Day Films developed aesthetic and economic strategies that created and addressed an audience that could produce themselves as a politically active community through their engagement with the films.

The following chapter by Sharon Daniel is set up as an advanced or experimental dialogue in which she comments on a male art critic's review of her own exhibited work. By intervening and responding to the critical commentary on her work, Daniel creates a rhetoric based on Henry Jenkins's idea of participatory culture's ability to bring new and multivocal aspects to cultural products. The layout of her chapter also indicates a lack of interest in the medium itself to the advantage of the contents of the work. It also seems to suggest that her work is not necessarily media specific, thus allowing it to take on transmedial aspects in its new form or manifestation. This part is closed with an interview between Elena Crippa, curator at Tate Modern in London, and Anna Backman Rogers. Together they discuss the autobiographical photography of Hannah Wilke and Jo Spence and, more specifically, how these two artists portrayed the ill and ageing female body.

Part two is devoted to documentary theories and examines, in particular, new theoretical approaches to documentary cinema. It opens with Gabrielle McNally's call for action through performative improvisation. The chapter discusses the mindful use of improvisational methods in women's autobiographical filmmaking as a means to establish a feminist documentary voice that lies outside of patriarchy and established Western notions of subjectivity, using intersections between improvisational theory and now well-established theories of the subjective voice in documentary.

INTRODUCTION

In her essay on Kim Longinotto, Rona Murray explores how Longinotto's mastery of emotion and address works to honour the complexity of her subjects, in light of the fact that Longinotto is a female author commonly associated with liberation. By focusing on voice and giving voice, and the deployment of Trinh T. Minh-ha's notion of 'speaking nearby', Murray considers how far Longinotto's filmmaking has enabled a speaking nearby in relation to her female subjects; she argues that the female subjects are able to sustain their subjectivity and agency in contradistinction to a potential objectifying, monolithic gaze.

The last chapter in this part is provided by filmmaker and scholar Aparna Sharma, whose essay focuses on the applications, epistemological and political implications of montage and haptics in her own documentary practice. The author argues that documenting local cultures and cultural practices constitutes a critical departure from dominant ideological and political discourses at play in the northeast region of India resulting as it is *viewed* as the *distant other* of the nation.

In the final part of this book, female authorship is set within the context of global identities.

Reading the films of Heddy Honigmann, Annelies van Noortwijk argues that through a paradigm shift from postmodernism towards what she proposes to refer to as meta-modernism, a new kind of poetics comes to the fore in which senses of 'sameness' and 'presence' and a drive towards inter-subjective connection and dialogue are pivotal. At the same time a turn to the subject, the real and the private, are the preferred strategies to address the central topics in contemporary culture: that of (often traumatic) memory and identity. Indeed, the re-evaluation of the female subject as an active, embodied and emotional individual is fundamental to such a shift.

Applying the idea of authorship, Boel Ulfsdotter problematises the effects of Mia Engberg's autofictional reiteration of her own memories in relation to narrative, aesthetic and cinematographic strategies in *Belleville Baby*. Sophie Mayer problematises the collective authorship and experimental documentary, using Tracey Moffatt's *Moodeijt Yorgas* as an exemplary piece of documentary filmmaking. The hybrid nature of *Moodeijt Yorgas*, which blends talking heads with oral histories presented through dance, music and optically printed effects, allows for a deepening of experimental documentary forms through a specifically non-white, queer feminist authorship. The author thus argues that Moffatt's film presents a challenge to traditional conceptions of the author/auteur, embedded in Euro-Western exceptionalist individualism.

Wakae Nakane explores how the Japanese filmmaker Naomi Kawase's mode of address, made manifest through empathic listening, emphasises participation *with* its women subjects rather than a narrative *about* them, and how this strategy therefore allows for a different realisation of the emotional and moral complexity of women on screen. Wakane concludes that this might be evidence to claim a discernibly 'female' style of documentary authorship if asserted with discretion, scrutiny and rigour.

In the part's last chapter, Catherine Summerhayes examines Mia Farrow's human rights directed photographs of children, both in the context of her status as a celitbrity activist, and from the point of view of her broad *oeuvre* as a well-known actress.

This part closes with an interview of Singing Chen and Wuna Wu, two Taiwanese documentary filmmakers. Together with Chris Berry, they discuss the local conditions of production for women documentarists in Taiwan today.

Together with its twin volume, *Female Agency and Documentary Strategies: Subjectivity, Identity and Activism*, this collection of essays is the first response to a call for an international scholarly study of female authorship and the documentary image. We would like to express our gratitude to Edinburgh University Press, especially Gillian Leslie, for giving us the opportunity to explore this topic. We also extend our appreciation to all contributors for having engaged with the remits of our project with such enthusiasm, generosity and outstanding expertise. We hope these books inspire both scholars and filmmakers to take the implications of our findings further.

Boel Ulfsdotter and Anna Backman Rogers
Gothenburg, January 2017

Notes

1. Stella Bruzzi, *New Documentary: A Critical Introduction* (London and New York: Routledge, 2000).
2. Michael Renov, *The Subject of Documentary* (London and Minneapolis: University of Minnesota Press, 2004).
3. Alisa Lebow, *The Cinema of Me: The Self and Subjectivity in First Person Documentary* (London and New York: Wallflower Press, 2012), p. 1.
4. Laura Rascaroli, *The Personal Camera: Subjectivite Cinema and the Essay Film* (London and New York: Wallflower Press, 2009), p. 3.
5. Ibid. p. 11.

PART ONE

DOCUMENTARY PRACTICES

1. WOMEN IN THE DIRECTOR'S CHAIR: THE 'FEMALE GAZE' IN DOCUMENTARY FILM

Lisa French

> A woman's vocabulary exists, linked to the feminine universe. I feel this occasionally in that I am inspired by a certain number of attractions, subjects which always draw me rather more than they would if I were a man . . . I don't want to make feminist cinema either, just want to tell women's stories about women.
>
> Agnès Varda[1]

INTRODUCTION

This chapter examines the concept of a 'female gaze' in documentary film with specific consideration of the work and viewpoints of women directors. I acknowledge every director is an artist in her own right, and I make the initial cautionary note that women directors make every kind of documentary. The aesthetic approaches, individual experiences and films of women directors are as diverse as their individual life situations and the cultures in which they live – so there is no implication that women are a homogenous or singular group (and gender is, of course, only one aspect of any individual's identity). Whilst acknowledging difference between women filmmakers, and conceding that any director would only be properly understood through her films and the world/s each woman constructs and represents, this chapter examines whether a film, as a creative artefact, is affected by the fact that the person making the film is biologically female and whether women directors feel that their gender has had any influence on their filmmaking. This has been compiled using data (including numerous interviews), mostly gathered in November 2014 at one of the most important festivals on the global documentary calendar: The International Documentary Film Festival Amsterdam (IDFA).[2]

In what follows, the key markers of a 'female gaze' in documentary film are discussed. These markers could potentially be found in the work of male directors and not found in the work of some women directors. I acknowledge that there are likely to be exceptions and therefore I am framing these observations as tendencies. However, it is the argument of this chapter that they are most commonly found in the work of women, particularly in combination, and that a 'female gaze' is a product of female gender. This chapter offers ways of understanding the 'female gaze' and examines the question of whether there is evidence that gender influences the work of female documentary filmmakers.

Foregrounding Female Subjectivity

The experience of gender, of living as a woman or as a man, is likely to affect any individual's subjectivity. The key marker of the 'female gaze' is the communication or expression of female subjectivity – a gaze shaped by a female 'look', voice and perspective – the subjective experience or perspective of someone who lives in a female body (female agency is privileged).

French filmmaker Agnès Varda has spoken of women filmmakers reflecting a world they see from the point of view of living life through the concrete experience of being female. In Marie Mandy's documentary *Filming Desire: A Journey Through Women's Cinema* (2000), Varda observed that:

> To be a woman is to be born in a woman's body . . . Simone de Beauvoir's view [that] we are nurtured into womanhood has to do with thoughts of the mind, [but] the fact remains we're born into a female body. How can that not be an essential fact whether you're a film director, cleaner, mother, whether you have children or not? We women inhabit a female body . . . The first feminist act is to say 'Okay, they look at me, but I can look too, it's to decide to look, not see the world and oneself through another's eyes.[3]

Varda's comments reflect a feminist politic in asserting a refusal to deny female subjectivity, for women to resist having their gaze colonised by 'another', and also the importance of having self-determination over representation. Her words underline the notion of difference caused by experiencing gender and allude to something that connects women. It implies a sensibility to female experience (as multifaceted as that might be). While the argument that subjectivity relates to the sexed body could be critiqued as essentialist, it is not the argument here that women have the same experiences in their lives or their bodies, but rather that gender causes an inflection which might be described as an awareness of 'Otherness' or difference, and that women share this and recognise it as a factor of the experience of patriarchal culture.

Would a Man Make a Film like That?

Scholar Gertrud Koch argued that there have been decades of debate that still has not resolved 'whether the female look through the camera at the world, at men, at women and objects will be an essentially different one'.[4] The question of whether it is possible to tell if a woman has made a film is a divisive issue. Some say that they can tell and others completely reject the idea. American director Barbara Kopple does not feel that we can tell whether a man or a woman made a film because there are films she feels would undermine that idea – the exceptions to the rule if you like.[5] English filmmaker Kim Longinotto has noticed such exceptions: for example, she cited the Swedish feature *Fucking Åmål* (Lukas Moodysson, 1998) felt to her like it was a film made by a woman.[6] Longinotto views it as difficult to generalise:

> I don't use the word masculine and feminine any more or male or female because ... when you're growing up you're told that's masculine or that's feminine, we're all questioning [that] ... For example, masculine's adventurous and confident and competent and practical, and women are becoming that or definitely wanting to be that, and women are meant to be intuitive sensitive emotional gentle and a lot of men are that and they're saying well, I want to be, I'm that.[7]

Longinotto is flagging the masculine and feminine as a cultural construction, but also that both sexes are oppressed by restrictions that do not allow both men and women to embody both or either of them as their natures determine.

Other filmmakers are strongly of the view that they can tell if a man or a woman made a film. Mina Keshavarz, one of the directors of the documentary *Profession Documentarist* (Abtahi et al. 2014), put it this way: 'I think that there is a difference between woman and man when they want to make a film or write something because ... we see around us different from the man because of our experience, because of our living.'[8] On the same question, her co-director, Nahid Rezaei, said that they did not decide to make something for women or with the gaze of a woman, 'but we wanted to be together and do something and ... we believe in the body of the woman'.[9] Rezaei observed that the great Iranian poet and film director Fourough Farrokhzad was asked many years ago if her poetry 'is the poetry of woman'? And her reply was 'Yes because I'm a woman, ... it's my life, my body, my thinking ... .'[10]

Peruvian-born Dutch director Heddy Honigmann has said, 'for sure, it is easier to know it is a man who has done it'. When asked if she felt there was a 'female gaze' she said that particular notion gave her problems but for her the idea of a 'feminine gaze' made more sense (acknowledging that some men have a feminine gaze). However, she said, even with Katherine Bigelow's *The Hurt Locker* (2008), she could tell it was made by a woman because she 'stays with the character . . . remains with him for a long time', adding (in response to my question of whether there is a 'female gaze'):

> space is something where you can feel there is a woman, length of shot you can feel there is a woman, [she] has more tendency to be more patient in looking, time passing. We [women] are used to wait . . . [we] wait for 9 months, for a man to say he wants to marry me, to wait looking at your mother while she is cooking [reference to her 2004 film *Food For Love – A Shtetl That's No Longer There*]. This waiting is in our blood and has great potential for making film.[11]

Leading filmmaker from Helsinki, Finland, cinematographer and director Pirjo Honkasalo believes she can tell whether a man or a woman made a film. During 2014 Honkasalo sat on the jury of a local Finnish festival and undertook an experiment to view all the films without looking at their credits (so without knowing if a man or woman made them). Of the thirty films in competition, she correctly guessed the gender of all the filmmakers, with no errors. She recalled, 'it was obvious, even from the animation. It was a surprise to myself.'[12] She interrogated her own gaze as a viewer to understand 'where did I read it?' For her, the markers were 'female aesthetics', which she located in attention to certain details and their movement within the frame. She also noted a gender difference in the treatment of certain themes, or a world view, so from this point of view it was an ontological difference she was reading. Whilst she couched these observations as generalisations, and noted it would need a deep study, she observed a differential in the treatment of subject. Examples she gave included that 'violence in women's films I think almost always has a social cause, and for men I think violence, it's kind of a challenge between two men'.[13]

In a similar vein, French/Belgian documentary filmmaker Marie Mandy has said, 'every story in life can be told from a man's point of view or a woman's point of view I guess and it's not the same – it's like telling a war from the point of view of the winner or the loser. It's never the same point of view. And it's interesting to have both . . .'[14]

Female Aesthetics

Honkasalo's observation of 'female aesthetics' is worthy of some attention here. The hallmarks of what might be understood as 'female aesthetics' have long been examined, particularly in relation to art and also to cinema.[15] Generally, aesthetics are understood to be the expressive, creative, formal or stylistic qualities of the work. To add 'female' into the equation infers that these elements might be understood as gendered.[16] Traits, patterns or qualities might trigger emotional or intellectual responses in audiences that encourage an understanding of, or through, something recognised as female. This 'female aesthetic' appears to trigger a recognition in female spectators; for example, Marie Mandy has said that 'from my experience as a spectator I can feel differences in films made by a woman and films made by a man most of the time, and I would say that the main difference regards identification ... I just have more pleasure because I can recognise things that really talk to me'.[17]

This circular quality, often accompanied by a lack of closure, is frequently a feature of documentaries made by women. Marie Mandy has observed:

> I think that in general women will tell the story in a more circular way. So that [it] means something more meandrous ... they ... interweave things, build a story with different layers but not always going from A to B. I think a lot of male films are driven by a strong A to B narration, which is not the case of most of the films made by women.[18]

In the film *Profession Documentarist*, which is constructed of a series of short films placed together to form a feature, there is a repeated lack of closure: the audience does not see the new house Sahar is moving into, nor is it revealed whether Mina gets her wish to go to film school; instead, they observe their reality as they live it at the time the film was made in Iran. Another Iranian documentary (short), by filmmaker Mahvash Sheikholeslami, *Murderer or Murdered (Qatel ya Maqtul* 2004), is based on interviews with women which she conducted in a Tehran maximum security prison. It captures women telling of their arranged marriages and violent lives, including stories of husbands who molested their children. This film has been described as having a 'lack of closure' and that 'this incompleteness is emblematic of the intractable social situations which women still find themselves in'.[19]

Whilst the imagery used by each female filmmaker will be as unique and diverse as they are as individuals, and no trait could absolutely belong to one gender, some theorists and filmmakers have identified and described (rather than locked down) what they understand as the commonalities of female aesthetics, often linked to the feminine. Fiona Probyn, for example, identified feminine symbols: 'fluidity, maternity, writing the body, silence, weaving metaphors'.[20] Lucy Lippard has distinguished a tendency for women to display 'obsessive line and detail, veiled strata, tactile or sensuous surfaces and forms, associative fragmentation, autobiographical emphasis'.[21] *NRC Handelsblad* film critic Dana Linssen has noted that women filmmakers share stylistic and formal qualities: 'I observed that to some extent, they all shared some traits that are traditionally called "feminine" ... observational, patient, empathetic, curious, sensitive, poetic and lyrical'.[22] Filmmaker Chantal Akerman said:

> I give space to things which were never – almost never – shown in that way, like the daily gestures of a woman. They are the lowest in the hierarchy of film images ... But more than content, it's because of the style. If you show a woman's gestures so precisely, it's because you love them. In some way you recognize those gestures that have always been denied and ignored.[23]

Indian filmmaker Nishtha Jain has observed similar qualities to Akerman. In her 2007 documentary *Lakshmi and Me*, which is about a woman in her house with a domestic worker, Jain captured 'little things'; it is a film she says is 'about gestures, it's about feudalism, it's about negotiating gender and class'.[24] According to Jain, the larger films do not deal with these kinds of subjects, which she says come to women 'more easily' and 'more naturally than to men': she says women make films that are generally 'more intimate, much more personal', they are 'about the domestic' because 'women do house chores, and they do raise children and it's the world they inhabit and that's what they want to talk about'.[25] They want to bring out the nuances of that world, they want to question that world', and so, Jain has observed, their films are 'quite different'.[26] Jain also sees women's films as having a specific aesthetic, as being 'much more tactile', 'about little things, about gestures and about feelings and emotions, it's not ... big concepts', it's about 'lived experience' and 'felt things'.[27]

Melissa Silverstein, founder and editor of *Women in Hollywood*, says 'men and women tell stories differently, not better, just different'.[28] Filmmakers also make this observation; Australian filmmaker Gillian Armstrong has further noted that, 'even though I don't like being labelled [a woman filmmaker], I do believe that women do see a lot of things differently'.[29] Marie Mandy identified autobiographical films as providing an example of difference:

> when directors make films about themselves or their families ... if you look at films made by men you will see that they occupy the screen a lot. They tell their story but they are on screen and we could do an exercise

and count the number of shots and so on where you have a woman dealing with an intimate story – family or autobiographical story. She would be more present with the voice; hands; reflection, but she won't just go and be there like that.[30]

A film does not have to be about or to feature women to show aspects of a 'female gaze'. The documentary *Startup.com* (Chris Hegedus and Jehane Noujaim, 2001), a film about two men who 'make it big' in a dot.com business, is an interesting one to note. Film critic Michael West wrote that 'we never see what sort of cars they drive. What did they buy when all those dollars were flooding in? Where did all the money go? No answer'.[31] The critic has missed the point and arguably the 'female gaze' of this film. The directors of *Startup.com* were not interested in the big story of cars and money; they were interested in the two men, a study of masculinity, and in human behaviour. Hegedus has said of it:

> I was very interested in making a personal story; a very personal story, . . . what interested me the most was the relationship [and] the generational difference between men at that age and I really loved that Tom and Kaleil had this really close friendship, that they weren't embarrassed to kind of hug each other and show emotion and say that they loved each other. [It] was particularly interesting for me to see and watch how they worked this relationship through business and friendship. And you know in the end, which do you compromise, the business or the friendship?[32]

Also relevant to this chapter is that this is a film focusing on men, but the filmmakers have expressed what interested them, which arguably evolved from a female sensibility or perspective.

FEMINISM AND REPRESENTATION

For some filmmakers the 'female gaze' embodies feminism. Today, and historically, there have been many feminisms or feminist movements. They feature differing priorities, often born out of their specific cultural locations and the situation of women in those particular societies. As Simone de Beauvoir wrote: '[s]urely a woman is, like a man, a human being . . . The fact is that every concrete human being is always in a specific situation.'[33] The issues that concern women directors vary from country to country as Kim Longinotto has offered: 'in Africa and Iran there is a war going on, people get shot in the head for going to school or they get locked in the house'.[34] Filmmaker Nishtha Jain has stated that living in a woman's body does influence her vision, but it is also culturally specific: 'whatever my lived experience is . . . [to be] living in a woman's body in India in itself comes with, with a lot of conflict';[35] and she believes that this is transmitted through her films which take up this specificity from a feminist (and female) perspective. For example, *Gulabi Gang* (Jain 2012) depicts women's activism in rural India in opposition to gender violence and oppression through following a central female character, the activist Sampat Pal Devi, a leader of an Indian activist group. They encounter the story of a sixteen-year-old who, married off at the age of only eleven, has been disposed of (murdered) by a husband who no longer wants her. The patriarchal society conspires to accept it – as they accept the notion that it would be alright to murder your sister if she married for love.

Jain has commented that for her, 'it's not a female gaze but a feminist gaze. And I think that makes much more sense to me', noting that men dominated production and therefore representation.[36] For Jain, it is an issue of representation and there are fundamental questions: 'how are we looking, how are the women being portrayed? How do men look at women? How do women look at women?'[37] Jain advocates making allowances and she wants to express this difference.[38] Feminist theorists have examined the idea of difference: Maggie Humm, for example, has observed that in feminism, difference is often taken to mean 'women have a different voice, a different psychology and a different experience of love, work and the family from men',[39] and it is this difference that is valued as not better or worse, nor inferior.

Women often make the point that they make films about women because those are the stories they are interested in, and that it is a natural thing to do – which is not to say they should make films only about women, only that they are more likely to do so. The implications of this argument are that having more women filmmakers will likely lead to more films about women, so equal participation in production arguably promotes diversity in representation. Indeed, research has shown women are more likely to tell stories about women and to employ women in the crew.[40] On this issue, Kim Longinotto said in response to whether she thinks her gender plays a role in her work: 'I think it does . . . [because, for her] the stories that seem to be good stories seem to be women's stories'.[41] Australian filmmaker Gillian Armstrong has similarly observed: 'the stories that I read and the stories that I react to, so often have a female character. And it hasn't been, and for my part, a political decision that I want to make a story about a woman, it's because I can see the world through her eyes.'[42] The implication of these statements is that women may be drawn to 'women's stories', and as women they will tell them from their gendered point of view: this is important to emphasise because the problem with not having the same numbers of men and women in key creative roles is that men have more opportunity to have stories they are interested in producing, which is a natural thing for them to do – but it can leave female-centred stories untold.

Resonant Themes

Informed by scholarship on filmmaking and gender, and watching dozens of films made by women directors at IDFA in 2014, I observed first hand a number of what I would call 'resonant themes' or defining features that I noticed characterised many of these documentaries and which I would argue are markers of a 'female gaze'. These included an interest in issues that particularly affect women (noting that women make films about all subjects); expressions of female experience or point of view (including women's social struggles or struggles for agency); a tendency to focus on emotions and psychological perspectives or interiority; a humanist interest (particularly in human behaviours and relationships); personal stories; and a strong interest in family or private spheres.

The apparent strong interest by female directors in issues that profoundly affect women is very strong in documentaries. American co-directors Rachel Grady and Heidi Ewing's film *12th & Delaware* (2010) depicts American women, some of them only children themselves, being confronted by anti-abortion protesters wielding photographs of mutilated aborted fetuses. The film illustrates the current challenge to women's reproductive rights. Leading Iranian director Rakhshan Bani-Etemad, who works in both fiction and documentary, made the film *We are Half of Iran's Population* (2009), which she describes as a story about problems concerning women (in particular, women's rights activists). She wanted to show 'problems that women had in common'.[43] Kim Longinotto has a long history of films that point to problems women face, including *Sisters in Law* (2005), a documentary that reveals violence against women living in Cameroon under Islamic (Sharia) law, highlighting rights issues for women and children. She has made a number of films about extraordinary women activists: *Salma* (2013) and *Pink Saris* (2010); and her film *The Day I Will Never Forget* (2002) tells the stories of Kenyan women faced with the practice of female genital mutilation. In Mahvash Sheikholeslami's *Murderer or Murdered* the interviewee on death row in a prison, Fatemaeh, tells how she discovered her husband abusing her daughter, causing her to strangle him 'out of fury and then to cut him up into pieces . . . what caused her savage behavior [was]: "he was naked on top of her. When he removed her bra and I saw my child's breasts exposed, I could not tolerate it any longer." She is executed soon after the filmed interview.'[44] In these films, the fact of being biologically female, and living your life in a female body, is distinctive from living it in a male body, and that fact highlights the experience of being female.

Emotion is another resonant theme or characteristic weaving its way into the structure of films by women filmmakers, as, for instance, in Bosnian Jasmila Zbanic's documentary *Images from the Corner* (2003). Zbanic constructs her film around a particular spot where a young woman was badly injured in the

1992 siege of Sarajevo. She traces the effect of this one small scar on the city and examines how this spot makes the young women *feel* when she goes there. Another example is Kim Longinotto's ambition for her practice: 'I want to make films which create a situation where the audience gets close to another individual, often from a completely different background, and feel a shock of understanding. I want the whole experience to be a strong and emotional one.'[45]

A prevalence of films with psychological interiors or interiority is common in documentaries by women. In *Profession Documentarist*, director Mina Keshavarz uses voice-over extensively, showing her shadow on the pavement, a woman holding a camera, the voice telling of her yearning to live abroad. The humanist focus frequently offers an intense focus on shifting relationships, particularly personal stories, often with domestic environments' private spheres, particularly the family. Heddy Honigmann's *Food For Love – A Shtetl That's No Longer There* (2004) explores the life history of her mother's family (all killed by Nazis in the 1940s), taking a horrific journey through an intimate time where a mother and daughter are cooking and talking. In *Good Husband, Dear Son* (2001) Honigmann takes her audience through a massacre in a small town outside Sarajevo through the recollections and voices of the widows, mothers and daughters – those who were spared the genocide that killed all the men and boys in their village. The interiority of these films directly connects to women's life stories and female experience, including of the filmmakers themselves.

An Advantage for Documentary Directors in Being Female

There is some evidence from women themselves that being female can be an advantage in gaining access to subjects within documentary filmmaking. For example, Barbara Kopple explained that she was not sure a man could have made *Harlan County* (Kopple 1976): 'people talked to me and they maybe told me things that they wouldn't tell a man because I like to do films that are very intimate'.[46] While at first she was regarded as a spy, she was eventually included, living with the miners on the picket line and being protected by them. Kim Longinotto has also described how her gender enabled her filmmaking process when she made *Pink Saris* (2010). The film involved Longinotto, her translator and sound recordist making the film in very close proximity with the subject (Sampat), and in that case, it was an advantage to Longinotto that she is a woman: 'we can't generalize but . . . in some instances . . . it is a real advantage if you are a woman'.[47] In that instance, it was a case of gender allowing the participants to be in close proximity and therefore growing a close relationship – something Longinotto felt would be much harder for a man to achieve in that context. Gillian Armstrong has said of her documentary *Smokes and*

Lollies (1976) that because she was a young woman making the film about teenage girls, the girls opened up to her and told her things they probably would not have told a typical filmmaking team at the time because in the 1970s the teams sent by broadcasters were generally men 'in suits'.[48]

Conclusion

As stated, the key marker of the 'female gaze' is the communication or expression of female subjectivity – a gaze shaped by a female 'look', voice and perspective – the subjective experience or perspective of someone who lives in a female body (female agency is privileged). The knowledge of gender difference, of living as a woman, is what connects women and the reason they often claim to identify with films made by women and recognise the gendered experience each variously captures in their 'female gaze' (as multifarious as that might be). Part of this recognition is due to visible female aesthetic approaches, world views, and treatments of subjects, themes, and the overall privileging of female subjectivity. Female documentary directors make all kinds of films with great success and it is important that within representation there are equal opportunities for their vision, which are, as Melissa Silverstein observed, not better, just different – they have a 'female gaze'.

Acknowledgements

The author of this chapter would like to thank the International Documentary Film Festival Amsterdam (IDFA), in particular Raul Nino Zambrano, who made this research possible, as did Mark Poole, who was the cameraperson for the interviews conducted at IDFA and elsewhere.

Notes

1. Agnès Varda, quoted in Alison Smith, *Agnès Varda* (Manchester: Manchester University Press, 1998), p. 92.
2. In November 2014 the author of this paper was IDFA's guest to undertake this research. They ran a special program called 'The Female Gaze' with 28 films included and many of the directors in attendance: <http://www.idfa.nl/industry/festival/program-sections-awards/female-gaze.aspx>. IDFA was motivated by a desire to celebrate the achievements of the many women whose successful careers have been launched at the festival, but they also noticed that whenever the question of the influence of gender has been discussed or researched, it has been in 'advertising, television and fiction films' – but not in the documentary form. Some other festivals, such as Sundance, have been monitoring their performance. IDFA undertook analysis of their gender record and released the statistics: <https://www.idfa.nl/en/article/65865/the-female-gaze>. I am greatly indebted to Raul Nino Zambrano from the IDFA programming department for his assistance with this research.
3. This statement cannot account for trans experience.

4. Koch, quoted in Teresa de Lauretis, *Technologies of Gender: Essays on Theory, Film, and Fiction* (Bloomington, IN: Indiana University Press, 1987), p. 134.
5. IDFA, 'The female gaze', *Industry Talk*, 22 November 2014.
6. Interview with Kim Longinotto, conducted by Lisa French, Amsterdam, 21 November 2014.
7. Ibid.
8. Interview with Mina Keshavarz, Sepideh Abtahi, Sahar Salahsoor and Nahid Rezaei, conducted by Lisa French, Amsterdam, 27 November 2014.
9. Ibid.
10. Ibid.
11. IDFA, 'Heddy H Retrospective' [Q&A following screening of *Food For Love – A Shtetl That's No Longer There* and *Good Husband Dear Son*], 25 November 2014.
12. Interview with Pirjo Honkasalo, conducted by Lisa French, Amsterdam, 23 November 2014.
13. Ibid.
14. Interview with Marie Mandy, conducted by Lisa French, Amsterdam, 24 November 2014.
15. Silvia Bovenschen, 'Is there a feminine aesthetic?', *New German Critique*, no. 10, Winter 1977, pp. 111–37; Teresa de Lauretis, 'Aesthetic and feminist theory: rethinking women's cinema', *New German Critique*, no. 34, Winter 1985, pp. 154–75.
16. There is no attempt to claim women all have any particular 'essential' attributes, but rather that they share gendered experience, and this has an impact on their creative outputs.
17. Interview with Marie Mandy.
18. Ibid.
19. Hamid Naficy, *A Social History of Iranian Cinema, volume 4: The Globalizing Era, 1984–2010* (Durham, NC: Duke University Press, 2011), p. 148.
20. Fiona Probyn, 'J. M. Coetzee: writing with/out authority', 2002: <http://english.chass.ncsu.edu/jouvert/v7is1/probyn.htm> (last accessed 31 January 2015). These are drawn from different feminists such as Irigaray and Cixous.
21. Lucy Lippard, quoted in Terry Barrett, *Criticizing Art: Understanding the Contemporary*, 2nd edn (Mountain View, CA: Mayfield Publishing Company, 2000), p. 49.
22. IDFA, 'The Female Gaze', *Industry Talk*, 22 November 2014.
23. Akerman, quoted in de Lauretis, *Technologies of Gender*, p. 132.
24. Interview with Nishtha Jain, conducted by Lisa French, Amsterdam, 20 November 2014.
25. Ibid.
26. Ibid.
27. Ibid.
28. IDFA, 'The female gaze', *Industry Talk*, 22 November 2014.
29. Interview with Gillian Armstrong, conducted by Lisa French, Sydney, 28 January 2015.
30. Interview with Marie Mandy.
31. Michael West, 'A dotcom tale of mucky greed shines on big screen', *Australian: Business News*, 31 August 2001, p. 36.
32. Interview with Chris Hegedus, conducted by Lisa French, Amsterdam, 20 November 2014.
33. Simone de Beauvoir, quoted in Toril Moi, *What is a Woman?* (New York: Oxford University Press, 1999), p. 8.
34. Interview with Kim Longinotto.
35. Interview with Nishtha Jain.

36. Interview with Nishtha Jain.
37. Ibid.
38. Ibid.
39. Maggie Humm, *The Dictionary of Feminist Theory*, 2nd edn (Michigan: Ohio State University Press, 1995), pp. 64–5.
40. Lisa French, 'Women in film: treading water but fit for the marathon', in Jane Campbell and Theresa Carilli (eds), *Challenging Images of Women in the Media: Reinventing Women's Lives* (Lanham, MD: Lexington Press, 2012), p. 42.
41. Interview with Kim Longinotto.
42. Interview with Gillian Armstrong.
43. IDFA, 'The female gaze', *Industry Talk*, 22 November 2014.
44. Naficy, *A Social History of Iranian Cinema*.
45. Loginotto, quoted in Kevin Macdonald and Mark Cousins, *Imagining Reality: The Faber Book of Documentary* (London: Faber and Faber, 1996), p. 379.
46. IDFA, 'The female gaze', *Industry Talk*, 22 November 2014.
47. Ibid.
48. Interview with Gillian Armstrong.

Filmography

Filming Desire: A Journey Through Women's Cinema (Filmer Le Desir) [Beta SP/DVD] (M. Mandy, SAGA Film, The Factory /ARTE/ RTBF TV, 2000).
Food For Love – A Shtetl That's No Longer There (Een Sjtetl die niet meer bestaat) [video] (H. Honigmann, Idéale Audience, 2004).
Fucking Åmål (Show Me Love) [35mm] (L. Moodysson, Memfis Film/Det Danske Filminstitute/Film Väst/ SVT Drama/Svenska Filminstitutet/Sveriges TC/Trollywood AB/Zentropa Entertainments, 1998).
Good Husband, Dear Son [video] (H. Honigmann, Appel & Honigmann/Interkerkelijke Omroep Nederland (IKON)/, 2001).
Gulabi Gang [DCP] (N. Jain, Final Cut for Real/Piraya Film A/S/ Raintree Films, 2012).
Harlan County [16mm] (B. Kopple, Cabin Creek, 1976).
Images from the Corner [video] (J. Zbanic, Deblokada/Ohne Gepäck Berlin, 2003.
Lakshmi and Me [DVD], dir. N. Jain, Deckert Distribution, 2007).
Murderer or Murdered (Qatel ya Maqtul) [DVD] (M. Sheikholeslami, Unknown Production Co., 2004).
Pink Saris [HDCam] (K. Longinotto, Vixen Films, 2010).
Profession Documentarist (Herfeh: Mostanadsaz) [DCP] (S. Abtahi, S. Barghnavard, F. Khosrovani, F. Sharifi, M. Keshavarz, S. Abtahi, S. Salahshoor, N. Rezaei, Independent, 2014).
Salma [HDCam] (K Longinotto, Channel 4, 2013).
Sisters in Law [digital to 35mm] (K. Longinotto, Vixen films/Film Four, 2005).
Smokes and Lollies [16mm] (G. Armstrong, 1:1 Films/SA Film Corp., 1976).
Startup.com [Mini DV: NTSC] (C. Hegedus and J. Noujaim, Noujaim Film/Pennebaker Hegedus Films, 2001).
The Day I Will Never Forget [Super 16] (K. Longinotto, Vixen Films/HBO/Cinemax Documentary Films, 2002).
The Hurt Locker [16mm & HDTV video transfer to 35mm] (K. Bigelow, Voltage Pictures/Grosvenor Park Media/Film Capital Europe Funds/First Light Production/ Kingsgate Films/Summit Entertainment, 2008).
12th & Delaware [HDcam] (R. Grady and H. Ewing, Loki Films, 2010).
We are Half of Iran's Population [Beta SP] (R. Bani-Etemad, Noori Pictures, 2009).

2. NEW DAY FILMS: COLLECTIVE AESTHETICS AND THE COLLECTION

Elizabeth Coffman and Erica Stein

New Day Films was founded in 1972 – on the cusp of sweeping changes in documentary and feminist filmmaking practice – by four documentarists who were unable to gain distribution in the bottleneck of the New York nonfiction filmmaking scene (Figure 1). Despite these challenges, their films about the everyday texture of women's lives were in demand with audiences as the women's movement grew across the country.[1] Today, New Day is one of the most financially stable nontheatrical distribution collectives in North America, boasting more than 165 members and $1m in yearly revenues.[2] Films distributed by the collective have been screened, broadcast and awarded around the world, studied in media journals, discussed at organising events, showcased in museums, and collected by libraries. New Day's collective (and its collection) provide compelling objects of study for the history of gender and documentary authorship.

In interviews spanning thirty-five years, from 1978 to 2015, founders (Figure 2) and newer members alike attribute New Day's success not only to its identity as a collective but also to two specific forms this category implies. First, New Day is a vehicle for self-distribution, wherein each member is responsible for the reproduction, audience engagement strategies, and direct marketing of their own film. Yet each member is also a part owner, and both individual profits and the cooperative's overhead are calculated through a share ladder – a transparent division of New Day's total profits – voted on by the members every year.[3] Second, while New Day's institutional identity and practices are derived from a model of participatory democracy and the pluralism it values,

Figure 1 New Day Films poster, 1973. Courtesy of Liane Brandon.

one of the collective's most prominent features is its highly unified presentation of its content – its films – on the Web, in promotional materials, and in other venues. New Day's titles, honoured with three retrospectives at the Museum of Modern Art in New York and recently acquired by Duke University's Archive of Documentary Arts, are marketed and often consumed as a historically significant, curated *collection* with a distinct house style. The complex play between individualised activism and collectivity threads through New Day's identity as both a dominant US independent educational film distributor and one of the few surviving feminist documentary collectives so important to the early 1970s.[4] This creative tension is also felt in New Day's current socially integrated business practices, which depend on branding its film titles as a curated collection, the participatory democracy implied by its by-laws, and its pioneering of digital distribution and exhibition possibilities.

Realist Polyphony

Cinema is rarely produced as a singular operation. The director may attract the most obvious credit for creative filmmaking choices, but the figure of the auteur does not begin to capture the collaborative forms of decision making and influence that occur at all stages of media production – both in the hierarchical, financially driven Hollywood production environment and the looser, idea-driven forum of the media collective. With opportunities behind the scenes and on screen in Hollywood still restricted for women in the 1970s, and 16mm Bolex and Sony Portapak cameras becoming readily available, women began to form media collectives. These collectives, such as New Day Films, Iris Films, and Women Make Movies (WMM), taught skills to women and other populations often denied access to production technologies while distributing materials that were viewed as being too controversial or aesthetically unusual for television or movie theatres.

Three years after its founding, New Day released *Chris and Bernie* (directed by Bonnie Friedman and Deborah Shaffer; USA: New Day Films, 1974), a short 16mm documentary about two single mothers who live together in order to afford raising their children. The young women, both divorced, have children under the age of six. Chris is trained as a nurse but is on welfare, while Bernie is trying to learn carpentry. As Chuck Kleinhans described in his 1975 review of the film in *Jump Cut*, 'We see Bernie building a stairway while she tells us, in voice-over, that she didn't want to be a secretary and fought the welfare bureaucracy to get into an OEO (Office of Equal Opportunity) carpentry training program that was "only for men".' The film evinces a documentary aesthetic that is neither expository nor overtly experimental – an observational slice of single parenthood and poverty in the 1970s. 'What we have in this new genre of political documentary, the discussion film,' Kleinhans

Figure 2   New Day founders Liane Brandon, Jim Klein, Julia Reichert and Amalie Rothschild, 1976.

continues, 'is the process and political struggle of everyday life.'[5] The film initially proved difficult to distribute, a challenge familiar to New Day's founders. Two of those founders, Julia Reichert and Jim Klein, who later received Academy Award nominations and Emmy Awards for their work, claimed that in the world of New York documentary filmmaking in the late 1960s and early 1970s, professional distributors barely paid filmmakers after the company took its cut and that some distributors, such as the Film-Makers' Cooperative in New York, were 'so into underground and experimental film that we could see our potential audience would never get that catalogue'.[6] Instead, Reichert and Klein, along with other founding members, Liane Brandon and Amalie R. Rothschild, developed aesthetic and economic strategies that addressed and created not only a wider audience interested in the women's movement, labour issues and political debates about reproductive rights, but also an audience that could produce themselves as a politically active community through their engagement with the films.

Reichert identifies New Day as a constitutive element of second-wave feminism:

> The whole idea of distribution ... was to help the women's movement grow. Films could do that; they could get the ideas out. We could watch the women's movement spread across the country just by who was ordering our films. First it was Cambridge and Berkeley. I remember the first showing in the deep South.[7]

Reichert also describes getting '30–40 bookings a month' in 1971–2 for one of the first and best-known New Day films that she directed with Klein, *Growing Up Female* (USA, 1971).[8] A chronicle of the social development of girls and women through a range of cultural, economic, and racial contexts, *Growing Up Female*'s initial bookings were at universities such as Harvard and Vassar College but then expanded to 'churches, nursing schools, technical schools' and 'junior colleges, Catholic high schools'.[9] For her part, Brandon recalls that, while it was a for-profit business (as it remains to this day), New Day negotiated fees with exhibitors on the basis of need,

> so that consciousness-raising groups and anyone we thought would be interested would have the tools to educate, organize, and spread the word. Different groups used [the films] in different ways – to educate, to plan 'actions' (if the group was so inclined), to plan screenings in schools, churches, union halls, local theaters, etc.[10]

As Brandon suggests, the exhibition venue and the films' content encouraged the audience to act as a collective, especially in their immediate response to the screenings. In 1975 Kleinhans named both *Growing Up Female* and *Chris and Bernie* as exemplary 'discussion' films that appeal to 'ordinary working people', and implied that discussions among audience members could lead to debate, dissent, or even organising.[11] At their height, these audience actions amounted to what Jane Gaines calls 'political mimesis', in which the bodies of the viewers and the bodies on screen are linked in a reproduction of actions.[12] The moment of political mimesis may occur through an orchestrated rejection or resistance to charged, overdetermined images on screen, such as dolls or pornography, the use of voice-overs or a dialectical recognition of the performance of gender, as in Liane Brandon's groundbreaking *Anything You Want To Be* (USA, 1971) and *Betty Tells Her Story* (USA, New Day Films, 1972) (Figure 3). The New Day films that helped the women's movement grow in the 1970s tended to show that, as Kleinhans argues about *Chris and Bernie*, 'small

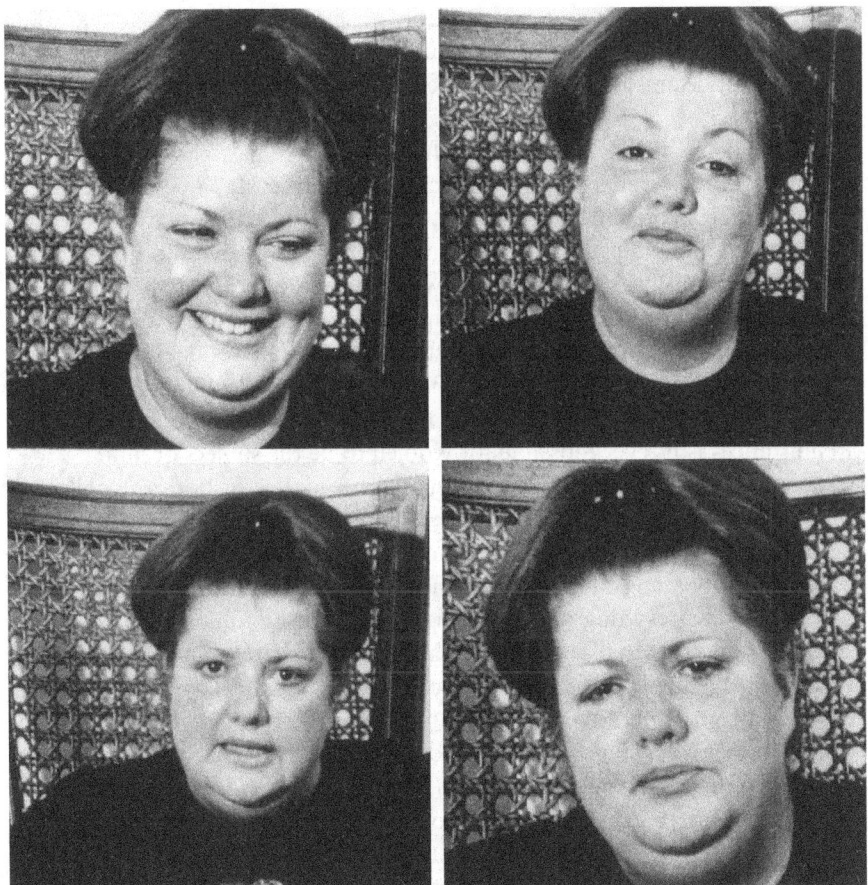

Figure 3 *Betty Tells Her Story* (New Day Films, 1972).

changes are no small thing. [They are] the very stuff of change, the foundation for those dramatic public and mass activities called demonstrations, strikes, and revolutions'.[13] This mirroring between the institutional structure of the organisation producing the films and the audiences viewing them had a crucial intermediary: the aesthetics of the films themselves.

New Day's aesthetic, and its articulation of that aesthetic with its status as a collective as well as the broader concept of collectivity, must be understood in the wider context of 1970s Anglo-American feminist film practice and theory. This connection is especially evident in a 1978 *New German Critique* roundtable discussion among editors, scholars, curators, and filmmakers about the status of feminist film theory.[14] After the discussion oscillates between the benefits of Marxist and psychoanalytic analyses of feminist film content for Hollywood and independent films, the editors pose the question of collectives. Is the collective model a more successful alternative for producing feminist content, they wonder, by involving female producers and evading the male-centred hierarchy of the studio system? Judith Mayne suggests, 'I think it's important to be more precise about what we mean by collectivity.' She describes the strategies of a worker's group that used video recording at a factory strike as one example that includes collective participation. But there are other ways to understand a 'collective aesthetic'. Mayne continues, 'The strategic interest of film collectives is, I think, a different relationship with what's being filmed or who's being filmed, which I hope would necessitate a different relationship between who's watching the film and who's made the film.'[15] As B. Ruby Rich notes, filmmaking is 'a dialectical experience' for women – from being the object of spectacle to suddenly producing it.[16] Rich's comment resonates with the most crucial problematic explored by feminist theorists and filmmakers in the 1970s, and for decades afterwards: under what circumstances is it (ever) possible for women to be the subject of film?

Women's ability to assume this position is a matter of both the collective and the aesthetic because the dominant film aesthetic uses classical narrative and structured looking positions to simultaneously reduce women to the bearer of the look and to the patriarchal construction of the feminine as other, as Woman. The resulting objectified figure was most famously elucidated by Laura Mulvey in her essay 'Visual pleasure and narrative cinema', published in 1975, and Mulvey joined figures such as Rich, Mayne, Claire Johnston, E. Ann Kaplan and others in calling for a filmmaking practice that could produce women both as the subject of film and as a collective. That is, a praxis that both communicates women as subjects and as a collective, a group structured and delimited by patriarchal oppression as well as diverse embodied experiences of race, class, gender and sexuality yet with the possibility of producing relations and works that exist outside of this structure and thereby helping to transform it. This complex goal produced multiple theories, praxes and texts.

The intervening years have collected, and perhaps (over)simplified them, into roughly two groups. The first marries psychoanalytic film theory to a modernist, allusive, experimental aesthetic in order to explore how social apparati, including film, construct women as Woman, and what some of the resulting consequences are. In the 1970s, this was the tactic of collectives such as WMM and films such as *Thriller* (directed by Sally Potter; UK: Arts Council of Great Britain, 1979) and *Riddles of the Sphinx* (directed by Laura Mulvey and Peter Wollen; UK: British Film Institute, 1977). At the same time, another strand of theory and praxis that stressed consciousness raising, organising and more directly Marxist action emerged in collectives such as the Boston Newsreel (of which New Day co-founder Liane Brandon was a member) or California Newsreel Film Collective, and films such as 'Up Against the Wall, Ms America' (Newsreel #22, 1968) and 'The Woman's Film' (directed by Louise Alaimo and Judy Smith; USA: California Newsreel Films, 1971).[17] These films, usually nonfiction, were known for using the documentary form to produce a transparent, realist style that explored individual women's experiences, and often studied the collectives they formed in order to change those experiences.[18]

New Day is one of the last remaining – and surely the most financially stable – organisations that made up this second strand, often referred to as 'the feminist realist' tradition. Perhaps because of this association with a kind of naïve realism, New Day's aesthetic has generally been read as the lack of one. In 1994, twenty years after the heyday of realist feminist documentary film and the rise of reflexive, formalist avant-garde work, Alexandra Juhasz set out to redefine realism as not simply a footnote on the road to the complexity of Trinh T. Minh-ha, Chantal Akerman and Tracey Moffat, but rather a politically viable adaptation of realist methods that both depicted acts of individual becoming and produced collective consciousness-raising.[19] At the outset of her article, Juhasz noted that

> perhaps the most disturbing consequence of [the academy's dismissal of realist feminist documentary] is the loss of these films for revaluation due to the economic relationship between film scholarship and alternative film distribution: only twenty years later, they are difficult, if not impossible, to find.[20]

At the close of the article, following a list of films screened at a 1992 Whitney Museum of American Art retrospective of feminist cultural objects, Juhasz notes that 'the distributors who handled many of these films are long out of business'.[21] Notably, while other exemplars of the realist style suffered economic collapse within twenty years of their founding, surfacing only in museum retrospectives that treat their aesthetic as indicative of a truncated path in a larger cultural movement, New Day has been the subject of three different film programs at the Museum of Modern Art, in 1983, 1996 and 2011. These exhibits, while they foreground New Day's most prominent early work, also feature new films on a variety of topics.

Juhasz's comments and MOMA's curatorial influence suggest that 'feminist realism' does constitute an aesthetic. In fact, the same year New Day had its first MOMA retrospective, which featured 'signature' New Day titles such as *Growing Up Female, It Happens to Us* (directed by Amalie R. Rothschild; USA, 1972), *Anything You Want To* Be (directed by Liane Brandon; USA, 1971) and *Chris and Bernie*, documentary scholar Bill Nichols published an article that suggested how this aesthetic should be understood.[22] Nichols identified a distinct mode he named 'the third style', which exhibits the influence of both expository and observational techniques while subordinating them to its use of interviews. In so doing, this mode transfers 'the voice of the documentary' from a central point of authorial enunciation in voice-over or in the camera's objective gaze to a decentralised and subjective experiential authority held by a variety of talking head interviewees.

New Day's films have long availed themselves of this technique, just as its institutional structure and distribution tactics function as analogues to it. From the beginning, New Day preserved and disseminated a wide variety of feminist creative output, and just as the exhibition contexts encouraged a range of responses to its films, so too were the aesthetics of the films themselves 'collective', employing a hybridised use of Nichols's 'third style' and offering many potential moments of recognition. Early New Day films present a range of women's everyday experiences, often using a collage aesthetic that precludes an identification of any one subject or experience as normative, while simultaneously insisting that each experience is delimited by a patriarchal society. Thus, the films retain a sense of the individual need and possibilities for collective support within a system, while showing the force of that system as it is felt on the individual level – similar to how self-distribution within a cooperative structure preserves the specificity of individual projects while allowing for their proliferation and recognition as part of a broader strategy, form or mode. The aesthetics of these films align with Jane Gaines's description of a radical remembering/viewing process for the film viewer, 'translating our interest in the viscerality of film-going' into 'the consequent radicalization of the spectator'.[23] Gaines reinvestigates how moving images achieve a radical audience response, how a film 'moves' a spectator 'to get up and do something'. She acknowledges that these questions are 'fraught with issues of measurement, causality, and disciplinary boundary', but suggest that critics should 'take a different tack':

> I want to see the historical bodies-in-action on the screen as having a mimetic relation to the bodies of the viewers. In this theorization, viewing

bodies re-produce the political movement imaged on the screen in the world of their present. Here the radical film has the power to make things happen because of this special screen/world relation that I call political mimesis.[24]

New Day's early work shows how a 'collective aesthetic', in this case one derived from Nichols's third style and informed by the conditions of production and exhibition, can help to achieve a politically mimetic film event. Films like *Growing Up Female* and *Chris and Bernie* effect a political mimesis that runs both from the screen to the audience and from the institutional structure to the screen.

This aesthetic is particularly evident in *Growing Up Female*, whose structured play of unity and disharmony chronicles the lives of women in the US from four to thirty-four. Although its subject is human development, the film is circular rather than linear, emphasising the issues presented as collectively, rather than individually, experienced. This results in extreme symmetry within and between segments, culminating in the linking of the opening scene and the film's final moments. This cyclic logic encompasses the suggestion that the film occurs within a day – the opening shots depict a mother taking her daughter to class and the closing shots show the daughter being picked up from school – binding the diverse lives of the subjects observed within a unifying temporal structure. This resonates with the film's audiovisual strategy, which produces the film's interviews as extremely ambiguous. The interviews feature the six primary subjects and those figures of authority who embody the institutions with the most impact on their lives. These figures often voice the conventional patriarchal wisdom surrounding feminine development. For example, the elementary school teacher in the opening segment notes in voice-over that little girls are 'mean', 'jealous' and 'competitive' in comparison with little boys, with whom they do not like to play. The voice-over is accompanied by a series of shots of the teacher's classroom. The master shots display mixed-gender groups of children playing together while two-shots and close-ups show little girls sharing with, grooming and comforting one another. The scene challenges one of Nichols's critiques of the third style, namely that it does not question or evaluate the authority of interviewees.[25] Here, the film utilises audiovisual montage to cast doubt on the teacher's assessment and to emphasise the selective and constructed nature of the social reality she reinscribes, implying its effects on a collective, as well as individual, level.

Growing Up Female further displays its third style traits by utilising something similar to Nichols's 'intertitles' – an apparently authorial voice that interrupts the traditional voice-over or interview – to suggest the complexity of its subjects' own experiences and perceptions. This is particularly noticeable in the segment featuring Terry, a sixteen-year-old African American aspiring cosmetologist from a small town. At the outset of her segment, Terry declares herself satisfied with her life goals and current romantic situation, both of which she professes should be primarily determined by her male partner, with whom she shares the screen. This view is reiterated by her high school guidance counsellor, who runs a course on marriage that stresses domestic sphere responsibilities for women, assumes that married women will work only in the home and that they will defer to their husbands in all matters of import. As her segment continues, Terry's discussion of her situation and goals becomes more nuanced, as when she suggests that her desire to find a boyfriend who would assume a dominant role in the relationship is at least partially due to the norms of her community. The segment concludes with Terry's completion of her marriage class and declaration of her intention to leave her town because 'the farther away I get, the better it might be'. The scene is accompanied by the Bob Dylan-penned 'I Shall Be Released' on the soundtrack, which connects Terry's desires to civil rights-tinged rhetoric as well as the liberationist aesthetics of the counterculture. Of course, this structure could be read as implying that this consciousness-raising film does not so much educate the audience as it produces its interview subjects as in desperate need of instruction by the filmmakers and the second wave feminism they represent. Such a reading resonates with the many critiques of *vérité* and direct cinema documentaries as inherently dismissive and even exploitative of their subjects, as well as with ethnographic critiques of emotional manipulation from musical soundtracks, even when positioned ironically.[26]

Despite moments of sound/image aesthetic intervention, as Juhasz observes, perhaps more 'often political producers are drawn to realist strategies'.[27] As both a feminist filmmaker and an academic scholar, Juhasz notes the ambivalence that she feels about including 'realist' aesthetic strategies in her video projects about women who are HIV positive while teaching the problematic patriarchal nature of making these same aesthetic choices in the classroom: 'it disturbs me that the theory I respect and use is often at odds with the media I make and watch.'[28] Juhasz argues for the importance of the interviews in *It Happens To Us*, which problematise assumptions about representation and identification. 'Words that have rarely been said by women out loud form a revisionist history that unifies *a range of positions* as one potential for a shared feminist identity.' By speaking these words on camera, from multiple 'positions', Juhasz suggests that a number of spectator identification points are possible, including 'the political action that this collective articulation of oppression will inspire',[29] the kind of relationship between screen and audience, the kind of aesthetic, that Gaines calls political mimesis. In this frame, early New Day films' focus on women in collective terms and observations on how individuals do and do not perceive themselves as part of this collective are used to develop a doubled vision, an aesthetic that simultaneously depicts the reality that creates women as Woman/object as well as the collective thought and action capable of revealing this reality as constructed.

Collective vs Collection

New Day's institutional culture and films, then, successfully achieve an aesthetic of collectivity. However, New Day has survived its original contemporaries in part by comprehensively marketing itself as a collection. As the story of New Day's founding suggests, the collective regarded both the ability to preserve a film with like-minded work and also to track the film's exhibition – as well as the impact of that exhibition – as its central purpose. This preservation feature lingers today, as New Day sells its works to educators and scholars as an impeccably curated collection, assuring its users of a certain level of quality (even predictability) and of bold, insightful content. This is evident in the cooperative's promotional materials and in its digital extensions, including the descriptions of films within its archive, MOMA's holdings of New Day films, as well as its three MOMA shows. While collective action and governance are hallmarks of both New Day and feminist politics in general, the collection as an organising structure tends toward an erasure of such possibilities. In her work on the collection, Susan Stewart argues that to collect is to forget, so that a collection stands for an entire experience, place or moment, while erasing differences among the collection's elements.[30] New Day's marriage of its economic and cultural survival as a collective to branding as a collection potentially complicates its ability to produce an aesthetic of collectivity.

Stewart's fears about the collection are potentially evident in all three MOMA shows, where New Day's status as a commercial concern and as an historical entity whose membership, output and politics have evolved over its forty-year existence is partially suppressed. New Day's relationship with MOMA dates back to 1982, ten years after the collective's creation. In that year, MOMA was approached by New Day as part of its tenth anniversary celebration and asked to participate.[31] The museum billed the collective in terms of both its feminist and activist roots and as 'a model cooperative of and for independent filmmakers [that] through its documentary films has participated in and charted many of the social changes in the United States over the last decade'.[32] The exhibit reflected New Day's current catalogue and history. However, the films were separated into programs that downplayed their historical difference and various political emphases in favour of shared topicality and audience.

The 1996 retrospective, also curated by Berger, followed a similar logic, and was publicised with reference to New Day as an historically important 'cooperative' entity yet without an account of its historical transformations.[33]

Thus, although New Day is acknowledged as a distributor, this is couched almost in terms of New Day being a kind of small peer to MOMA, pre-selecting and collecting worthy works that the museum will now 'screen' for maximum importance and interest before screening them for its audience, even as the 'venerable New Day artists', many of whose films are exactly those housed in MOMA's archives, are separated from their work, which is not individually named or attributed. By presenting itself as an archival collection in both internal and external sites, New Day takes on the ability to construct itself – not its films, directors or history – but the institution itself as an object (worthy) of study, the fact of whose existence itself testifies to the success of its projects and its organisational practice. The museum's celebration of New Day diffuses the idea of historical evolution – from a somewhat exclusionary second wave feminist outlook to one engaged with an entire range of social justice issues – in favour of the image of an ahistorical archive of educational film.

New Day's embrace of the collection – and MOMA's parallel acknowlegement of New Day's own curatorial practices – does recapitulate several of the qualities that make this form inimical to the collective aesthetic and at odds with the kind of political mimesis attempted by New Day's preferred exhibition contexts, yet it is key to its institutional branding. While collections may reinforce some ideological erasures, they can also help to mediate a certain strand of public memory by countering 'social amnesia'.[34] Forty years after New Day Films contributed to a national discussion about gender equity and stereotypes, a social and political 'backlash' to these concerns has grown.[35] While the collection may tend to erase history, new digital storage models can act as a kind of counter archive that allows for collective – even mimetic? – engagement with the past. New Day's recent donation of materials to Duke University's Archive of Documentary Arts displays some of the potential of such models. Kirston Johnson, the archive's head curator, described how 'Our collecting informs the history of documentary arts just as much as [the collections]'.[36] Because the Duke collection is interested in the filmmaker's creative process as well as in distribution history, they include ancillary prints and materials along with exhibition film and video prints.[37] For instance, the sales and rental invoices from the New Day collection may help to track the importance of film exhibition for the early establishment of Women's Centers around the country. Johnson also plans to complete oral history interviews with the New Day founders to complement the archive's holdings, a co-archival or ethnographic act that starts to mimic the initial stages of documentary production. New Day's archival moment relates to the present digital revolution in that both allow for easier access to representations of our collective past, representations that may help reorder earlier assessments of forgotten, ignored or misremembered histories.

Collecting Small Changes

The aesthetic strategies displayed in many of the founding films and the mimetic tactics employed by their directors remain key components of New Day's activity today, although membership, the aesthetic modes employed, and the films' exhibition contexts have all diversified. New Day's pioneering digital distribution platform weaves together the cooperative's past and future by emphasising the discussion aesthetic of many of its films. The platform simultaneously renews and reinvents possibilities for how 'discussions' may occur: in single-channel and interactive screenings among a geographically scattered, sometimes atomised audience.

New Day Digital, spearheaded in 2008 by New Day filmmakers Paco de Onís, Jeff Tamblyn and Peter Cohn, was an early streaming platform for independent documentaries hosted by Seattle Community Colleges television.[38] Recognising the collaborative opportunities of the digital platform, New Day has chosen to promote films that facilitate the forging of connections, dissemination of memories or sharing of political strategies among digital visitors. Some of the most compelling interactive documentary projects connected with New Day filmmakers are *Granito: How to Nail a Dictator* (directed by Pamela Yates; USA, 2011) and Rebecca Snedeker and Luisa Dantas's *Land of Opportunity* (USA, 2010). Through their content platforms, these New Day documentaries allow for collective commentary and interactive feedback surrounding issues of poverty, education and citizenship – a logical expansion from New Day's beginnings with discussions of films that feature critiques of patriarchy.

The digital platform suggests that the logic of the collection can help progressive media achieve its ends. This is particularly evident in *Granito*, which both performs and unravels the processes of history (Figure 4). Co-produced by Skylight Labs, New Day Digital leader Paco de Onís, Pamela Yates and Peter Kinoy, *Granito* recuts footage from an earlier documentary that Yates and Kinoy worked on, *When the Mountains Tremble* (directed by Newton Thomas Sigel and Pamela Yates; USA: New Day Films, 1983). The original film covered the Guatemalan genocide by interviewing corrupt government officials as well as indigenous rebel armies. Traveling with the leftist guerillas, a young Yates profiled Inés – whose name was actually María Magdalena Hernández – a Mayan guerrilla fighting for fair wages, property rights, and the recognition of her people. *Granito*'s title is taken from Hernández's own fateful words in *When the Mountains Tremble*: 'We are making a big effort, each contributing our tiny grain of sand, our *granito*, so that our country can be free', words and images that *Granito* returns to repeatedly.

Granito suggests the ways in which a collection can be compatible with the aims of the collective, just as *When the Mountains Tremble*'s collecting and

Figure 4 Director Pamela Yates in the Guatemalan Highlands with the crew filming *Granito: How to Nail a Dictator*. Photo: Dana Lixenberg.

recording of the conflict was itself a political act: the preservation of the events depicted in the film contradicts the regime's official narrative of its actions and locates the actions of the rebel armies in a wider context. The film was used as a politically mimetic object within and outside of Guatemala, most notably in the case of Yates's 1983 interviews of former dictator Efraín Ríos Montt. Yates records Ríos Montt bragging about his responsibilities, 'I control the army', a statement that was used as forensic evidence at his trial for genocide in May 2012. In its turn, *Granito* reopens this history in its engagement with *When the Mountains Tremble*, turning the form of the collection against its expected uses. Distributed digitally by New Day and contextualised within a complex social media environment predicated on presence, *Granito* is characterised by the digital prostheses that so often accompany the contemporary film collection, as well as by shared aesthetic decision making practices from the staff of Skylight Pictures and Labs.

On New Day's website, Yates describes how the 'collective concept' behind the co-production, direction and editing of *When the Mountains Tremble* and *Granito* allowed her, de Onís and Kinoy (Skylight Pictures) to develop 'our approach to political documentary storytelling'.[39] This 'collective concept' continues with the social media updates to the memorial website that accompanies *Granito*, 'Every Memory Matters' (a multimedia project that Skylight identifies as a 'platform', developed at the Bay Area Video Coalition Producers Institute).[40] The memorial website includes Yates's description of Hernández in 1980, months before her death. After contact from Hernández's brother on Facebook, Yates and de Onís posted a letter from her that they found in their files, as well as many other emotional memorial documents and photos, on 'Every Memory Matters'. As a result of the ongoing interactive storyworld of *Granito* more outreach initiatives and two new interactive platforms, 'IJCentral', on the international criminal court, and 'Anatomy of a Trial', examining the 'strategies behind the historic 2012 Ríos Montt genocide trial', have been developed or are in development by Skylight Labs. With the support of New Day Films, Skylight continues to provide compelling examples of how women's storytelling history may achieve social justice through the outreach strategies and aesthetic and institutional strengths of both the collective and the collection.

Notes

1. Liane Brandon, email message to Elizabeth Coffman, 3 August 2012. Brandon is an award-winning filmmaker and cofounder of New Day Films along with Julia Reichert, Jim Klein and Amalie Rothschild. See 'Liane Brandon', New Day Films, <www.newday.com/filmmaker/42> (last accessed 9 October 2015).
2. Beverly Seckinger, email message to authors, 8 September 2014. Seckinger is a filmmaker and producer affiliated with New Day Films. 'Beverly Seckinger', New Day Films, <www.newday.com/filmmaker/132> (last accessed 9 October 2015).
3. For information on the share ladder, application processes and distribution practices, see New Day Films' website, <www.newday.com/content/apply-join-us> (last accessed 17 August 2015).
4. While New Day is notable simply for its decades-long operation, the collective is perhaps even more remarkable for its continued adherence to its original economic model and mission, especially when compared to WMM. Like New Day, WMM recently celebrated its forty-year anniversary as a women's film collective. The biggest difference between the two distributors today is that New Day has continued to operate successfully using collective and sustainable decision-making models, while WMM's comeback is more the product of a single individual's (Debra Zimmerman) efforts to develop it into an organisation that is more focused on independent film distribution. See Debra Zimmerman and Patricia White, 'Looking back and forward: a conversation about women make movies', *Camera Obscura*, no. 82, 2013, pp. 147–55; B. Ruby Rich, 'The confidence game,' *Camera Obscura*, no. 82, 2013, pp. 157–65.
5. Chuck Kleinhans, '*Chris and Bernie*: the virtues of modesty', *Jump Cut*, no. 8, 1975, p. 6.
6. Quoted in Julie Lesage et al., 'Interview with Julia Reichert and Jim Klein: New Day's way,' *Jump Cut*, no. 9, 1975, p. 21.
7. Lesage, 'Interview with Julia Reichert and Jim Klein', p. 22.
8. Kleinhans, '*Chris and Bernie*: the virtues of modesty', p. 6.
9. Lesage, 'Interview with Julia Reichert and Jim Klein', p. 22

10. Brandon, email message to Elizabeth Coffman, 3 August 2012.
11. Kleinhans, 'Chris and Bernie: the virtues of modesty', p. 6.
12. Jane Gaines, 'Radical attractions: the uprising of '34', Wide Angle, 21/2, 1999, p. 103.
13. Kleinhans, 'Chris and Bernie: the virtues of modesty', p. 6.
14. Michelle Citron, Julia Lesage, Judith Mayne, B. Ruby Rich and Anna Marie Taylor, 'Women and film: a discussion of feminist aesthetics', New German Critique, no. 13, Special Feminist Issue, Winter 1978, pp. 82–107.
15. Ibid. p. 96.
16. Ibid. p. 87.
17. See John Hess, 'Notes on U.S. radical film, 1967–90', Jump Cut, no. 21, November 1979, pp. 31–5; 'Brandon tells her story: back in the (New) Day of social issue films', Documentary Magazine, International Documentary Association, <http://www.documentary.org/magazine/brandon-tells-her-story-back-new-day-social-issue-films> (last accessed 12 December 2016).
18. A third potential group currently receiving attention were early proponents of more direct interactivity, systems theory and followers of Gregory Bateson's concept of cybernetics. Writers and videomakers such as Beryl Korot and Phyllis Segura, and collectives, Raindance Corporation and Videofreex, were drawn to video in large part because of the creative, interactive potential for recording, playback and feedback between subjects and cameras. Phyllis Segura references talking with William Burroughs about a 'band' of people spread across a road, all with video cameras recording the same thing from a variety of perspectives, in 'Creating radical software: personal account', Rhizome, 28 April 2015.
19. Alexandra Juhasz, 'They said we were trying to show reality – all I want is to show my film: the politics of the realist feminist documentary', Screen 35, no. 2, Summer 1994, pp. 171–91.
20. Juhasz, 'They said we were trying to show reality', p. 173.
21. Ibid. p. 190.
22. Bill Nichols, 'The voice of documentary', Film Quarterly, 36/3, 1983, pp. 17–30.
23. Gaines, 'Radical attractions: the uprising of '34', p. 111.
24. Ibid. p. 103.
25. Nichols, 'The voice of documentary', pp. 25–7.
26. Such critiques are epitomised by Calvin Pryluck's review of direct cinema and cinéma vérité's aesthetics in 'Ultimately we are all outsiders: the ethics of documentary filming', Journal of the University Film Association, 28/1, Winter 1976, pp. 21–9.
27. Juhasz, 'They said we were trying to show reality', p. 174.
28. Ibid. p. 176.
29. Ibid. pp. 182–3.
30. New Day curates via a long-established process of voting by committee. See <https://www.newday.com/content/apply-join-us> (last accessed 18 February 2016). Susan Stewart, On Longing: Narratives of the Miniature, the Gigantic, the Souvenir, the Collection (Durham, NC: Duke University Press, 1984), pp. 151–3.
31. Isabel Hill, email message to Erica Stein, 4 August 2012.
32. Stuart Klawans, 'The Museum of Modern Art presents a birthday tribute to New Day Films, New York, Film Press Office, Museum of Modern Art, May 1983.
33. MOMA program describes, 'For the twenty-fifth anniversary of New Day Films, the Department of Film and Video has organised two programs from the cooperative's recent acquisitions, and a retrospective of eleven films and videos by venerable New Day artists, including Ralph Arlyck, Joyce Chopra, Jane Gilooly, Isabel Hill, Julia Reichert, and Amalie S. Rothschild. Also presented are some of New

Day's earliest films, from MOMA's archives.' Graham Leggat, 'Fall advance schedule of film and video programs', New York, Film Press Office, Museum of Modern Art, August 1996, p. 32.
34. Francis X. Blouin, Jr and William G. Rosenberg, *Processing the Past: Contesting Authority in History and the Archives* (Oxford: Oxford University Press, 2011), p. 110.
35. In 2010 Harvard University students organised a 'Feminist coming out day' in response to the perceived 'backlash', which also references Susan Faludi's *Backlash: The Undeclared War Against American Women* (New York: Random House, 1991). See <http://feministcomingoutday.com/>.
36. Phone conversation with Elizabeth Coffman, 19 December 2012.
37. Liane Brandon confirmed that the combination of the library's ability to preserve and screen film as well as the Sally Bingham collection helped to convince New Day founders to select Duke University for their archive donation. Liane Brandon, in discussion with Elizabeth Coffman, July 2012.
38. Beverly Seckinger, email message to authors, 17 February 2013.
39. Pamela Yates, quoted in *Granito: How to Nail a Dictator* (USA, New Day Films, 2011), <www.newday.com/film/granito> (last accessed 17 August 2015).
40. 'About the project', *Granito: Every Memory Matters*, <http://www.granitomem.com/acerca-del-proyecto/> (last accessed 3 February 2016). And Skylight media platforms, <http://skylight.is/media/#platforms> (last accessed 3 February, 2016).

Filmography

Chris and Bernie [film] (Bonnie Friedman and Deborah Shaffer, USA, New Day Films, 1974).
Growing Up Female [film] (Julia Reichert and Jim Klein, USA, New Day Films, 1971).
Anything You Want To Be [film] (Liane Brandon, USA, 1971).
Betty Tells Her Story [film] (Liane Brandon, USA, New Day Films, 1972).
Thriller [film] (Sally Potter, UK, Arts Council of Great Britain, 1979).
Riddles of the Sphinx, film, (Laura Mulvey and Peter Wollen, UK, British Film Institute, 1977).
Up Against the Wall, Ms America [film] (Newsreel #22, USA, Third World Newsreel Film Collective, 1968).
The Woman's Film [film] (Louise Alaimo and Judy Smith, USA, California Newsreel Films, 1971).
It Happens to Us [film] (Amalie R. Rothschild, USA, New Day Films, 1972).
Granito: How to Nail a Dictator [film] (Pamela Yates, USA, New Day Films, 2011).
Land of Opportunity [film] (Rebecca Snedeker and Luisa Dantas, USA, New Day Films, 2010).
When the Mountains Tremble [film] (Newton Thomas Sigel and Pamela Yates, USA, New Day Films, 1983).
Granito: Every Memory Matters [website] (Pamela Yates, Peter Kinoy and Paco de Onis, USA, Skylight Labs, 2011).
Dictator in the Dock [website] (Pamela Yates, Peter Kinoy and Paco de Onis, USA, Skylight Labs, 2013).
IJCentral [website] (Pamela Yates, Peter Kinoy and Paco de Onis, USA, Skylight Labs, 2008).
Anatomy of a Trial [website] (Pamela Yates, Peter Kinoy and Paco de Onis, USA, Skylight Labs, (in production)).

3. MORE THAN ONE

Sharon Daniel

This is a multi-vocal essay. It is an attempt to both describe, and in a sense, embody the philosophy and methodology on which I have built my practice as a new media documentary maker. The first section, The Personal is Political, looks at the relation between politics and aesthetics in conversation with Jacques Rancière, Kimberlé Williams Crenshaw, Gail Vanstone and others. In the remaining four sections, Convictions, Place, Body and Perspective, I use an essay written by Belgian Art critic, Pieter Van Bogaert, in response to an exhibition of my work at STUK Kunstencentrum, as a kind of way-finder to guide you through a body of work that examines systems of justice and punishment. Van Bogaert's essay acts as an armature which supports fragments of texts, or lexia – examples of anecdotal theory based on actual testimony taken from four documentary projects – along with various ruminations on their concerns and content.

The somewhat unusual structure and layout echo that of the non-linear and interactive documentary projects – so that here, as in the works themselves, your navigation can proceed as form of inquiry informed by multiple voices – an inquiry that provides a parallel experience to that of the author's encounter with and response to those voices. You needn't read every lexia, nor should you try to read in a particular order. The essay is a site for you to traverse. Its argument embodied in its design.

You may well wonder how the formatting of this essay is related to the focus of the collection where you find it. Does the structure make an argument about authorship that is specifically female? Possibly, but I am more concerned about the political efficacy of my work than its gendered-ness. I must admit that I have been troubled by the notion of the specificity of the female in the documentary image and authorship that the title of this publication implies. I am female, a feminist and a politically and socially engaged artist concerned principally with challenging multiple modes of oppression – social and environmental injustice, state violence, structural inequality – in which gender inequality plays a role. My goals are not exclusively feminist, feminine or female, but my approach may well be informed by the various forms of exclusion I have experienced as a woman – and the body of work I attempt to explain in what follows may well take the form that it does, in part, because of that experience.

'POLITICS IS THE STRUGGLE OF AN UNRECOGNIZED PARTY FOR EQUAL RECOGNITION IN THE ESTABLISHED ORDER. AESTHETICS IS BOUND UP IN THIS BATTLE BECAUSE THE BATTLE TAKES PLACE OVER THE IMAGE OF SOCIETY – WHAT IT IS PERMISSIBLE TO SAY OR SHOW.'[1]

In the battle over the image of society undertaken in the late 60s, second wave feminists articulated a shift from individual struggle to collective action.

The Personal Is Political

It was an assertion that personal problems should be seen in political terms – that women were not consistently the victims of violence, abuse and discrimination because they were stupid, weak, mad, hysterical, having a period, pregnant, frigid, over-sexed or 'asking for it', but because they were subject to gender-based oppression.

More broadly, as Kimberlé Williams Crenshaw observes, 'This process of recognizing as social and systemic what was formerly perceived as isolated and individual has also characterized the identity politics of African Americans, other people of color, and gays and lesbians, among others.'[2]

It meant taking the focus off individual responsibility and recognizing women as a subjugated 'class'. It meant that to speak both from primary experience (as an individual with a particular perspective) and as part of a **Class** of shared experience, constitutes a political act. Speech acts of this kind, carried into the register of representation, have the power to transform the public sphere.

It's a phrase that is often quoted and generally misunderstood. It was first published in *Notes from the Second Year: Women's Liberation* (1970), as the title of an essay by Carol Hanisch. Hanisch's essay was a response to criticism of 'consciousness raising' sessions held during the early women's liberation movement, where women discussed the impact of sexism in their daily lives. Critics claimed such sessions were merely 'group therapy', not political action. Hanisch argued that by equating personal testimony with political speech feminist 'consciousness raising' produced an analysis of structural inequality. IT REQUIRED MORE THAN ONE WOMAN'S STORY. By multiplication personal narrative is transported into the realm of politics – this is what multi-vocality effects - at first, incrementally, but over time and through accumulation, significantly.

I believe that this transformation can be affected by documenting an issue as a larger 'site' of socio-political and economic experience - rather as A SINGLE STORY or individual narrative. In my process I work to collect a significant amount of direct testimony from a given 'site' and then I design an interface structured in a manner that will circumscribe that 'site' as articulated by my participant/interlocutors/cocreators. Rather than building a single road across that site to get from point A to point B (or the beginning of an argument to its resolution), THE DATABASE design maps out an extensive territory — say, 100 square miles -- and the interface sets the viewer down within the boundaries of this territory -- allowing her to find her own way — to navigate a difficult terrain, to become immersed in it, and, thus, to have a transformative experience. The interface and information design constitute a form of 'argument', (as writing does for a scholar), and a user's navigation becomes a path of 'inquiry' (a distillation and translation of the encounter through which the speech of the participants emerge). THE DATA AND INTERFACE are framed by what I think of as anecdotal theory (after Michael Taussig and Jane Gallop), which combines narratives drawn from my encounter with my interlocutors, annotated research and analysis. The passages of ANECDOTAL THEORY, which can be found in the introductions and conclusions as well as dispersed throughout the works, create a point of entry that allows the audience to become immersed in the 'subjective plurality' that is manifest in the 'site'. Taken together, the recorded interviews or conversations, the information and interaction design and theoretical framework, materialize the Rancièreian 'political', creating a space of 'dissensus' both for participants and for viewers — one that introduces new subjects into the field of perception.

IT TAKES MORE THAN ONE STORY

'It is impossible to talk about the single story without talking about power...How [stories] are told, who tells them, when they're told, how many stories are told, are really dependent on power. Power is the ability not just to tell the story of another person, but to make it the definitive story of that person...

The consequence of the single story is this: It robs people of dignity. It makes our recognition of our equal humanity difficult. It emphasizes how we are different rather than how we are similar.'[3]

In the space circumscribed by subjectivising speech and transformative understanding there exists a productive tension between the particularities of individual histories, that are in one sense the most compelling aspects of narrative persuasion, and the force capacity of the collective voice – where one voice, an individual story, is intended to stand in for a class of subjects, there is a dangerous and disabling tendency to identify the subject as a case of a tragically flawed character or unusually unfortunate victim of aberrant injustice – rather than one among many affected by structural inequality. When multiple voices speak, in a manner that is intimate and personal, collective and performative, from the same experience of marginalisation, the scale and scope of injustice is forcefully revealed.

AS AN ARTIST I join with impacted communities in telling their truths and together we engage in a call and response with larger publics in an effort to change the conversation about race and crime – to effectively challenge the goals of mass incarceration. I want to use my skill and experience as a researcher, ethnographer and artist to collect, interpret and connect evidence of institutional racism and, by leveraging aesthetic expression, create a humanly compelling and factually concrete, intersectional analysis of structural violence – one that will raise awareness of the multi-dimensional, interlinking forces of discrimination and show that change must be radical and comprehensive to be effective.

I have been engaged for a number of years in developing new media documentary projects that reveal social and economic injustice across a spectrum of public institutions — with a particular focus on the criminal legal system. I've collaborated with legal, human rights and public health NGOs that have introduced me to individuals from the populations and communities that they serve.

This has allowed me to build interactive interfaces to online audio archives of conversations I've recorded with those most severely impacted by structural racism and inequality. They provide testimony and evidence of how state institutions, social structures and economic conditions connect in a causal chain that fosters and perpetuates social injustice.

When I talk about my work I always point out that I see my self as a context provider... rather than a content provider. I provide the means, or tools that will induce others to speak for themselves, and the context in which they may be heard

I engage with groups of participants who live at the margins, outside the social order, and attempt to create a space for the assertion of their political subjectivity. The process of subjectivation occurs both in speaking and being heard. For injection drug users living outside the norms of society in the shadow of the criminal justice system, and women trapped inside the prison system, the statements they make, and allow me to record, are acts of juridical and political testimony. If amplified and contextualised, their speech can turn the capacity for empathetic response toward broader social and personal CONVICTION.

*The **scriptrix narrans** is a different sort of auteur, committed to breaking out of the constraints of traditional narrative, that is to say patriarchal, supportive of hierarchies, divisions, etc. She is one who, facing in one direction, enables those she films to likewise become **scriptrix narrans** and, who, facing in the other direction, produces what Roland Barthes describes as scriptible, writerly, as opposed to readerly, texts. And in doing this Varda also renders her viewers (readers) **scriptrix narrans**. She exhorts her audience to become what Paula Rabinowitz describes as "**subjects of (potential) agency and actors in history**". I want to consider what the effect of shifting to new/digital media might have on this ecriture.*[4]

I have come to see all of my work as part of a larger effort to examine and address structural and environmental racism. Ours is a country founded on the near extermination of one race of people and the enslavement then subsequent mass incarceration of another. Expressions of State Violence are as varied as they are pervasive manifest in environmental injustice, as much as in police violence enacted against people of colour, and the epidemic of injustice within the criminal justice system.

For poor communities of colour, every experience of public life, every interaction with a public institution, and every venture into public space is perilous — from predatory mortgage lending and the deliberate destruction of Black economic power in segregated cities like Baltimore, MD; to militarized and policed public schools in New Orleans, where black students are handcuffed, expelled and even jailed for minor behavioural infractions and 'status' crimes like suspected gang affiliation; to the poisoning of people of colour in toxic fence-line communities like Port Arthur, Texas, and failed industrial towns like Flint, Michigan; to the epidemic of police violence against unarmed blacks on the streets where almost daily an African American is murdered by police.

CONVICTIONS

Convictions was the title of Sharon Daniel's exhibition at STUK. It is a misleading, ambiguous title, which can be interpreted in at least two different ways. It can be read as the verdicts of guilt handed down to those who are accused, or as beliefs in a given system. These meanings are interchangeable, and that is what this exhibition invites us to do: to change locations, put yourself into other characters, spaces and situations. It means setting yourself aside, as well as bringing yourself to the fore, stepping back and approaching. Each change of place creates a different meaning. Each meaning creates its own truth.

Convictions brings together four recent works: *Public Secrets*, *Blood Sugar*, *Inside the Distance* and *Undoing Time*. In the first work, Sharon Daniel focuses on the public secrets of prison. The second work is about the secret public of drug users. The third and fourth works are about the fluidity and complexity of subject positions, on each of these four works, it is the interchangeability or reversibility of the ideas of public and/or secret to which the artist gives space. She gives them a body. Something that makes them tangible and visible. She creates an exchange, an interchangeability, that both comes from and leads to a change of place, body and perspective.¹

America has become a carceral landscape where a society built upon the assumption of white supremacy contains, marginalises, and jeopardises people of colour. The regime of criminalisation of black life and subsequent incarceration of black bodies is so pervasive that it is tantamount to a form of ethnic cleansing. Urban ghettos on the south side of Chicago and predominantly black sub-urban communities like Compton or Ferguson are, in a sense, equivalent to prisons and jails — like islands in a penal archipelago. Black men are imprisoned at a rate six times that of white men. Women of colour are the fastest growing segment of the prison population. Determinate sentencing laws in many states have increased and fixed extraordinarily punitive sentences for behaviours that are most common among poor people of colour — behaviours that have become crimes of survival. As a result of 'three strikes and you're out' laws across the nation, which require longer terms for those convicted of any felony if they have previous convictions for 'serious' or 'violent' crimes, inmate populations have expanded exponentially. Even the burglary of an unoccupied dwelling and simple drug possession are considered 'serious' crimes under these laws and can lead to life sentences. So-called 'gang-related' offenses and sentencing 'enhancements' essentially punish poor people of colour for living in poor neighborhoods and criminalise their associations with other poor people of colour. Inside prisons, administrators use gang 'affiliation' (which can be assigned arbitrarily on the basis of the slightest contact with another so-called 'gang affiliate') to justify the torture of solitary confinement for periods of 20 years or longer — a kind of 'social death' sentence.

"Prison plays a major role here. PUBLIC SECRETS is a website constructed around conversations with detainees at the Central California Women's Facility, the largest prison for women in the United States. BLOOD SUGAR is an online archive of conversations with past and present drug users. Most of them sooner or later come into contact with the prison system (one in four prisoners in the United States is serving time for drug-related offenses). The prison is a place. It is space – too much (too many prisons for a society) and too little (too few cells for the prisoners). It is a space that serves as a model: punishment is intended to deter, as a lesson or as correction. The building is intimidating. It is a symbolic space: invisible, hidden behind high walls. Inside, invisible guards watch, hidden behind monitors, cameras and mirrored windows. Here, the space removed from view, and thus kept secret from the public, is made concrete – not with images, but with words: the only cameras in the prison are those of the prison guards. Public Secrets includes 500 fragments of conversations with prisoners. Their voices and stories embody the women inside the prison, but Daniel's own voice is equally important."

PLACE

Public Secrets is built on the concept of the aporia.

There are three principle branches of navigation:

 INSIDE | OUTSIDE,
 BARE LIFE | HUMAN LIFE,
 PUBLIC SECRET | UTOPIA.

Each branch is structured as aporia. Each aporia frames multiple themes and threads elaborated in clusters of narrative, theory and evidence.

Together they explore the space of the prison - physical, economic, political and ideological - and how the space of the prison acts back on the space outside to disrupt and, in effect, undermine the very forms of legality, security and freedom that the prison system purportedly protects.

A three million dollar razor wire fence separates California Correctional Women's Facility from the middle of nowhere, its site is an agri-business desert between Los Banos and Chowchilla, where there are three prisons within thirty square miles.

Past the metal detector, through two electronic gates, under the gaze of the gun towers, there is an uncannily suburban, perfectly manicured, lawn. Between the fence and the visiting room I follow a rose-lined path surrounded by razor wire glinting in the relentless heat – this space is a counter-site intended to reinscribe the symbolic order of the space of the prison as safe, calm, domesticated.

The prison is an anamorphosis, like the 'memento mori' in Holbein's painting *THE AMBASSADORS*, in which a smear, or 'blot' mars the illusion of three dimensional space. When seen from the proper perspective - a specific location outside the space depicted in the painting - this 'blot', or smear resolves into the image of a skull. Recognition of the blot-as-skull reverses one's reading of the symbolic order of the painting.

The lawn and rose garden are only visible to those who come to the visiting room from the outside – an orientation that is both physical and political. Despite the razor wire border inside and outside "in-determine" each other. This is apparent in the way the prison 'acts back on' the space outside it.

Inside, beyond the visiting room, the sun-baked yards are bare, treeless, there are no roses. Outside, beyond the edge of agri-desert impoverished communities of colour are eviscerated, and the prison industrial complex expands. Anyone, prisoner or police, who enters the space of the prison moves about in a 'zone of indistinction' between outside and inside, exception and rule, licit and illicit, public and secret...

Before I started visiting the California Correctional Women's Facility (CCWF) in 2002 I held, on an intellectual level, a rather typical, liberal distaste for the idea of prisons but, like many, I had not seriously questioned my assumptions about justice and punishment. I assumed that those who were being punished had committed crimes and that by and large the punishment they received would be just. I imagined that cases of prosecutorial malpractice, racial bias, human rights violations and wrongful conviction were the tragic, but rare stuff of investigatory journalism and documentary film. But after spending time at the prison – after meeting the women inside and, visit after visit, hearing one after another testify to the same injustices, the same egregious, pervasive, human rights violations -- the weight of the evidence, the repetition, the shared experience threaded through the vast amount of testimony, changed my assumptions and destroyed my complacence.

Years ago, I walked through a metal detector and into the Central California Women's Facility, the largest female correctional facility in the United States. It changed my life. I went, as a legal advocate, with the non-profit, human rights organisation, Justice Now, documenting conversations with women prisoners at CCWF in an effort to unmask the well known, yet still secret injustices that result from our society's reliance on prisons to solve social problems. The stories I heard inside challenged my most basic perceptions - of our system of justice, of freedom and of responsibility. After our interviews the women were subject to strip search and visual body cavity searches. For these women our conversations were acts of ethical and political testimony - testimony that challenges the underlying principles of distributive justice and the dehumanizing mechanisms of the prison system.

Just like in Blood Sugar, Daniel gives herself a place among the people whom she interviews and consequently moves between the objective and the subjective. This moving back and forth between spaces and positions is crucial. These works move from the artist to the prisoner (Public Secrets), from the addict to the caregiver (Blood Sugar), from the offender to the victim (Inside the Distance), from the inside to the outside (Undoing Time).

Daniel seeks her own place amongst all these characters and spaces. She is not a neutral figure, but she creates ample space for the others. She refers to herself as a "context provider." The "content" comes from the other (which she also is herself).

LIFE INSIDE

READ **"I AM INNOCENT AND I WILL BE EXONERATED"** MORE ▶

INSIDE/OUTSIDE

"I DIDN'T LEARN TO TAKE CARE OF MYSELF."

"THEN I WAS ABLE TO GET THE HEROIN AND ABLE TO SELL IT, WHICH MAKES MONEY."

"I'M 24 YEARS OLD, I'M DOING A LIFE SENTENCE... JUST FOR BEING A DRIVER"

"I WAS PREGNANT ON MY CASE..."

"I FIGURE THAT SOMEWHERE ALONG THE LINE WE ALL HAVE BEEN PUSHED AWAY IN OUR LIFE..."

"I WANTED TO GET OUT OF THE HOUSE SO BAD..."

"HE TOOK THE KEYS, HE THREW THE KEYS TO ME. SO MY ROBBERY IS FOR THE SET OF CAR KEYS..."

"FOR A LONG TIME, I THOUGHT EVERYBODY DRANK."

"I WENT TO JUVENILE FOR THE FIRST TIME, I THINK WHEN I WAS PROBABLY ABOUT 11 OR 12..."

"WHAT CAUSED ME TO GET INVOLVED WITH DRUGS? THE MEN AND BEING POPULAR..."

"YOU CAN ALWAYS REMEMBER A POINT WHERE SOMEBODY SAID, 'I NEED HELP,' AND THEY DIDN'T GET IT."

LIFE OUTSIDE

"I WAS SENTENCED TO 34 TO LIFE FOR PETTY THEFT."

"I PUT A CHECK IN MY ACCOUNT FOR A SO-CALLED FRIEND – THIS A FRIEND THAT'S AN EX-CONVICT AND ALSO A DOPE-FIEND..."

OUTSIDE ▲

The 'site', or space of dissensus, produced through the project PUBLIC SECRETS consists of the testimony of incarcerated women, taken from conversations recorded over a period of six years. Their statements reveal the secret injustices of the war on drugs, the criminal justice system and the prison industrial complex. These narratives of first-hand experience represent the kind of 'speech situation' that Rancière argues constitutes all the 'diverse historical instances of politics'. And PUBLIC SECRETS performs a further Rancièrian 'staging of equality', or disruption of the hierarchical status quo, by bringing the voices of these incarcerated women into dialogue with those of other legal, political and social theorists such as Giorgio Agamben, Michael Taussig, Walter Benjamin, Fredric Jameson, Catherine MacKinnon and Angela Davis. While this is a dialogue that I have constructed, by design, between interlocutors whose perspectives originate from very diverse social locations, for me all of their voices emerge out of a shared ethos and converge in critical dissent.

The databases in Public Secrets, Blood Sugar and Inside the Distance are spaces in which to navigate and to transform. These transformations are important. The accents, the content and form of these stories change according to the way the user moves through them. By making new connections, new relationships occur that continually infect one another.

Three databases are now completely accessible online at
publicsecret.net
bloodandsugar.net
insidethedistance.net

This too is a way of making public what is hidden. It makes secrets public, but it also connects to secret publics. The Internet may seem like a public space, not every public has access to it. That is something Daniel learned from her work with prisoners and addicts.

...sometimes the recordings end abruptly.

Visitation is called for the count at 3:30pm. The door opens – conversation stops. The guard comes in. I turn off the recorder and gather my things quickly. The woman I am speaking with is taken back inside. She may be forced to endure a pat search, a strip search, even a visual body cavity search which could be performed by a male guard. It is entirely up to the guard. I try not to think about this as I walk out into the afternoon heat. It angers and disgusts me. I feel guilty and relieved. I am free to go.

As I walk down the rose-lined path I try to think about my plans for the evening. I imagine going out for a drink, shopping, a movie – pleasure and choice. I actually started thinking about it early this morning – before I left the house. I always do - before a visit - in anticipation and hesitation - I recognize the refugee, the prisoner, that I am.

There are wild rabbits on the lawn at this time of day. They must come in from the desert. They have no difficulty passing through the 3 million dollar razor wire fence. The gates open for me, one after another. I pass through the metal detector and I'm outside - released. On the black top parking lot the car has become a convection oven. We open the doors to let it air out but a voice over a loudspeaker from one of the guard towers insists we move on.

We speed down the farm road toward Los Banos and strip-mall fast-food – by the time we pull up at the Dairy Queen a Friday night high school football game is beginning across the street – One of the legal advocates is interested in the game – her high school played against Los Banos high. The marching band begins to play...

I wonder – what sort of topological deformation makes it possible for these two spaces to exist in such proximity. Does this picture of middle class play and complacence depend on the existence of suffering and oppression at the prison?

While we stand and listen to the cheering across the street I try to remember a quote – it was... 'If you have come here to help - you are wasting your time – if you have come because your liberation is bound up with mine, then...'

I can't recall the wording exactly – but I know my life is bound to the lives of these women. I can't be free until they are free. None of us can really be safe until they are safe. No citizen can honestly claim their inalienable rights until all people can share in them.

The atrocity that has come to be known as 'mass incarceration' is possible because it is a public secret – a secret kept in an unacknowledged but public agreement not to know. The public perception of justice – the figure of its appearance – relies on the public not acknowledging that which is generally known. This is the ideological work that the prison does.

'Before atrocities are recognised as such, they are authoritatively regarded as either too extraordinary to be believable or too ordinary to be atrocious...if it's happening, it's not so bad, and if it's really bad, it isn't happening...'[19]

Feminist Legal Scholar Catherine MacKinnon has analysed the cultural pattern by which we are able to deny, ignore and assimilate atrocities that occur locally and globally on a daily basis. When something is both too violating and too ordinary or pervasive to be acknowledged the public secret is in play. Its structure is that of an aporia – an irresolvable internal contradiction...

There are several references to Giorgio Agamben in this work. The Italian philosopher and author of Homo Sacer makes (by way of Aristotle, Arendt and Foucault) a distinction between "bare life" and "human life" between "zoe" and "bios".

In the first, the body is what remains, the last thing to hold onto. In the second, the body acquires political rights in order to live, work, function and make decisions within a society.

The data bodies in Public Secret, and the audio bodies in Blood Sugar, are in many cases lost bodies, throwaway bodies, worthless bodies.

(Agamben writes about an extreme form of imprisoned bodies in Remnants of Auschwitz, the third part of his Homo Sacer cycle).

And yet, each event, each body, carries the "affective potential" for things to turn out differently

BODY

Daniel creates in-between space, space that connects. She seeks out spaces that remain hidden. She refers to Alice's looking glass: it is by way of the looking glass that Alice found her way to Wonderland, that 'other' space. She also refers to Michel Foucault's 'heterotopias,' the other spaces that exist, non-utopian, other spaces that are actually possible.

Alice's looking glass is an in-between space. Compare it to our skin, which creates a bridge from the outside to the inside of the body. Think of the needle that the drug user pricks through the skin. It makes a hole, which immediately fills up again. This in-between space is elastic, thin, physical, (in)tangible.

Bodies play an important role here. They form a database within the database, as carriers of hereditary, genetic, social and cultural material. The perfect body does not exist. Each body is a carrier of defects that generate contaminating connections. These lead to detours and explorations, and this makes the body itself a space. A battlefield, more specifically, on which a war is being fought: the "war on drugs," which for Daniel is also a "war on race," "on gender," "on class." She calls it a war against the mentally ill, impoverished, depressed, weakened and addicted body of the socially different. That body, its form and its formation, is what you carry with you all your life."

'The needle junkie is a magician who can work the conjuring trick of making a hole and simultaneously fixing it.'[11]

The depth of the skin is an unimaginable paradox. The distance from the surface to its opposite side is minutely fathomless. The skin is both surface and organ – boundary and bridge – it is simultaneously the site of the sense of touch and the seamless enclosure that separates self from other. Everything happens at the surface. The needle pierces its outer, protective layer (the epidermis), perforates a lattice of nerve endings and passes through the connective tissue of the vascular dermis. Its penetration is a kind of sleight of hand – the act itself doubling back on the meaning of the word: to 'pierce,' to 'permeate,' to 'infiltrate,' and to 'understand.' The needle performs a logical and a topological inversion – making a hole and closing it – opening a continuous surface to its other and its opposite. The familiar distinction between outside and inside dissolves like the reflection that absorbs, first, Alice's hand, and then her whole body as she passes through the looking glass.

WHAT DO WE HOLD AGAINST THE DRUG ADDICT?

Her dissent – that she rejects community through the violence of 'non-address', her refusal to participate, her exile from reality.

Her ethics of choice – that she chooses destruction, powerlessness, fascination.

Her narcissistic self-enclosure – that she embraces a technology of alienation, forgetting, and denial, and that by doing so she reveals nature's insufficiency in the face of pain.

Her libidinal economy – that her autonomy, 'like the charm of the cat', is a social menace – that her pleasure is taken in an illusion, an experience without truth.

Her compulsion to repeat – that the structure of addiction is that of seduction and non-satisfaction, the illicit, promiscuous cycle renewed every day.

Her incorporation of violence – that she willingly injects the foreign into her body, interiorizing the alien, embracing contagion, self-medicating.

Her impenetrable irresponsibility – that she is de-socialized, that 'no single word of the addicted subject is reliable, and therefore [s]he escapes analysis altogether'.

What do we hold against the drug addict?

That she releases uncontrolled signs of impurity, corruption, and contamination, into the public sphere – that in her there is no distinction between need and desire – that no one is safe.

'In prison, THESE BODIES become state property. There are punishments for damaging or crippling that property.

These bodies are poorly maintained and assimilated into an economic system.

The silent witnesses to this process are the products that Daniel uses in Undoing Time.

Beverly Henry, one of the characters in a video in the work, stitched these flags in prison for 55 cents per hour.

This new economy of the prison as a sweatshop (it has a name: the "prison industrial complex")

has resulted in an increased demand for prisoners, for bodies without rights –

easily made into cheap labor."[12]

'Like Betsy Ross, I sew American flags. But I do my work for 55 cents an hour in an assembly line inside one of the largest women's prisons in the world. I was sentenced to prison for 15 years after being convicted of selling $20 worth of heroin to an undercover cop. I sew flags to buy toiletries and food.

From the time I was a little girl, I was taught to put my hand over my heart when pledging allegiance to the flag. I emphatically believed in the values of independence, freedom and equality the flag represents. But as time went on and I grew older, I learned that these values do not apply equally to all Americans. As a black girl, I attended segregated schools without enough resources to provide a quality education. As an adult, I struggled continuously with drug addiction, but there were no resources available for me to get help. Instead, I was sent to prison. My experience resonates with the historical reality for black people. We always have had unequal access to resources that would have allowed us to provide for our families and make our communities prosper. Nearly one-fourth of all black folks in America live below the poverty line, twice the national average. America has become a country that imprisons those it fails, blaming poverty, drug addiction or homelessness on individuals rather than recognizing and addressing the conditions that give rise to them. And we, as Americans, pledge allegiance to the flag I sew, dedicating ourselves to "one nation, under God, indivisible, with liberty and justice for all". To honor this flag at the start of this year, we must resolve to make America a country where all people can thrive.' by Beverly Henry [13]

'ALL THESE BODIES *move and make other bodies move. They not only stimulate an economy, they generate migrations.*

ALL THESE BODIES *function through exchange and becoming other. They insist on understanding the incomprehensible. You cannot understand everything, but each bit, every small piece of a story brings you a step closer to the other. You cannot know everything: Daniel's interfaces seem to be created to get lost in and to explore. A complete overview is impossible. What remains are small overviews, a collection of personal stories...*

PUBLIC SECRETS IS CONSTRUCTED AROUND DICHOTOMIES...

public secret and utopia, human and bare life, inside and outside – that slowly dissolve, as misleading as they are interchangeable. Along the way, it becomes clear that in every piece of utopia, there also hides a public secret. In every human life, there is also a bare life, and in every inside, there is also an outside. The one cannot do without the other. The one cannot escape the other.

THIS LEADS TO THE UNAVOIDABLE CONCLUSION IN EACH OF THESE WORKS: WE ARE ALL PRISONERS (OF CAPITALISM). WE ARE ALL ADDICTS (AS CONSUMERS).

Every desire remains unachievable; the prisoner within yourself is frightened of the freedom that possibly awaits; the addict does not desire to get high, but desires the needle, the promise of getting high; as a consumer, you do not so much want to possess, but to desire. Each desire achieved extends the frontier of that same desire.

*These works embody our inability to understand. Instead, they call on feeling. A feeling of recognition: of the addict, the prisoner, the offender, the victim, the mediator in yourself. The introduction of feeling, of recognition, goes through the self. This is the power of the personal reflections on prison and drug users that Daniel makes part of her work. Herein also lies the power of her reference to the insulin injection that her father, as a diabetic, gives himself twice a day in order to survive. That is his drug, the drug with which his daughter has learned to live.'[14]

I met Beverly Henry at the Central California Women's Facility [CCWF] in 2001. Through many years of her incarceration Beverly worked for the Prison Industry authority in a textile factory that produces United States flags. Over the years that I visited CCWF I recorded many conversations with Beverly. Her voice is heard throughout Public Secrets - and the history of her struggle with addiction, is one of the most powerful accounts of the causal relations between poverty, addiction and incarceration I have heard. Beverly spent 40 years locked inside California state prisons. Like more than 70 percent of women in prison in California, she served all of this time for nonviolent, drug-related offenses.

PERSPECTIVE

'THERE IS NO "REAL WORLD" THAT FUNCTIONS AS THE OUTSIDE OF ART... THERE IS NO "REAL WORLD". INSTEAD, THERE ARE DEFINITE CONFIGURATIONS OF WHAT IS GIVEN AS OUR REAL, AS THE OBJECT OF OUR PERCEPTIONS AND THE FIELD OF OUR INTERVENTIONS. THE REAL ALWAYS IS A MATTER OF CONSTRUCTION, A MATTER OF "FICTION"...'[15]

An interview is a performance of something true but not necessarily or always factual. It takes flight, lands somewhere between emotional truth and constructed memory, is always inflected by the context of the interlocution and the potential for misrecognition.

I don't assume that the men and women who allowed me to record our conversations at the needle exchange and in the prison, offered natural, objective descriptions of an unambiguous reality. An interview is always an affective encounter.

The definition of 'affect' includes, 'assume' and 'pretend'. The interview is a 'fiction', as articulated by Rancière, – not the opposite of 'real' but a reframing of the 'real' – a way of 'building new relationships between reality and appearance, the individual and the collective'.[16]

The personal narratives of those trapped in poverty and addiction are a very particular form of 'fiction' in this sense. They resist translation into rational linear form – they loop and repeat – they are both horrifically compelling in their individual accounts of personal tragedy and astonishingly similar across the board.

Addict's stories, especially, can be frustrating and incomprehensible. This is part of the nature of the disease. Their historical trajectories aren't logical. They don't advance in a traditional narrative arc or resolve in a satisfying conclusion. To understand and empathize, to hear and accept, a listener must be moved beyond the logic of cause and effect and into the realm of affect. Taking affect and 'fiction' seriously may be the point where 'real' 'politics' begins.

'INSIDE THE DISTANCE

begins in Leuven – far away from Henry's California. Here Daniel works with the mediators, university criminologists, the staff of the Suggnomè mediation service, and the police who work with offenders and victims.

Back in California, she continues her work with actors who perform the various roles from her conversations in Leuven.

Now and then, we see the mediators from the videos in Inside the Distance. But the roles of the victims and the offenders (and in many cases the mediators as well) are assumed here by the actors. This reenactment is important. It once again leads to that interchangeability of views. Everyone can play the role of the offender, the victim, and the mediator. We are all accomplices. There is no outside to this network of connections.'[17]

The conversation takes place across a table.

Victim and offender gauge the distance over which they face each other: the dimensions are not fixed – a span (of time), an expanse (of space) – reach, withdrawal, restraint.

Crime is a social phenomenon – conflicts, estrangements, violations, at once, create distance and proximity.

After the trial, the conflict is over – or so it appears at a distance – but not for the victim or for the offender. The act, the crime, brought them into a relationship that is, as yet unresolved. They each have questions – Why me? What have I done? What actually happened? How did I react? Who am I in this case?

Paradoxically, they need each other's help to find the answers.

In boxing 'the distance' refers to the scheduled length of a fight, nine rounds, twelve, for the boxer, as for all of us, the goal is to stay standing, to win, inside the distance.

In the space of mediation 'the distance' is materialized in the length of a table – the time of a meeting. This encounter becomes a kind of reenactment – not a reconciliation but a reconsideration of a fact.

They recall the event, rehearse it's details measure the intervals, the gaps – struggle to revise the plot – to remember who they were and recognize what they have now become.

After all, at some level, at some moment –
we are all victims, we are all offenders.

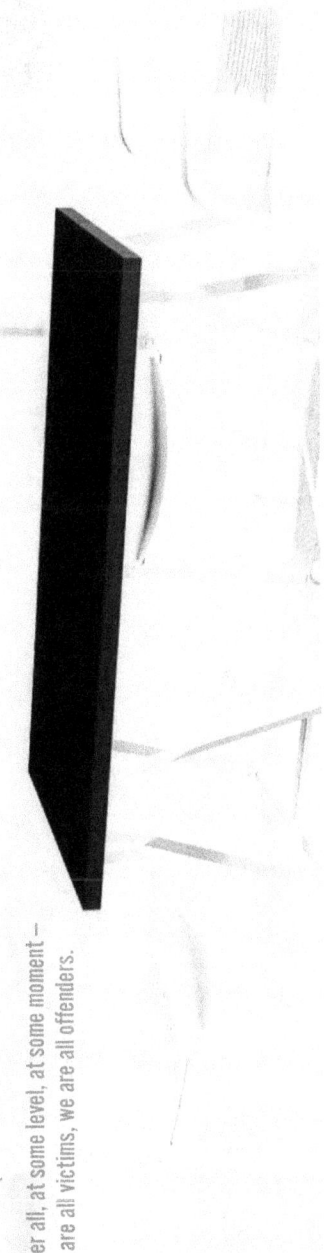

This is where the character of* BEVERLY HENRY *reappears.

She is the shadow behind the actors who play the different roles and effectively change places as they do. She is the drug user who becomes the prisoner who becomes the mediator, and ultimately becomes an actress. But it never gets really clear who the offender actually is. Is it herself (she who injects her own drugs: is that her crime)? Is it her boyfriend (who introduced her to drugs: does that make her a victim)? Is it the state (that makes using drugs a crime to be punished and not an illness to be cured)? It is this aporia, this undecidedness, that each of these works confronts us with, time and again. And it is to these questions that Daniel forces us, time and again, to formulate answers of our own."[8]

Notes

1. Ben Davis, 'RANCIÈRE for Dummies', Artnet Magazine, <http://www.artnet.com/magazineus/books/davis/davis8-17-06.asp> (last accessed 3 May 2017).
2. Kimberlé Crenshaw, 'Mapping the margins: intersectionality, identity politics, and violence against women of color', Stanford Law Review 43, no. 6, 1991, pp. 1241–99.
3. Chimamanda Adichie, 'The danger of a single story', transcript of TED Talk, <https://www.ted.com/talks/chimamanda_adichie_the_danger_of_a_single_story/transcript?language=en>, 2009 (last accessed 3 May 2017).s
4. Gail Vanstone, 'Scriptrix narrans: digital documentary storytelling's radical potential', conference paper given at Visible Evidence XXIII, 11 August 2016.
5. Peter Van Bogaert, 'Public secrets and a secret public', in Art and Social Justice: Inside the Distance (Ghent: Grafische Cel, 2014).
6. Ibid.
7. Ibid.
8. Van Bogaert, 'Public secrets and a secret public'.
9. Catherine A. MacKinnon, Are Women Human?: And Other International Dialogues (Cambridge, MA: Harvard University Press, 2006).
10. Van Bogaert, 'Public secrets and a secret public'.
11. Marek Kohn, Narcomania: On Heroin (London: Faber and Faber, 1987).
12. Van Bogaert, 'Public secrets and a secret public'.
13. Text of Op-ed written by Beverly Henry for publication on the 254th anniversary of the birth of Betsy Ross.
14. Van Bogaert, 'Public secrets and a secret public'.
15. Rancière, Jacques, Dissensus: On Politics and Aesthetics, trans. S. Corcoran (London: Bloomsbury Academic, [2010] 2015).
16. Ibid.
17. Van Bogaert, 'Public secrets and a secret public'.
18. Ibid.

INTERVIEW: 'THE FINAL PROJECTS OF HANNAH WILKE AND JO SPENCE' – A DIALOGUE BETWEEN ELENA CRIPPA AND ANNA BACKMAN ROGERS

ABR: In their projects, *Intra-Venus*, *The Picture of Health* and *The Final Project*, Hannah Wilke and Jo Spence respectively turned the camera on their own vulnerable and dying bodies. Wilke in particular was plagued with the accusation of narcissism throughout her career. In your view, is this a critique that is frequently levelled at women who self-document and to what extent do you think the work of Wilke and Spence counteracts or confronts this reading of their work? Both artists seem to be profoundly aware of the gaze and how they, as photographic subjects, might be read by an observer.

EC: Both Spence and Wilke were well aware that in any given context men and women are social actors, reproducing or defying learned and accepted behaviour and accepted typologies to do with gender. They both used performance in order to embody and produce images that challenged conventions on the role, tasks and demeanour that women should themselves perform in order to be socially acceptable. They both turned their camera towards themselves, for all or most of their adult life and career. However, Spence's way of holding her body and performing her sexuality, as she analyses in *Beyond the Family Album*, reflected both her insecurities – her feelings that she lacked beauty, that her breasts were too large, as well as her ongoing poor health – and her desire to understand one's image and self-image in relation to the 'invisible class and power relationships into which we are structured from birth'.[1] Spence's work was not readily susceptible to accusations of narcissism. On the other hand, Wilke's work, from sculpture to performance, was richly tactile (about the folding and unfolding of forms), gestural and sensuous. She was aware of her beauty and performed an erotic, self-empowered woman. She exposed her lived desire and pleasure by focusing not so much on the image of the body – as in the case of Spence – but on its way of being and unfolding, comfortable with itself. What seems to be truly transgressed in Wilke's performance and depiction of her self is that it says I am comfortable if not in love with myself.

As a viewer I personally feel empowered by it. Whatever the origin of the criticism of those who accused Wilke of narcissism,[2] it is problematic on at least two levels. It relies on assumptions about the way in which women can or cannot behave and, as such, they are prescriptive and constrictive – if not fascist, as Wilke stated. Equally if not more importantly, for all that Wilke (or Spence, for that matter), may have said about the relationship between their life and work, these accusations completely fail to realise that what these artists produced is art, not reality. This is a recurrent problem in the discussion of political and feminist art. In these works, the artist might use her body in order to propose, chastise, play with or make fun of particular ways of being and engaging with reality, but they are still artworks, not life.

ABR: Indeed there is a consistent assumption, at the heart of which is a misogynist agenda, that a woman is too close or approximate with her own body to be able to analyse, critique or say anything about herself. In fact, it strikes me that there is a great deal of resonance between responses levelled at Wilke in particular and the denigration or castigation of self and body that so many young women receive online – I am thinking specifically of social media platforms such as Instagram and how some people seem to take this as an invitation to criticise and denounce the bodies of young women. I am still not convinced that there is a political ethos to phenomena such as the selfie, for instance (although Amalia Ulman has, of course, created some fascinating work in this regard in her 'Excellences and Perfections' project), because I do not feel this element of 'performance' is at work or manifest in most instances. For me, the political component is vital to both the projects of Wilke and Spence. These last projects that centre on illness seem in particular to be about subjectivity in (de)formation. Do you agree?

EC: Both Spence and Wilke's work is consistently feminist because it focuses on sex and gender and performance and is motivated by a desire for progressive change in the way women feel able to appear and behave and in the way they are judged as a result of it. When it comes to Spence's *The Final Project* and Wilke's *Intra-Venus*, there is a sense they move 'inwards', that the images they produce are less readily social critiques. And in a way they are so – and for good reasons. Both artists were progressively weakened by their illness and had to spend considerably more time looking after themselves than engaging in broader socio-political issues. If we can say that political work is such because it is socially concerned, are their last works still so, or are they more akin to self-healing and self-preservation? I feel strongly that they remain socially concerned, and this is very simply because the work was from the beginning, or from a certain point through its making, conceived for public display, to be shared with others. It seems to me that in these works the feminist mantra whereby the personal is political is, if anything, enhanced. This is because with these projects the two artists decided to make public and share what remained a taboo in respect to what aspects of one's personal art should or could be made public: illness and death.

Nonetheless, in relation to your notion of subjectivity in (de)formation (if I understand this correctly), the works of both artists are rather different. In the case of Wilke's *Intra-Venus*, and particularly the tapes, there is a clear sense of documenting the process of change, mutilation and loss undergone by the body through illness and therapy. The comparative view of tapes from different stages in the development of the illness and at different moments in the artist's life allow one to distinguish the person from the illness and yet reconcile them. Similarly, through the diverse way in which she portrays herself in photography, Wilke defies monolithic ways of presenting and self-representing oneself when ill – as stoically accepting and fighting the illness, or passively surrendering to it. For me this is political in a way that is consistent with her previous work – the artist is imaginatively playing with a received notion of the way in which one has to perform for society. To me there is a strange, if inverted correlation with her earlier 'S.O.S' series – here the body was young and healthy, and yet – in the process of its public display and consumption – it was scarred, or in any case dramatically marked.

In the case of Spence's *The Picture of Health* project, the work aims to address the way in which the health system dispossesses patients of their body and choice, and is a call to regain agency in the treatment of one's own physicality and wellbeing. Things changed with her later, terminal illness, leukaemia, which for the artist represented the ultimate crisis of self-representation. As Anne Boyer has recently pointed out, this is largely because of the difficulties of representing illness 'without reproducing the reductive heroics or violent sentimentalities attached to sickness'.[3] In *The Final Project*, she responded to this crisis not by representing her debilitated body but by creating images that adopted masks, skeletons and still life as its subjects, or rendering an already dematerialising body, floating in a pool. After having deconstructed identity (the self as the product of class and power relationships), and after having explored the complex plurality of one's subjectivity through phototherapy, *The Final Project* seems to let go of the very core of Spence's practice – her self and its representation – and indeed be concerned with the dissolution (rather than deformation) of the self. There is no flesh, no visible illness, no deformed or deforming body.

ABR: In fact, I was very struck by the superimposition of the body onto nature in Spence's final project – almost as if this is not merely about a process of depersonalisation, but also a complete levelling out. That is interesting to me – that she spent her career examining the ways in which gender and class intersect as a relation of power and ended her career with a work that centres on death as that which delivers parity on all bodies. And of course, before this final work she looks at the ways in which the medical system turns people into patients as an act of depersonalisation; yet, whereas there is a defiance to both her earlier work and, I think, to that of Wilke's final project (in which she seems, despite the documentation of her illness, to remain radically herself precisely because her presence is so insistent), there seems to be an acceptance of inevitable disappearance in Spence's final images. They are very poignant indeed – almost unbearably so.

In this regard, Tamar Tembeck has suggested that these kinds of images encompass a 'performative dimension' since the 'pathographic image is tied to its function as a pharmakon'.[4] Would you agree that these projects serve recuperative and healing functions even as they address terminal illness? Might self-documentation/authorship (or autopathography) be seen as a form of control over an incurable illness? Spence in particular spoke of her work as 'phototherapy' and 'activism' and feminists have long viewed, after Audre Lorde, self-care as a radical act.

EC: I think this is probably correct, but in different ways. Wilke was interested in the representation of the flesh and its vividness – and remained so when she became ill. Rather than revulsive, her illness, physical deformation and limitations were developments worth staging, recording and displaying. My mind relates this to her earlier photographs of her younger self and her mother, terminally ill with cancer, and yet portrayed as full of grace – as retaining a vital energy that was saved despite the physical scarring through self-determination but also through relationships of care and love with others, like with her daughter. There is a sense of wanting to preserve one's grace and that this can only happen through nourishment, by oneself as well as others. And in this respect I think that Wilke's (as well as Spence's) collaboration as well as dependence on her partner and friends in order to make these works, as well as look after herself, is key to their quality and our understanding. For Wilke, documenting her body through her illness means affirming that that body continues to deserve love, care and attention. I am not sure this process would give control over an illness, but to me it has an important healing function when it comes to one's psychological journey of acceptance and self-preservation.

The photograph in which Spence appears bare-chested, with tinted glasses and the writing above breast: 'Property of Jo Spence?' is a declaration of control over the health system, rather than control over the illness. After having opted out of orthodox medicine, Spence said that she felt that documenting the changing/deforming condition of her breast helped her come to terms with a reality that she admitted to finding initially shocking and abhorrent. Coming to terms with the illness, accepting one's deteriorating physicality, rather than attempting to control it, is certainly what I see in these pictures. Phototherapy, as I understand what Spence and Rosy Martin did, did not relate so much to Spence's illness, but to a new investigation of the performance of self as multiple and fragmented.

ABR: So, the idea – and act – of self-care is a very powerful one. Wilke does find some kind of aesthetic or artistic redemption in illness and death and I wonder that there is something deeply feminist in this; namely that the stakes are raised when one documents the female body in such a way that defies normative expectations of the 'beautiful female body'. I feel that while Wilke's earlier work displays a profound awareness of the other's gaze, she retains or reclaims her body for herself in this final project. The act of love she extended to her own mother in her illness is here extended towards herself, perhaps? Whereas, as I intimated earlier, Spence's work that centres on illness seems to address the systematic and systemic dehumanisation, or depersonalisation, of the body in illness. As such, her earlier and later work are deeply imbricate because of the manifold ways in which she deconstructs power and explores how power works to create and contain bodies as a disciplinary technology.

I would like to return to the effect of the gaze; we have discussed how the projects of both Wilke and Spence are inherently performative (especially in relation to gender) and it seems to me that what plays out here is a hyperawareness of performing *for* someone – as such, identity comes into being the moment we are *something for someone*. What is the nature of the gaze, both that of the artist and that of the viewer, when we consider these photographs? Does this art have a transformative effect on the gaze? I am thinking, in particular, of Spence's reversal of the 'clinical or medical gaze' and Wilke's studied and determined gaze towards the viewer in her self-portraits. Both Spence and Wilke seem to address the objectification of the medical subject (its reduction to diseased body parts). The persistence of the artist's subjectivity and gaze seem to fight against the body's decline and obliteration and their almost fetishistic framing of scars and wounds seemingly serves to critique the way in which the medical gaze turns a subject into a patient?

EC: I think the three projects you list at the beginning are in this respect rather different. Spence did *The Picture of Health* when she was ill but still had the energy and capacity to engage more broadly with political issues. These are striking self-portraits. Some are very tough images, of self-humiliation and self-deprecation, the crudeness and directness of which served to propose a response that is not of pity. If anything, as Spence acknowledged, there was at least partially a level of self-flagellation. When she realised *The Final Project* Spence was much frailer, explaining that she was barely able to look after herself, let alone address 'big' social issues. The work becomes more about the representation of her perception of dissolution and death. The ill or decaying body is not the focus of it. Wilke's *Intra-Venus* differs from both of Spence's projects.

Some of the photographs from Wilke's *Intra-Venus* and Spence's *The Picture of Health* share a sense of defiance and irreverence in the face of how an ill, mature woman should behave, in the assumption that illness should be hidden and lived with dignity. Some of the pictures of both projects are loud, in your face, and irreverent. Other images from *Intra-Venus* though, as in those where she plays Marilyn Monroe and many others, Wilke's work greatly differs from Spence's in what Nancy Princenthal defines as the life affirming moments of raw beauty. The body ages but not the mind ...

ABR: So, something like the making public of a body that, in terms of 'old-fashioned propriety', we thought should be kept private? The politicisation of the personal and the personalisation of the political.

Notes

1. Jo Spence, *Putting Myself in the Picture, A Political, Personal and Photographic Autobiography* (London: Camden Press, 1986), p. 20.
2. See Joanna Frueh, 'Hannah Wilke', in Thomas H. Kochheiser (ed.), *Hannah Wilke: A Retrospective* (Columbia, MO: University of Missouri Press, 1989), p. 41.
3. Anne Boyer, 'The kind of pictures she would have taken: Jo Spence', *Afterall*, no. 42, Autumn/Winter, 2016.
4. Tamar Tembeck, 'Exposed wounds: the photographic autopathographies of Hannah Wilke and Jo Spence', *Racar* XXXIII, nos 1–2, 2008.

PART TWO

DOCUMENTARY THEORIES

4. THE FEMINIST VOICE: IMPROVISATION IN WOMEN'S AUTOBIOGRAPHICAL FILMMAKING

Gabrielle McNally

Bill Nichols introduces his reader to documentary modes by forewarning that 'definitions of documentary are always playing catch-up' and that these definitions need to be reconsidered regularly.[1] Documentary has never been, and will never be, only one thing; its definition is fluid and always changing. The one consistency in documentary about which Nichols speaks is his concept of 'Voice', the filmmaker's ultimate power over the form of the work. He describes Voice as: 'The selection of shots, the framing of subjects, the juxtaposition of scenes, the mixing of sounds, the use of titles and inter-titles – all the techniques by which a filmmaker speaks from a distinct perspective on a given subject'.[2]

Likewise, this documentary voice also has the power to name – labelling actions, objects, concepts and thoughts, potentially transforming them for the viewer.[3] This correlates with the scientific model: the goal of any human in any interaction with an object – film – should be full intellectual control over that object.[4] Power as subject is enacted through naming, designing and controlling objects.

However, women, who do not find themselves in a position to speak freely, cannot easily adopt this form of Voice as their own. The patriarchal construction of the documentary mode of filmmaking closes meaning for female subjects, particularly those whose goal is self-reflection and autobiography in film form. The history of the female form-as-object on screen and the silencing of women's self-identified experience in the documentary film canon creates a non-space for female autobiographical documentary filmmakers. As philosopher Luce Irigaray states, 'Because woman is considered as either a castrated version of, or compliment to, man, there is no room in patriarchy for her to exist as a subject.'[5] At this point, female filmmakers continue to use the same vocabulary of making as that of the oppressor: one that establishes a relationship of power-to, the ability to perform, and power-over, a freedom contingent on circumstances that women simply do not have.[6] The use of this paternal language separates the relationship of the body from the mind, relegating interaction with the world and subjective meaning and identity to a series of sign systems. Feminist autobiography stands against this cultural construction and questions the authority of single-perspective representations of women.[7] As Audre Lorde states, we can locate revolutionary change in identifying 'that piece of the oppressor which is planted deep within each of us'.[8] Women need to discover and employ a new language which does not necessarily include words but rather a corporeal experience of self and process.

Traditionally understood as an object at which the viewer is intended to gaze, the woman filmed has been 'closed in silence so long/she doesn't know the sound of her own voice'.[9] The female body does not act but is acted upon. Viola Spolin speaks about the relationship between performance of self and the fear of rejection when presenting the self:

> Having thus to look to others to tell us where we are, who we are, and what is happening results in a serious (almost total) loss of personal experiencing . . . We function with only parts of our total selves.[10]

By 'avoiding the "objectivist" stance', by 'entering [one's] own subjectivity into the research'[11] and by using one's body as a tool for autobiography, including a relationship to the camera as an extension of physicality and performance in front of the lens, women can reconstruct themselves by deconstructing the patriarchal language 'that reduces' them to objects.[12] Through realising this pre-existing bodily knowledge, women can discover their own physical ability and undergo positive change through the improvisational process of autobiographical filmmaking.

Drawing connections between improvisational studies and documentary filmmaking in general has not been formally conducted. The obvious relationship between existing in the moment, going with the flow and other proverbial definitions of documentary and similar theories in improvisation seems almost too simple to expound on. Documentary *is* film's engagement with improvisation. Perhaps the reason is clear – documentary, as Nichols states, is always changing and adapting.[13] Technological advances and content evolution make documentary difficult to define as a process. However, the political agenda of some documentary, particularly that with autobiographical content, already works in a revolutionary manner, similar to the work marginalised groups do in other artistic forms of improvisation. The linking of the documentary process and its inherent improvisational techniques can create a new form, one that exists outside of the well-established, patriarchal documentary system, structure and agenda. Through the organisation of female practitioners and re-appropriation of improvisation, women can 'challenge the world that (sadly) exists' and create a medium outside the purview of capitalism.[14]

Improvisation in the United States developed as a multi-dominant form of both visual and sonic expression out of the African diaspora and is deeply embedded in the history of American race relations.[15] Understandably, the key tenets of improvisation: adaptability and invention, 'are the weapons of the weak'.[16] The labeling of improvisation as a primitive musical practice became an imperialistic tool imposed on black jazz musicians working through polyphony and relationships of power and freedom.[17] This figuring of the black improviser as a con man or trickster was an attempt to devalue improvisation as a method for music-making. However, in African American culture, the trickster 'also embodies survival techniques in the face of the oppressor'.[18] These practices have found their ways into other forms of self-expression including dance, theatre and visual art to be utilised in a similar way: as a means to create with an alternative theory of agency outside of the oppressive Western structure.

Improvisation as a black invention was appropriated by whites and renamed experimental, chance, aleatoric and indeterminate to be used in artistic expression.[19] The whitewashing of improvisation into mainstream America also instigated its transition from a verb, an action, into a noun, a name to call a certain method.[20] The privileging of the noun form of improvisation stagnates the political agency improvisers have for change. By returning improvisation to its original meaning, the *act* of improvising as opposed to its theoretical *product*, marginalised groups, including women, can gain access to the opportunity for action that improvisation provides not outside but 'in dialogue with the Western social system known as patriarchy'.[21] Because *no one* is mindfully practising improvisation in documentary, women improvisers could define the new standards, dispensing with the notion that men control and delineate art practice, allowing the practitioners of improvisation to address their own oppression and develop new means for a revolution of subjectivity.

Revolutionary and political improvisation begins with an *idea*, a structure, something present within the improviser that 'may or may not have been consciously intended'.[22] The act of improvisation refers to spontaneity, risk-taking, the ability – and desire – to change within a structure or set of rules which is itself constantly changing.[23] However, improvisation is more than a social relationship or a dialogue of sharing. The accessibility of improvisation and its ability to build community creates a sense of connectedness among the practitioners and it is within this connectedness and shared power that political change can occur.[24] Improvisation shares many principles with anarchism, part of its political appeal. David M. Bell refers to these four core concepts of anarchism as: freedom and non-dominance; mutuality; difference; prefiguration and open-endedness.[25] By utilising these concepts, artists in other media have found ways in which improvisation can create new opportunities for political and social resistance.

Nietzsche considered improvisation to be the 'pinnacle of pleasure'.[26] Along with the desire to enact political and social change, improvisation can and does implement self-change in the practitioner. Through improvisation, women can become, as Irigaray argues is necessary, 'speaking subjects in their own right'.[27] Improvisation, like self-awareness, is not a form, but rather an ongoing practice. Hungarian psychologist Mihalyi Csikszentmihalyi refers to the state of being in an improvisation as flow. While in flow, women have no active awareness of control and only in reflection on the process do they become aware that their 'skills were adequate for meeting environmental demands', thus leaving them with a 'positive self-concept'.[28] It is through this process that female improvisers might develop a heightened regard for themselves. This pleasure can be just as important and changing as an overt political engagement. Finding self-pleasure outside of the confines of patriarchal structure *is* a political statement, made even more radical when experienced by women and/or people of colour.

Improvisation as a mindful method of self-expression in documentary film would function as a potentially radical form of alternative community formation and resistance to pre-existing structures in filmmaking. Many of the improvisational forms in jazz, avant-garde theatre, and dance could easily be adapted by feminist filmmakers. As such, improvisation is useful as a tool for individuals that have little or no access to material resources and education.

Many theorists have already discussed the relationship between political revolution and collective musical improvisation found in jazz. No one musician leads the collective, the individual musicians perform by their own accord and with different intentions, and the results of the performance are thus entirely open-ended. Jazz traditionalist and trumpeter Wynton Marsalis proclaims: 'Jazz is music of conversation, and that's what you need in a democracy. You have to be willing to hear another person's point of view and respond to it.'[29] Rebecca Solnit adds that jazz is 'a mode of being in the world ... suspicious of either/or viewpoints'.[30] Through a mindful use of improvisation, feminist filmmakers could develop filmmaking collectives and collaborations as a practice of anarchy, working together outside of the capitalist, patriarchal system.

Improvisation also has a rich and well-documented history in avant-garde theatre and dance. In direct opposition to the standard hierarchical structure of commercial theatre, feminist and minority groups instead share collective responsibility for decisions, script development, and leadership roles behind the scenes.[31] By challenging the imposed structure and processes of established, mainstream repertoires, utilising improvisation functions as a political action of collective agency. Improvised performance of females in theatre can also become political actions and performances of agency.[32] Women working in autobiographical documentary, and the performance of self, particularly, could employ these working methods.

The dance form Movement Improvisation (MI) is rooted in concepts of bodily agency and possible alternatives to the theories of individual and collective agency.[33] MI works against the notions of pre-established choreography and instead relies on the relationships and dialogues between individual dancers and dance in order for the choreography to evolve over time. At its inception in the 1960s to 1970s, Contact Improvisation, one form of MI, focused on the body's ability – regardless of gender – to be both strong and sensitive simultaneously and, through interaction with other bodies, develop a new language in the moment to express the multiple subjectivities of the dancers. As the form entered the 1990s, 'the content of the dance tended toward explicitly stated politics of identity, in terms of gender, sexual preference, race, and ethnicity'.[34] Including both implicit and explicit political action, autobiographical filmmakers, through partnering with other people and also the equipment as bodily extension, have many tools for political statements at their disposal.

Marginalised voices disappear when the documentary canon valorises the auteur model: the subject/filmmaker in control of the situation telling the audience what to know and think. This also speaks to the notion of patriarchal (and auteuristic) notions of ethnography. 'Having thus to look to others to tell us where we are, who we are, and what is happening results in a serious (almost total) loss of personal experiencing.'[35] Bill Nichols argues that what we need instead is 'History from Below'.[36] Nichols continues, 'Karl Marx once said, "They [the working class] cannot represent themselves, they must be represented."' This is a statement to which much documentary film and video production by those who have been the presumed victims of the documentary tradition – women, ethnic minorities, gays and lesbians, people from the developing countries – gives the lie.[37] Yet, the minorities Nichols lists are usually relegated to one or two chapters in film theory and history textbooks. Marginalised, colonised and other oppressed individuals need a working method that falls outside of the traditions of documentary storytelling. The current model only furthers the oppression.

Because freedom and power are mutually exclusive – one must have power in order to be free and vice versa, female documentary autobiographers struggle to engage their domination over the film form. Irigaray argues that the only power women have accessed historically is through maternal care.[38] Relating this concept to Voice, the supposed power over children can be understood similarly to the supposed power over film form: decisions made change and alter the child/film for better or for worse. This relegated feminine power creates a struggle for women in documentary wanting to work outside of its patriarchal structure. In order for women to have any sense of power or control, that control must be of a different kind than that which Nichols defines. Improvisation allows for the circulation of power through collective actions as a redefinition of the notion of hierarchy in the making of documentary film, allowing for multiple perspectives, iterations and themes. Improvisation and the interaction between filmmaker and other redefines relations of power to become a 'point of counter-identification against systems of control, hierarchy and subordination'.[39] Through improvisation, feminist filmmakers can create an ecology of knowledges that breaks down the notion of a singular Grand Narrative.

Autobiographical documentary provides the experience of history from below – displaying 'what one person might experience and what it might feel like to undergo that experience'.[40] This notion is familiar to marginalised artists as many tire of hearing others speak for them (or not about them at all) and the opportunity to speak for oneself from an emic viewpoint can become an action of agency. However, at this point, the Voice and language used has still been that of the patriarchal establishment. Women and other minorities have struggled to find a location for their Voices that reads differently. Instead, these filmmakers need to 'appropriate and subvert [the] language'.[41] As Nathanial Mackey states, 'A revolution of the word can only be a beginning. It initiates a break while remaining overshadowed by the conditions it seeks to go beyond.'[42] Mackey is speaking specifically about re-appropriating words indicating colonialism in Caribbean folk culture, but the same idea applies: through a denial of Voice and subjective centring, female autobiographical filmmakers can create a new language, one that prioritises process over mastering and naming.

To think verbally instead of subjectively or objectively creates a new space in which the process can take precedence. Documentary *making* is a process that includes an agent of action, the filmmaker. The word *film*, normally indicating a complete, recorded product, returns to its verb form – *to film*. Considering this in relationship to improvised music, the performance of the improvisation in the present is merely recorded for future reflection. Like music, the meaning of film 'lies in its doing'.[43] The relationship shifts between the active and passive Voices to a centred Voice in which the focus lies on the subject and the verb as opposed to the subject and the object. Instead of a filmmaker creating a film, the filmmaker and the film work together. The filmmaker is not the subject but rather the agent of the action. By shifting focus from the documentary *record* ('rekərd; noun: indicating evidence, something written down) to *record* (rə'kôrd; verb: repeat, to commit to memory), one creates a medial position. Improvisation in autobiographical filmmaking moves the process even more toward the relationship of the agent to the film.

Hans-Georg Gadamer, in writing about hermeneutics, defines this medial position as middle-voiced-ness, a process through which a dialogic engagement with various other subject/objects occurs, an incredibly applicable concept in the making of feminist autobiographical film. To dialogue is middle-voiced; it indicates neither a subject nor an object but rather a process. This concept is heavily theorised in documentary, but by use of a different language. Nichols writes about the observational, participatory and performative modes of documentary, in which the filmmaker's interactions with the film's subjects become more direct, personal and complex.[44] In this case, Nichols refers primarily to social actors, the individuals with whom a filmmaker engages in front of the camera.

The primary social encounter in documentary, the interview, can easily become a relationship based on domination in which the filmmaker/subject interrogates the interviewee/object. Approaching the interview instead through a middle-voiced dialogue creates a space in which both individuals are constructed as Others and through the process, both dialoguing and listening occurs from both parties. This ability to speak and listen, call and respond, directly relates to improvisational forms in music, theatre and dance. To call/respond in an interview setting continually puts the filmmaker/agent into question and allows the process to shape and be shaped by the relationship.[45] By embracing improvisation, 'new, unexpected and productive cocreative relations [can develop] among people in real time ... promoting a culture of collective responsibility, dispersed authority, and self-active democracy'.[46] As a practitioner of Movement Improvisation, Kent De Spain refers to this as a transpersonal encounter: 'not the personal, nor the interpersonal, but that which is beyond either of those categories'.[47] By Othering the self *and* the social actor, both individuals can feel that they belong and have something to contribute to their shared experience.

Middle-voiced-ness challenges the language used by the oppressor in that every noun is either subject or object, in which case women predominantly find themselves as objects. By focusing on the verb, women can resist becoming objects but are also not attempting to define themselves in terms of the patriarchal dichotomy of subject/object and active/passive meaning making. Instead the process allows female filmmakers to ask questions and attempt to understand themselves and their locality. De Spain states:

> Once you enter the state [of improvisational attention], things happen for you faster than you can think them. My consciousness rides along with the action, as opposed to directing it from a position of power ... My 'mind' is interactional without being dictatorial.[48]

The agent is 'within [her] actions, yet without being passive'.[49] This method instills female autobiographers with mediality and creates a space in which they can engage with their film without the deterministic sense of mastering the film form in order to set forth their own identity. The idea of *being* indicates something static: a fixed permanent state. Instead, the improvisational process calls for a renewed awareness that *to be* is actually a verb and a process.[50] This connects to the feminist idea that identity, particularly gender identity, is neither fixed nor completely in flux.[51] Keith Sawyer states that in group musical performance, the key characteristics are improvisation, collaboration, and *emergence* (my emphasis).[52] Through this enacting of self-transformation, women documentary autobiographers Other themselves willingly, identifying their self as a verb instead of a noun.

Much of the empowerment and self-transformation that occurs in the process of improvisation comes from the improviser's embracing of risk and failure, vulnerability and trust. The approach to improvisation is, as Csikszentmihalyi indicates, the result of 'pure involvement' without any considerations or concerns about the results.[53] In the process, the filmmaker would submit control, not act, but also not be acted upon. Susan Leigh Foster eloquently describes this non-active/non-passive voicing as 'shit happens'.[54] This level of vulnerability entails a responsibility to the self as well as the other. This vulnerable-making and risk-taking creates change within the improviser. Through the risk, one can recognise their former way of thinking as particular to the self, relating greatly to Gadamer's expansion of horizons in which improvisers are made aware of their individual perspective as differing from another's.[55] When a woman has the opportunity to teach herself through a moment of vulnerability, the agency she identifies in herself is itself a political action.

A binary exists in documentary filmmaking that indicates the high regard with which the documentary tradition upholds the *auteur* and denounces the collaboration. It is instinctive to consider the film director an auteur, leader, and to attribute group creativity to a single person's genius.[56] Instead of looking at the relationship between the auteur and collaboration as a binary, one should view it as a spectrum on which improvisation also resides. In autobiographical improvisation, a *facilitator*, not auteur, creates a structure in which the improvisation and collaboration will take place. Kent De Spain describes the feeling of being in the moment during a facilitated collaboration: 'Sometimes I am acting, sometimes I am responding, and sometimes I am being acted upon – and it reveals so much about how we interact with the world around us.'[57] Through this dialogism and poly-vocality, the agent of the film becomes a part of a larger dialogue and relinquishes control to the process.

Film itself is a relational medium; everything happens through relationships and collaboration. The autobiographical improvisation is a site of negotiation and interaction from improviser to improviser as everyone involved undergoes the same process of potential growth and change. As Fischlin argues, in improvisation 'the key to the self is found through how it encounters difference'.[58] Viola Spolin discusses the issues with the leader/group dynamic in improvisatory theatre practices:

> A healthy group relationship demands a number of individuals working interdependently to complete a given project with full individual participation and personal contribution. If one person dominates, the other members have little growth or pleasure in the activity; a true group relationship does not exist.[59]

This can easily be equated to the documentary film crew. The director/agent of documentary film should neither lead nor follow but instead move with the other individuals working through the same process, offering opportunity and structure for collaborators to explore and fail or succeed.

It is through the 'incessant confrontation with *now* that leads to the "naked intimacy" of intense communication' that is necessary to evoke personal or political change.[60] This form of conversation has its place in many modes of artistic improvisation including call/response jazz form and situation/response choreography. To engage on this level of dialogue, one must look beyond one's individual horizon and become a part of a fusion of horizons, as defined by Hans-Georg Gadamer. One's own horizon is established by a 'historically-determined situated-ness' and one's ability to look beyond it depends on many factors, particularly persistent forms of domination in society.[61] The ability to fuse horizons and interpret the Other, develops a new language, one that is created by both engaged parties.[62] By reaching out to the Other, female autobiographical filmmakers undergo an identity shift which is always expanding outward. This shifting and merging, call and response, can be most easily ascribed to a situation in which a female autobiographer surprises herself by filming something unintended. With this new knowledge, the filmmaker has learned, grown, and can try to recreate the dialogue with film again in other ways. Likewise, dialogic engagement with social actors or other crew members may force the filmmaker to uncover some new, unintended truth.

Documentary filmmaking has colonised the filmmaker. Much like ballet may colonise the dancer's body in which techniques impose a set of strict and often dysfunctional rules and behaviours on movement, technique training can also limit or curtail possibilities for expression and creativity.[63] This is a technocratic age in which technical ability, production value and aesthetics control filmmakers' options for festival acceptance, distribution and positive reaction. Instead of making film solely out of enjoyment or need, Susan Leigh Foster states that most contemporary artists are making work that:

only enhances the growth of capital and the all-consuming power of the state. In these models, all individual choices merely maintain the appearance of independence. On closer scrutiny, however, the structuring of individual initiatives reveals their prior co-optation by governmental or capitalist channels through which power exercises its control.[64]

Instead, we must discover a new language, one that does not replace the documentary encounter with the technological understanding needed to record it.

Improvisation is more concerned with social and political matters than aesthetic ones. In a way, the quality of the image – or lack thereof – makes the documentation of the process appear more genuine.[65] The pursuit of perfection can affect the improviser's ability to engage in the present moment.[66] The improvisational relationship between the filmmaker/agent and the camera calls for feminist documentarists to unlearn conventional techniques and discard codified procedures. This provides an opportunity for those not immersed in the technology to begin its utilisation, democratising the form by allowing its use by unskilled practitioners. Much like the technological developments that occurred during the establishment of *cinéma-vérité* and kino-eye theory, the filmmaker/agent uses the camera with the possibility of 'making the invisible visible, the unclear clear, the hidden manifest . . . making falsehood into truth'.[67] *Cinéma-vérité* supposedly tells the truth because of the type of equipment used: light, portable, consumer-friendly and inexpensive. Easy-to-use, consumer-friendly cameras allow for the action more easily to merge with awareness inside the process. 'Flow seems to occur when tasks are within one's ability to perform.'[68] By focusing on the exchange between the filmmaker/agent and the film itself, both the film and the improviser are put into question and create a dialogue of embodied agency and documentation of political action.

The improvised film product is the documentation of an interchange between the filmmaker and the film that relates directly to ideas of dialoguing: neither is the same coming out as they were going in.[69] By having a document of embodiment, one can refer back to the improvisational process. In the stopping and retrospection, conveniently recorded by the camera, one can observe how much the world has changed because of the encounter.[70] Gadamer states, 'The work of art is the expression of a truth that cannot be reduced to what its creator actually thought in it.'[71] To address this, one needs to consider the true function of the documentary form. As William D. Routt questions, is the experience of documentary the experience of an *attempt* at truth (my emphasis)?[72] Documentaries cannot be *about* truth but are themselves a subjective truth of experience for the filmmaker. The truth is in the process, not in the final film form.

During editing, the manipulations of improvised autobiographical film, liveness becomes fixed much like the contested recordings of live improvisational music performances. The commodification of improvisational records feeds into the capitalist ideas of production and distribution,[73] a situation 'inherently at odds with improvisational narratives of experiment and autonomy'.[74] Instead, the composition of a document, the process of selectively storing and organising information accumulated from the process of improvisation allows for both the filmmaker/agent and the viewer to move beyond the autobiographical ideas present within the piece without having to reinvent the form with every encounter.[75] The experience of flow from before the process of improvisation, through the process, and into the composition of the final record all indicate part of the same process in which the dialogue between the filmmaker and film continues and both are shaped by and shape each other.

The preservation of the event allows for others outside of the process to engage on some level with the autobiographical material present and to perhaps find their own sense of change, personally or politically. Improvisation has the potential to empower 'those who witness it as well as those who perform it'.[76] One must keep in mind the relationship between the process and the result as a continuation of the process and a way for the process to be experienced by those outside of the original encounter. The true goal of *cinéma-vérité*, Routt explains, was to utilise technology in 'order to tell a truth which the human senses alone could not attain'.[77] The experience as an ongoing process challenges the typical understanding of documentary as static knowledge. Three stories intertwine in every documentary: the filmmaker's, the film's, and the viewer's.[78] Only by including the viewer's story can the process continue beyond the completion of the documentation/product resulting from the feminist autobiographical improvisation. Although improvisation occurs only in the present, it can affect more lives, particularly the lives of future viewers, through its historical reference. These feminist autobiographical films can become documents of 'hope, resilience, and determination' that exist indefinitely as the record of a moment of agency and political revolution.[79]

By making correlations between improvisation and feminist autobiography, documentary filmmakers can address the potential for new creative methods of self-expression and self-exploration. Improvisation is proven to create a sense of power, agency, and self-worth by incorporating these methods developed in other forms of feminist art practices. Feminist filmmakers can create a new Voice and neutralise the documentary Voice of power and control. No filmmakers are currently using improvisation (or at least writing about it) in the ways mentioned here. This chapter is a call to arms, an invitation to explore new methods of working and to share those findings with the world.

Everything necessary for a successful adoption of improvisation as a method exists relatively inexpensively and is user-friendly. Like the early days of jazz, the improvisation of women's autobiographical filmmaking can utilise simple tools such as cell phone cameras, little to no editing, and free distribution. The mindful use of improvisational filmmaking could find its home in social media; YouTube, Facebook Live, SnapChat and Instagram are forms of distribution and sharing that exist outside of the capitalistic distribution structures of documentary and already function as repositories of History from Below. On these sites, one can find videos of Syrian families evacuating their country, global spectators witnessing terrorism in the streets, and American citizens recording the murder of their loved ones by police – all legitimate examples of improvisational filmmaking, regardless of intent.

Rzewski states, 'The difficulty of living in the present moment is somehow related to the difficulty of creating an egalitarian society.'[80] Improvisation as a working method invites practitioners into a space of community, empowerment and political change. As Fischlin ponders, 'Were people able to mobilize their everyday lives in the momentum, the spirit of dialogue and inquiry, associated with improvised musical performances . . . imagine what could happen.'[81] Through the utilisation of improvisation as a method of feminist autobiographical documentary praxis, filmmakers can take a step in the direction towards a future promising personal growth and both social and political change and define their work outside of standardised, patriarchal means.

Notes

1. B. Nichols, *Introduction to Documentary* (Bloomington, IN: Indiana University Press, 2010), p. 15.
2. Ibid. p. 5.
3. A. Breen, 'Between the covers: feminist, anti-racist, and queer performance art in Australia', in K. Blee and F. W. Twine (eds), *Feminism and Anti-Racism: International Struggles for Justice* (New York: NYU Press, 2001), p. 164.
4. C. R. Nielsen, 'Hearing the other's voice: how Gadamer's fusion of horizons and open-ended understanding respects the other and puts oneself in question', *Otherness: Essays and Studies*, 4/1, 2013, <http://www.otherness.dk/fileadmin/www.othernessandthearts.org/Publications/Journal_Otherness/Otherness__Essays_and_Studies_4.1/Gadamer_on_Hearing_the_Other_s_Voice.pdf> (last accessed 13 January 2016), p. 5.
5. E. Waterman, 'Naked intimacy: eroticism, improvisation, and gender', *Critical Studies in Improvisation*, 4/2, 2008, p. 2 (last accessed 21 August 2015).
6. D. M. Bell, 'Improvisation as anarchist organization', *Ephemera: Theory and Politics in Organization*, 14/4, 2014, p. 1014.
7. G. Raaberg, 'Beyond fragmentation: collage as feminist strategy in the arts', *Mosaic (Winnipeg)*, 31/3, 1998, p. 11. Available from AcademicOneFile (last accessed 12 July 2015).
8. A. Lorde, *Sister Outsider: Essays and Speeches by Audre Lorde* (Berkeley, CA: Crossing Press, 2007), p. 123.
9. N. Shange, *for colored girls who have considered suicide / when the rainbow is enuf* (New York: Bantam, 1980).
10. V. Spolin, 'Seven aspects of spontaneity', in R. Caines and A. Heble (eds), *The Improvisation Studies Reader: Spontaneous Acts* (London: Routledge, 2015), p. 407.

11. C. Brown, 'Inscribing the Body: Feminist Choreographic Practice', unpublished PhD thesis, University of Surrey, 1994, p. 202.
12. Breen, 'Between the covers', p. 164.
13. Nichols, *Introduction to Documentary*, p. 15.
14. Bell, 'Improvisation as anarchist organization', p. 1026.
15. G. E. Lewis, 'Improvised music after 1950: Afrological and Eurological perspectives', *Black Music Research Journal*, 22 (supplement), 2002, pp. 215–46.
16. D. Fischlin, A. Heble and G. Lipsitz, *The Fierce Urgency of Now* (Durham, NC, and London: Duke University Press, 2013), p. xvi.
17. R. Wallace, 'Writing improvisation into modernism', in R. Caines and A. Heble (eds), *The Improvisation Studies Reader: Spontaneous Acts* (London: Routledge, 2015), p. 188.
18. Ibid. p. 189.
19. Ibid. p. 192.
20. N. Mackey, 'Other: from noun to verb', in R. Caines and A. Heble (eds), *The Improvisation Studies Reader: Spontaneous Acts* (London: Routledge, 2015), p. 245.
21. Waterman, 'Naked intimacy', p. 1.
22. A. Hamilton, 'The aesthetics of imperfection', *Philosophy* 65, 1990, p. 331.
23. Wallace, 'Writing improvisation into modernism', p. 188.
24. S. Banes, 'Spontaneous combustion: notes on dance improvisation from the sixties to the nineties', in R. Caines and A. Heble (eds), *The Improvisation Studies Reader: Spontaneous Acts* (London: Routledge, 2015), p. 134.
25. Bell, 'Improvisation as anarchist organization', p. 1013.
26. G. Peters, *The Philosophy of Improvisation* (Chicago, IL: University of Chicago Press, 2009), p. 141.
27. N. Shor, 'This essentialism which is not one: coming to grips with Irigaray', in A. J. Cahilll and J. L. Hansen (eds), *French Feminists: Critical Evaluations in Cultural Theory* (New York: Routledge, 2008), p. 127.
28. M. Csikszentmihalyi, 'A theoretical model for enjoyment', in R. Caines and A. Heble (eds), *The Improvisation Studies Reader: Spontaneous Acts* (London: Routledge, 2015), p. 155.
29. Matthew Goodheart, 'Jazz and Society: Freedom and Individuality in the Music of Cecil Taylor', unpublished Master's thesis, Mills College, Oakland, CA, 1996, part 1.
30. R. Solnit, *Hope in the Dark: Untold Histories, Wild Possibilities* (New York: Nation, 2004), p. 103.
31. Y. Yarbro-Bejarano, 'Chicanas' experience in collective theatre: ideology and form', in R. Caines and A. Heble (eds), *The Improvisation Studies Reader: Spontaneous Acts* (London: Routledge, 2015), p. 125.
32. J. D. Smith, 'Playing like a girl: the queer laughter of the feminist improving group', in R. Caines and A. Heble (eds), *The Improvisation Studies Reader: Spontaneous Acts* (London: Routledge, 2015), pp. 261–77.
33. S. L. Foster, 'Taken by surprise: improvisation in dance and mind', in R. Caines and A. Heble (eds), *The Improvisation Studies Reader: Spontaneous Acts* (London: Routledge, 2015), p. 402.
34. Banes, 'Spontaneous combustion', p. 138.
35. Spolin, 'Seven aspects of spontaneity', p. 407.
36. Nichols, *Introduction to Documentary*, p. 206.
37. Ibid. p. 215.
38. L. Irigaray and H. V. Wenzel, 'And the one doesn't stir without the other', *Signs*, 7/1, 1981, pp. 60–7.

39. A. Durant, 'Improvisation in the political economy of music', in C. Norris (ed.), *Music and the Politics of Culture* (London: Lawrence and Wishart, 1989), p. 270.
40. Nichols, *Introduction to Documentary*, p. 206.
41. Waterman, 'Naked intimacy', p. 2.
42. Mackey, 'Other: from noun to verb', p. 249.
43. Bell, 'Improvisation as anarchist organization', p. 1011.
44. Nichols, *Introduction to Documentary*, p. 157.
45. Nielsen, 'Hearing the other's voice', p. 1.
46. Fischlin et al., *The Fierce Urgency of Now*, p. 198.
47. K. de Spain, *Landscape of the Now: A Topography of Movement Improvisation* (New York: Oxford University Press, 2014). P. 82.
48. Ibid. p. 168.
49. P. Eberhard, 'The medial age or the present in the middle voice', *International Journal of the Humanities*, 3/8 (2005/2006), p. 125.
50. Ibid. p. 128.
51. Nielsen, 'Hearing the other's voice', p. 10.
52. K. Sawyer, 'Group creativity: musical performance and collaboration', in R. Caines and A. Heble (eds), *The Improvisation Studies Reader: Spontaneous Acts* (London: Routledge, 2015), p. 91.
53. Csikszentmihalyi, 'A theoretical model for enjoyment', p. 154.
54. Foster, 'Taken by surprise: improvisation in dance and mind', p. 402.
55. Nielsen, 'Hearing the other's voice', p. 11.
56. Sawyer, 'Group creativity: musical performance and collaboration', p. 91.
57. De Spain, *Landscape of the Now*, p. 72.
58. Fischlin et al., *The Fierce Urgency of Now*, p. 70.
59. Spolin, 'Seven aspects of spontaneity', p. 408.
60. Waterman, 'Naked intimacy', p. 1.
61. P. Auslander, 'Toward a hermeneutics of performance art documentation', in J. Ekeborg (ed.), *Kunsten A Falle: Lessons in the Art of Falling* (Horten, Norway: Price Museum, 2009), p. 95.
62. Nielsen, 'Hearing the other's voice', p. 15.
63. K. Barbour, *Dancing Across the Page: Narrative and Embodied Ways of Knowing* (Chicago, IL: University of Chicago Press, 2011), p. 73.
64. Foster, 'Taken by surprise: improvisation in dance and mind', p. 402.
65. Auslander, 'Toward a hermeneutics of performance art documentation', p. 93.
66. De Spain, *Landscape of the Now*, p. 84.
67. W. D. Routt, 'The truth of the documentary', *Continuum: The Australian Journal of Media and Culture*, 5/1 (1991), p. 3.
68. Csikszentmihalyi, 'A theoretical model for enjoyment', p. 152.
69. Routt, 'The truth of the documentary', p. 7.
70. T. Etchells, 'Play on: collaboration and process', in R. Caines and A. Heble (eds), *The Improvisation Studies Reader: Spontaneous Acts* (London: Routledge, 2015), p. 431.
71. H. G. Gadamer, 'Aesthetics and Hermeneutics', *Philosophical Hermeneutics*, 104, 1976, p. 1.
72. Routt, 'The truth of the documentary', p. 2.
73. Wallace, 'Writing improvisation into modernism', p. 195.
74. Fischlin et al., *The Fierce Urgency of Now*, p. 134.
75. F. Rzewski, 'Little bangs: a nihilistic theory of improvisation', *Current Musicology*, 67/68, 1999, p. 378.
76. Foster, 'Taken by surprise: improvisation in dance and mind', p. 403.
77. Routt, 'The truth of the documentary', p. 4.

78. Nichols, *Introduction to Documentary*, p. 94.
79. R. Caines and A. Heble, 'Prologue: spontaneous acts', in R. Caines and A. Heble (eds), *The Improvisation Studies Reader: Spontaneous Acts* (London: Routledge, 2015), p. 2.
80. Rzewski, 'Little bangs: a nihilistic theory of improvisation', p. 385.
81. Fischlin et al., *The Fierce Urgency of Now*, p. 202.

5. SPEAKING ABOUT OR SPEAKING NEARBY? DOCUMENTARY PRACTICE AND FEMALE AUTHORSHIP IN THE FILMS OF KIM LONGINOTTO

Rona Murray

Kim Longinotto's female authorship has long been recognised for its engagement with 'transnational feminism' because her films focus on women subjects in a variety of non-Western contexts. Patricia White has specifically identified Longinotto's practice as 'transnational' rather than 'globalising', a recognition still relevant for this analysis of the complexity and struggle of these cross-cultural relationships.[1] This article wishes to explore these ideas further through Longinotto's specific adaptation of the documentary form, returning to these difficulties of speaking 'about' or speaking 'nearby' women situated in other cultures, an idea drawn from the writings of Trinh T. Minh-ha. A particular focus is on how Longinotto's work is uniquely placed in its control of emotion, apparently combining a rallying cry against social oppression while still retaining an affective confessional intimacy. Her films have borne remarkable witness to a wide variety of hidden voices, the witnessing of the 'outsiders or the disenfranchised', according to Belinda Smaill.[2] These include those caught in systems of power, such as the girls undergoing female genital mutilation in Kenya (*The Day I Will Never Forget*, 2002) or women seeking divorce in Iran (*Divorce Iranian Style*, 1998). There are the voices of a community: women working with abused and traumatised children in South Africa (*Rough Aunties*, 2008) or living as men in Japan (*Shinjuku Boys*, 1995). In certain films, women leaders emerge, such as Vera Ngassa, a lawyer prosecuting male and female abusers in Cameroon (*Sisters-in-Law*, 2005) or Indian women's rights campaigner Sampat Pal in *Pink Saris* (2010). Finally, in an unusual American setting, she follows community activist Brenda

Myers-Powell, who works among prostitutes and vulnerable young women in Chicago (*Dreamcatcher*, 2015).

Longinotto's focus on injustice earned her the prestigious BBC Grierson Trustees Award in 2015.[3] The trust characterised her as follows:

> The creator of numerous ground-breaking films which focus on and explore the lives of women across the globe, throughout her career she has consistently given voice to those who have no voice living in some of the world's most repressive and hostile societies.[4]

This prevailing perception of Longinotto's work raises a question about the 'asymmetrical power relations' that Inderpal Grewel and Caren Kaplan recognised as needing persistent scholarly attention.[5] In her expanding *oeuvre*, it is relevant to ask whether Longinotto's mastery of emotion and address works to honour the complexity of her subjects. Chandra Mohanty confronted the failure of First World/Western scholarship to take account of difference and the tendency to produce an 'ethnocentric universalism' in 'certain analyses'.[6] In her film practice, has Longinotto avoided literalising the moment of the white, Western objectifying gaze or, as damaging, constructed a homogenising gaze, appealing to a 'global' form of emotion? This will be the difference between being able to 'speak nearby' her subjects rather than 'speak about' them across the transnational divide.[7]

Longinotto's Career

Longinotto's career, in the Western system of filmmaking and distribution, has been marked by sustained success since the 1970s,[8] including a BAFTA (*Divorce Iranian Style*), Prix Art et Essai at the Cannes Film Festival (*Sisters-in-Law*), the Grand Jury prize for *Rough Aunties*, the Sundance Film Festival directing award (*Dreamcatcher*) and the Special Jury Prize at the Sheffield International Documentary Festival (*Pink Saris*).[9]

Biography can play a significant role in exploring a filmmaker's emotion, even if its tendency to literalise motivation is problematic in relation to film study. Longinotto's extremely repressive childhood and schooling[10] and her experience of gang rape whilst studying filmmaking at the UK's National Film and Television School, can make a context for the character of her stories of oppression. Longinotto consistently resists a victim narrative[11] and focuses on survival and recovery, an increasing focus of contextual publicity. Longinotto's transparency about these experiences reflects her own commitment to the importance of communal and shared witnessing to resist, rightly, unjust feelings of shame.[12] She is the documentary maker who is focused on unsilencing those repressed as an 'honest witness bearer' who knows herself what it is to suffer in silence.[13]

In uncovering hidden histories, Longinotto's documentaries assume a ready pattern for what constitutes a 'woman's picture' or feminist documentary.[14] However, it is her 'craft' as a documentarian which forms the current focus, a form which itself foregrounds ethical questions of speaking for or about others.[15] Longinotto's observational style tells stories as much as compiles histories of women's experiences and the emotions attached to these fictional forms tend to globalise these experiences. Does this act to preserve complexity and to recognise 'asymmetrical power relations'?

Longinotto and the Craft of the Documentary Voice

The form of observational documentary shapes Longinotto's textual voice and comes with its own set of practices and discourses, consistently foregrounding questions of filmmaker impartiality. Mark Cousins identified her as 'amongst the purest of Britain's documentary classicists'[16] and her approach has been likened to the Direct Cinema style of Frederick Wiseman. Her perceived use of 'realist conventions' within observational documentary, rather than the self-reflexive style adopted by many modern documentarians, is seen by Belinda Smaill as enabling Longinotto to collaborate with her subjects, even to demonstrate a 'collusion with particular individuals'.[17]

Before considering the style in more detail, it is important to note that Longinotto's practice is, in fact, the result of several well-established collaborations behind the camera. Operating the camera, she has typically worked with a sound recordist (frequently Mary Milton) and producers, such as Ziba Mir-Hosseini (*Divorce Iranian Style*), Florence Ayisi (*Sisters-in-Law*) and Amber Latif (*Pink Saris*). This small team has helped to characterise the tone of Longinotto's films, of 'narrative intimacy and its emotional connection', according to Sophie Mayer.[18] Patricia White noted how the crew could 'effect their actual shooting by communicating without words', which White saw as imbued with 'female coding' and quoted Longinotto's characterisation of her technique as a '"gentle" way of filmmaking'.[19] Ollie Huddleston, as her male editor, breaks into this all-female production group and it is his right of veto which Longinotto herself credits as a crucial element in the 'craft and art' of her filmmaking.[20]

Observational simplicity and direct emotion arise out of a collaborative craft incorporating fictional conventions. Biography can indicate that Longinotto was always driven by storytelling[21] and Japanese and Iranian filmmakers directly inspired her.[22] Examined in the light of this poetic sensibility, Longinotto's form of observational documentary draws quite overtly on established melodramatic modes in cinema. Her authorial voice, for the purposes of this analysis, is a blend of the generic structures used, both of documentary and of fictional melodrama. In the relationship of subject, filmmaker and the spectator constructed by Longinotto and her collaborators, the nature of those 'repressive' and 'hostile' societies will be demonstrated, via Longinotto's technique, to be closer to home than imagined.

Bill Nichols' work on documentary is useful here, by the way he characterised 'voice' as 'not restricted to any one code or feature, such as a dialogue or spoken commentary'. For Nichols, it was 'akin to that intangible, moiré-like pattern formed by the unique interaction of all of a film's codes'.[23] Giving voice to her subjects' lives will, in Longinotto, be effected through this interaction. Her particular 'moiré-like pattern' is a result of choices regarding sound, camerawork and editing creating a conduit for emotion in Longinotto's construction of a 'human eye' in documentary. Can this hold the complexity of 'transnational feminism' in its emotional address?

The 'Human Eye' and Participant Voices

Part of Longinotto's 'purity' is the screentime and direct address allowed to her participants. Sophie Mayer argued that this shooting style created 'the electrifying sense that we are present in the room' because the filmmakers let the subjects 'speak to each other for a long time, Longinotto's single camera moving between speaker and listener'.[24] In conjunction with this is the emergence of language which communicates the 'human eye' behind the camera. Moving away from conventional biography as a context, this presence is a different, but equally crucial, personalisation of address.

Writing on observational documentary in 1978, Annette Kuhn emphasised the way in which the camera speaks in the 'first person' and identifies itself as 'one man's truth'[25] and demonstrates avowedly 'personal points of view'.[26] In Longinotto, who dispensed quickly with voice-over (used in a limited way in films such as *Divorce Iranian Style*), this 'human eye' emerges in various forms of movement, from the whip-pan to small visual adjustments by the hand-held camera, representing the presence of a personal response to a statement or a change in situation. Editor Ollie Huddleston is instrumental in preserving these gestures. Rather than 'tidying' up a 'messy' (in Longinotto's words) movement, Huddleston likes to leave this movement in, implying that these appeal to him as the first spectator.[27] What this 'messy' style reveals is the camera's tendency to move 'off-centre'. In *Hold Me Tight, Let Me Go* (2007) (set at the Mulberry Bush School in Oxfordshire, England) it is the severely emotionally disturbed children who draw Longinotto's camera, often to the exclusion of their adult carers from the frame. In the action of the long take, the children hold screentime as they articulate their frustrations. Subjects draw her eye or even command camera movement, as in *Runaway* (2001), a film about the

Reyhaneh Centre in Tehran, for young girls who have run away from their families. Setarah, who has been abused but is relentlessly positive, comforts her new friend Parisa and rhapsodises that their future is going to be so much better: 'We're also in the winter of our lives. Listen it will pass and then spring will come.'[28] Longinotto, perhaps at Mir-Hosseini's silent bidding,[29] effects a small instinctive adjustment to the camera to reframe Setarah in this speech, making her central to the frame and giving this young, romantic woman centre stage.

In these shifts and movements of her camera – the readjustment of point of view or the movement off-centre – there is a demonstration of the separation of the camera from the operator. We are no longer watching directly through a 'neutral' gaze; instead we simultaneously watch Longinotto's reaction to Setarah's passion and we respond to *her* emotion as well as her subject's. The resultant relationship – of camera, filmmaker and spectator – is an interesting one for Western spectators. Kuhn characterised the 'space' of Direct Cinema as 'marked out by a particular form of spectator-text relationship which holds the spectator in the same position of observer as the camera operator *and* the camera'.[30] Direct Cinema, as it 'offers its address in the first person', then 'moves that first person between that of the camera operator and that of the spectator'.[31] Longinotto's work shows that there is a variety of effects via this relationship of subject, filmmaker and spectator and this connection across different temporal spaces.

Pink Saris provides a key example of this. A young girl, Rekha, of the Untouchable caste, awaits a decision about her marriage to a boy of higher caste. They have run away together and she is now pregnant, and therefore faces ruin, even death, since he has subsequently abandoned her. In the negotiations, headed by Sampat Pal with the boy's family, this girl has subsisted in the background of the camera shot. As her distress overwhelms her, Longinotto follows her away from the action so that the spectator, too, becomes her ally. Later, the camera 'waits' with Rekha in advance of her wedding ceremony. This silent girl, who has briefly remonstrated regarding her treatment only to be hushed, asks the off-screen documentary crew if she can go away with them, to where they have come from. It is a truly affective moment for the spectator; the tension between observing and participating is communicated. An off-screen voice, presumably producer Amber Latif's, reminds her that it is her wedding day, a statement receiving Rekha's ambivalent shrug.

In that moment, the appeal made to the Western spectator is complex. Could she be 'saved' and taken to a 'modern' and 'liberated' London? At the marriage, presided over by Sampat Pal and attended by her followers, the Gulabi Gang, a feeling of foreboding pervades the action. Rekha refuses to look at her husband during the ceremony and is shot looking offscreen in the concluding marriage 'portrait.' Rather than characterising this young woman as saved

Figure 5 'Can't you take me with you?' Rekha in *Pink Saris* (Ginger Productions/ Vixen Films, 2010).

from disgrace and ruin, Rekha appears now subsumed by the limits of her world. Interestingly, Rekha delivers her above request with a wry smile (Figure 5). There is, arguably, a specific address to the female spectator through this knowing smile, which provides a link to solidarity on equal terms and not the 'liberated-victim' asymmetry expected.[32] Here, perhaps, is a moment encapsulating the complex 'transnational feminism' that Patricia White saw as discoverable in Longinotto's work.

THE 'HUMAN EYE' AND THE 'STAR WITNESS'

Longinotto's human eye thus constructs a variety of spatial relationships to her female 'protagonists'. Longinotto claims a desire for her own disappearance as a subject: 'I want you to forget me, so there is nothing between you [the audience] and them, so it looks like a fiction film.'[33] However, Nichols has expressed a suspicion in relation to the potential, within the purely observational form, for the presence of a strong character – the 'star witness' – to unbalance the documentary 'voice': 'Characters threaten to emerge as stars – flashpoints of inspiring, and imaginary, coherence contradictory to their ostensible status as ordinary people.'[34] Nichols advocates the return to the documentary mode which 'asserts its own voice in contrast to the voices it recruits and observes'.[35]

Longinotto's work demonstrates how variable the relationship between author and subjects can be in practice. Vera Ngassa in *Sisters-in-Law* is uncomplicated as the clear protagonist and heroine.[36] By contrast, Sampat Pal is a more difficult and complex protagonist, whose relationship to the girls she rescues seems often to be as manipulative as it is nurturing. Longinotto and her team follow her around the villages as she adjudicates on cases of domestic violence, marital oppression or young couples who are facing parental opposition to their desire to marry. Sampat Pal has herself broken taboos by her relationship with an educated man of higher caste, being herself of low caste.

Sampat Pal's relationship with the camera can be seen in the context of Longinotto's later film, featuring a less complex character in *Dreamcatcher*. Brenda Myers-Powell has founded the Dreamcatcher Foundation in Chicago, to support young women on the streets, and aims to bring them into forms of recovery and rehabilitation. Myers-Powell is a former prostitute herself. There are marked similarities between these two women. Their commitment to their charges verges on a personal, emotional need: Sampat Pal embraces one, Renu, wiping her tears and pledging to be her mother. In the same way, Myers-Powell breaks down at the thought that a personal, medical operation is going to take her away from 'my girls'. However, in each film a different spatial relationship between Longinotto and the protagonist emerges. Longinotto's camera remains at a distance from Sampat Pal, shot consistently in long or medium long shot as she works. Myers-Powell, however, is embraced with an intimacy throughout; Longinotto's camera follows her into the bathroom and the bedroom where she is looking for 'her hair' – the wig she wanted to wear for that day: 'I felt like that hair – it was fun, it was springy. I'm throwed off.' At the bathroom mirror, Longinotto is close upon Brenda's face as if they are two women sharing their ablutions. It makes perfect sense of Longinotto's ready acknowledgement of her own emotional engagement; she described how seeing Brenda was like 'love at first sight'.[37]

Longinotto's personal emotion[38] constructs a portrait of Brenda that is everyday and intimate. In the power of Brenda's personality onscreen, there arises the 'star witness' that Nichols so distrusted. Longinotto's camera distance seems again to bring in the emotion of the human presence behind the camera. By contrast, her distance from Sampat Pal reflects a possible response to her repeated grandstanding and domination of the diegetic soundtrack. Perhaps Longinotto's 'human eye' cannot 'help' but indicate how much more personally comfortable some forms of feminine leadership are compared to others.

Longinotto and Emotional 'Storytelling'

If these differences in the camerawork make us conscious of the documentarian at all times, Longinotto still moves towards fictional storytelling in the films' structures. The idea of 'aporia'[39] is associated with Hollywood melodrama, a term from Greek tragedy applied by Douglas Sirk retrospectively to his own films, capturing an idea of the unresolvable impasse at their conclusion. For him, 'there is no real solution of the predicament of the people'; a happy ending 'makes the crowd happy' but for Sirk it functioned differently: 'To the few it makes the *aporia* more transparent.'[40] Of *Imitation of Life*, Sirk stated: 'You don't believe the happy ending, and you're not really supposed to.'[41]

Ranging over a diverse set of cultural contexts, Longinotto makes them universally accessible through the workings of fictional narration and devices such as *aporia*. Longinotto clearly has an intention here: 'to allow the audience to make a sort of leap where they can feel what the person in the film is feeling, through cultures'[42] and through the 'melodramatic narrative flows'[43] of these stories to connect spaces, albeit temporarily. As demonstrated above, the action of her personal response and 'human eye' is an essential liberatory tool in constructing a plurality of voices, 'multiple Is'.

A tension arises between the documentary 'truths' of the situation and the melodrama of the story being told. This is apparent in *Runaway*. Mrs Ghamsogar and her team demand written assurances from fathers and brothers regarding future treatment if the girls return home, and are seen attempting to persuade some of the youngsters to reconstitute their own lives independently, with support. This reveals a progressive note, which might surprise a Western audience. Yet, this is destabilised by the note of *aporia* which is struck repeatedly in the endings to each of the girls' mini-narratives. As Maryam leaves, for example, she turns back and seems to notice Longinotto's camera pointed at her from inside. The camera angle is adjusted, again connoting the human presence and consciousness operating it. Maryam reacts – seeing her new friends – and waves, smiling happily and confidently.[44] Within the walls of the home, fathers and brothers tell their women how important they are and sign agreements to effect better treatment. Yet, standing by Longinotto's camera and watching them leave, the spectator feels overwhelmingly conscious of letting them go into an uncertain future.

Longinotto's frequent use of the freezeframe, usually on a moment of happiness or success also works, surprisingly, to enforce a sense of *aporia*. Notably, *Rough Aunties* ends with the embrace of a newly adopted orphan by her new sister, a moment of rescue and hope; as a temporal 'freeze', it is a passing moment in the ongoing flow of narrative of good and bad. Similarly, whilst Longinotto brings careful balance to her portrayal of Sampat Pal, who testifies movingly to the difficulty of her life towards the end of *Pink Saris*,[45] a moment of complexity remains in the closing shots of her new charge Renu, expressing her hopes to help her 'new mother' entwined in Sampat Pal's tight embrace.

Here, the personal and responsive human eye threatens to give way to a Western, objectifying gaze through the action of *aporia*. It is striking that the conclusion of her less complicated relationships, with Vera Ngassa and Brenda Myers-Powell, reflect a personal, emotional relationship with these women.

Figure 6   Brenda sings to her girls in *Dreamcatcher* (Green Acres Films/ Vixen Films, 2015).

In *Dreamcatcher*, Longinotto gives Brenda the closing moments, as she sings Stevie Wonder's 'Always' to the young girls she seeks to educate and protect (Figure 6).

As she sings unaccompanied, it is an affective moment, an act of her love for them and an assertion of her positive hope for their future. The film endorses it by creating a sound bridge from her voice into an instrumental arrangement on the non-diegetic soundtrack over its closing titles, a soaring adaptation which honours and amplifies her emotion, taking it outside the diegesis.

Authorship, Emotion and Transnational Feminism

What is the significance of this understanding of Longinotto's ability to render women's invisible lives with such effective emotion as a female filmmaker? If she seeks to disappear, her camerawork is still marked by her humanity, one which I have argued above often brings the spectator temporarily into the same temporal space as the subject. In its affective ability, Longinotto's work raises issues at the heart of transnational feminist thinking and its abiding concern with the relationship of emotion and difference.

Emotion has become part of the politics of cultural difference and, as discussed above, emotion has played a significant role in Longinotto's work. Her choice of subjects is politically charged, in her collaborations in postcolonial settings, and means she has to be judged as a feminist as well as a female author. What does Longinotto's work add to 'transnational feminist practices'[46] of relationships between women across the globe? Carolyn Pedwell has stated that this humanising through individualising might 'divert attention away from analysis of wider structures of power which condition transnational encounters'.[47] Breny Mendoza theorised the distinction between 'global sisterhood' and 'transnational feminism' by directly referring to the 'romanticising of feminist global relationships' and the need to avoid assuming 'essential' distinctions between First and Third World women.[48] In the situations of rescue represented by Longinotto's films, there is very little systemic analysis of what has led to these failures.[49] Both White and Smaill have questioned the role of emotion in her films with contexts of spectatorship perceived as playing a key role, White describing how the successes represented in *Sisters-in-Law* may, for US audiences, be reduced to a '"you go, girl" style of comeuppance', part of a wider 'marketing of documentary humanism' and 'effacement of feminism in the public sphere'.[50] Smaill's work also recognised that the action of empathy can 'in effect, reinforce existing cross cultural assumptions and hegemonic relations of value'.[51] Moving into a Western/First World setting with *Dreamcatcher*, her film arguably still eschews these 'wider structures of power'. Even as Kimberlé Crenshaw's concept of 'intersectionality' offers discursive language to address these complex relations.[52] Might Longinotto's individuality and personal emotion ultimately fail the development of 'transnational feminist practices'?[53]

Speaking Nearby?

Longinotto's particular filmic style – the 'gentleness' and 'narrative intimacy' that is perceived critically – should be examined in the light of those questions of difference. Chandra Mohanty, in 'Under Western Eyes: Feminist Scholarship and Colonial Discourses' (1988), singled out for criticism Western scholarship's creation of the 'composite, singular "third-world woman" – an image which appeared to be arbitrarily constructed but nevertheless carried with it the authorising signature of western humanist discourse'.[54] Additionally, this 'monolithic' imagining tended to produce 'the (implicit) self-representation of western women as educated, modern, as having control over their own bodies and sexualities, and the "freedom" to make their own decisions'.[55]

I have suggested above that Longinotto may enforce these monolithic stereotypes through her practice of empathy. As questions of honouring difference pervade feminist scholarship,[56] does Longinotto's practice escape censure through an ability to 'speak nearby'? The critical writings of Trinh T. Minh-ha help to theorise further the function of space and voice here, to see how far Longinotto *can* 'speak nearby' her subjects rather than to 'speak about' them.[57] Trinh, as a non-Western subject herself, acknowledged her own difficulties in 'disentangling Difference' but suggests that the 'process of differentiation ... continues, and speaking nearby or together with certainty differs from speaking for and about. The latter aims at the finite and dwells in the realm of fixed oppositions ...'[58] Trinh seems to answer some of the questions above, arguing that the 'work of decolonisation will have to continue within the women's movements'[59] but seeking plurality of identity was a goal, 'the existence of multiple "I's" and multiple "Others"' as represented in her own film *Reassemblage* (1983).[60]

Emotion, as feminist scholars have demonstrated, is at the heart of these questions of difference. Sara Ahmed has stated that pain may be one which 'cannot be accessed directly, but is only ever approached'.[61] Clare Hemmings argued that 'empathy' has a complex role in relating to other cultures; it may lead to 'sentimental attachment to the other, rather than a genuine engagement with her concerns' or, more destructively 'a cannibalisation of the other, masquerading as care'.[62] She also questions the tendency to naturally articulate it with femininity and to see it as an aspect of female authorship. This would be a form of 'speaking about'. Hemmings proposed a form of bearing witness which 'does not assume a common position or even the possibility of one, but it does assume the recognition of the other as subject'.[63] Crucially, Hemmings called up an idea of 'affective solidarity' drawing on 'a broader range of affects – rage, frustration and the desire for connection' as 'necessary for a sustainable feminist politics of transformation'.[64] For the purposes of this analysis, this can be both the emotion of the filmmaker and subject. If Longinotto's 'multiple Is' can express 'emotional' agency, then Longinotto's own 'craft' of emotion – not least through her fictional structures – is speaking nearby and not about.

Hemmings's proposal regarding 'affective dissonance' is particularly pertinent in relation to Longinotto's films, the point at which a socially situated subject may recognise 'the dissonance between my sense of self and the possibilities for its expression and validation'.[65] This enables a different reading of Longinotto's work; one in which emotion is engaged at the point of difference. The long take and her spatial sensitivity allow the subjects, as described above, to reveal their own anger through resistance. In those moments and spaces, her work begins to 'speak nearby' rather than 'speaking about'. Returning to the figure of Rekha, her request to be taken away is precisely that 'affective dissonance' – an awakening of consciousness of the differences between her own self and her situation in her own society. Hemmings stressed that this awakening does not necessarily lead to action.[66] In Rekha's case, the impossibility of this is painfully visible in *her* ambivalent attitude in the following marriage scene. These formulations leave the complexities of the situation intact but allow expression of Rekha's subjectivity. This is neither consciously expressed by Rekha herself, nor one endowed by the action of the documentarian's camera; thus, we begin to escape those relationships of power – from Western to non-Western subjects – which have troubled this form of practice.[67] It *is* a form of 'speaking nearby' – a cross-cultural relationship. It is one which has to be recognised to be a finely balanced constructed space, constantly threatening to implode.

It also helps us to look for other 'multiple Is' at work in Longinotto's films. These are many kinds of people constrained by their circumstances. Some are emotionally invested in the patterns of their society, who look for individual forms of hope, like Setarah in *Runaway*; some who bring their rage to bear on the structures and the system, like Sampat Pal in *Pink Saris*. Or there are those who are directly engaged with changing systems from within, like Vera Ngassa in *Sisters-in-Law*. Longinotto's style (with her collaborators) allows for revelations of 'affective dissonance' within her subjects and, at these moments, their voices direct the action of the camera. Thus, pupil Robert in *Hold Me Tight, Let Me Go* ignores the praise being offered by his teacher, enjoying playing music on his (awarded) CD player. The film ends with a freezeframe of this moment of rebellion. His refusal to enter the system of socialisation is delivered with a grinning assertion: 'I can't hear yer', a joyous moment of 'affective dissonance' subject, filmmaker and spectator can share.

Conclusion: Gentleness, Intimacy and Rage?

Looking at Longinotto's films as a body of work, it becomes apparent that her approach problematises the Grierson Trust's 'Western' view of which societies are deemed to be 'repressive' and/or 'hostile'. Many similar issues of 'asymmetric power relations' are present in her Western-based documentaries. An objectifying gaze might equally be present for American affluent audiences and their reaction to the 'underclass' living on the streets of Chicago in *Dreamcatcher* or for the middle-class/educated British spectator observing the situation of the children at Mulberry Bush School. This reconstitutes our understanding of difference. Belinda Smaill identified Longinotto's films as negotiating binaries within non-Western societies.[68] From the above analysis, Longinotto's approach is consistent across continents. Women in Iran, transgender groups in Japan, children in rural England are joined as they occupy clear situations of difference within their own societies; in both Western and non-Western cultures, it is Longinotto's intention to empathise with the powerless, speaking nearby.

In Hemmings's terms, the action of Longinotto's own experience of injustice uncovers how individual biography works alongside the transnational nature of her feminist authorship. In answer to Kira Cochrane's friendly, tentative speculation that her repressive and traumatic childhood was an influence on her filmmaking perspective, Longinotto responded with laughter and good-humoured ambivalence: 'I don't know, that would be neat, wouldn't it?'[69] Biography has played around the edges of this analysis, but Longinotto's comment reminds any critic that her own story cannot explain her crafting of a specific language to unsilence others.

It might be tempting to replace one singularity – her 'transnational feminism' – with another, her search for justice borne out of her own experience of pain. What is significant is that Longinotto has fashioned her personal 'rage' into these intimate portraits. This self-effacement is part of her craft[70] which crucially ensures that it is her subjects' emotion and not her own which prevails. In 2016, Kimberlé Crenshaw still needs to call for activists to 'say her name' as part of necessary activist rage against police brutality.[71] Longinotto has been allowing those 'names' their own voice and identity – rebellious, humourous, complex. Her films offer the possibility of a temporary imaginative connection to those who are situated differently, remaining in the spectators' minds long after the film's ending. Similarly, the effects of *aporia* enable conflicting emotions to be held together – after all, these films, as Sirk stated, are not supposed to make us feel happy. Why should they, in the face of injustice or continuing struggle? Her 'craft' of simplicity and self-effacement, her performativity *with* rather than *in front of* the camera, is her means of advocacy. Thus, this soft-spoken, warm and humorous documentarian demonstrates how activist anger can reside effectively in gentleness and intimacy.

Notes

1. Patricia White, 'Cinema solidarity: the documentary practice of Kim Longinotto', *Cinema Journal*, 46/1, 2006, pp. 120–8. White's analysis draws on Inderpal Grewel and Caren Kaplan's influential statement of the work of 'transnational feminist practices' which recognise 'asymmetrical power relations' and 'involve forms of alliance, subversion, and complicity within which asymmetries and inequalities can be critiqued'. Inderpan Grewal and Caren Kaplan, 'Postcolonial studies and transnational feminist practices', *Jouvert A: Journal of Post-colonial Studies*, 5/1, Autumn 2000.
2. Belinda Smaill, 'The documentaries of Kim Longinotto: women, change, and painful modernity', *Camera Obscura*, 24/2, 2009, p. 43.
3. Previous recipients include John Pilger, Sir David Attenborough and Molly Dineen.
4. The Grierson Trust, *The BBC Grierson Trustees' Award to be presented to Kim Longinotto*, 2015, <http://www.griersontrust.org/about-us/news/2015/trustees-award-kim-longinotto.html> (last accessed 1 November 2015).
5. Grewel and Kaplan, 'Postcolonial studies and transnational feminist practices', 2000.
6. Chandra Talpade Mohanty, 'Under Western eyes: feminist scholarship and colonial discourses', *Feminist Review*, 30, Autumn 1988, p. 64. The language itself, as Mohanty considered, has to be subject to challenge and refinement. I am using the terms Western to connote First World vs. so-called Third World, whilst recognising its troubled history in relation to postcolonial nations. See Mohanty, '"Under Western eyes" revisited: feminist solidarity through anticapitalist struggles', *Signs*, 28/2, 2003, pp. 499–535.
7. Trinh T. Minh-ha, *Woman, Native, Other: Writing Postcoloniality and Feminism* (Bloomington, IN: Indiana University Press, 1989), p. 104.

8. Her student documentary *Pride of Place* (1976), about her own boarding school, was shown as part of the London Film Festival.
9. Longinotto's films are available from *Women Make Movies* in the US, <http://www.wmm.com/>, and from The Royal Anthropological Institute in the UK, <http://www.therai.org.uk>.
10. *Pride of Place* helped towards her school's closure nine months later, based on the pupils' onscreen testimony. It caused her former head teacher to denounce Longinotto as a 'traitor'. In an interview after the release of *Pink Saris*, Longinotto laughed and described that moment as 'thrilling ... I think I was more excited about that than anything else.' Melanie Scagliarini, 'Kim Longinotto: surviving with a smile', *Ceasefire Magazine*, 12 April 2011, <https://ceasefiremagazine.co.uk/kim-longinotto> (last accessed 12 February 2016).
11. Catherine Fowler, 'The day I will never forget: an interview with Kim Longinotto', *Women: A Cultural Review*, 15/1, 2004, pp. 101–7.
12. Kira Cochrane, 'BFI Directors Q&A', *Dreamcatcher* [DVD], Dogwoof Ltd., 2015.
13. Mark Cousins, '*Divorce Iranian Style/Runaway*. Two films by Kim Longinotto and Ziba Mir-Hosseini', Second Run DVD, 2009, p. 4.
14. Annette Kuhn's analysis, in 1982, still encapsulates a dual objective now for a 'woman's picture': 'films that were not just about women, ordinary working women, housewives, mothers, but were also by women (1982, p. ix). Annette Kuhn, *Women's Pictures: Feminism and Cinema* (London: Routledge, 1982).
15. See Sarah Cooper, *Selfless Cinema? Ethics and French Documentary* (Leeds: Legenda, 2006).
16. Cousins, '*Divorce Iranian Style/Runaway*', p. 4.
17. Smaill, 'The documentaries of Kim Longinotto', 2009, p. 44.
18. Sophie Mayer, '*Gaea Girls* and *Shinjuku Boys*. Two Films by Kim Longinotto and Jano Williams', Second Run DVD, 2010, p. 10.
19. Ibid. p. 10.
20. Sheffield Doc/Fest 2010: Kim Longinotto and Ollie Huddleston Masterclass. Sheffield Doc Fest, 2010, <https://www.youtube.com/watch?v=oEwuX9Clm0Y>.
21. Longinotto has discussed her enjoyment of a summer job telling stories to children in parks. See Quentin Falk, 'Interview with Kim Longinotto', *BAFTA Guru Academy* Magazine, October 2007, <http://guru.bafta.org/kim-longinotto-interview> (ast accessed 20 November 2015).
22. Of Kurosawa's women, Longinotto has stated that: 'They're always there, and they're beautiful, but they're very silent, and they're always in the background' (see Mayer, '*Gaea Girls* and *Shinjuku Boys*', 2010, p. 4) and, in Iran, she was interested in the contrast between the images produced by current-affairs television documentaries, and those in the work of Iranian fiction film-makers. See Cousins, '*Divorce Iranian Style/Runaway*', 2009, p. 9.
23. Bill Nichols, 'The voice in documentary', in Bill Nichols (ed.), *Movies and Methods: Volume II* (Berkeley and Los Angeles, CA: University of California Press, 1985), pp. 260–1.
24. Mayer, '*Gaea Girls* and *Shinjuku Boys*', p. 9.
25. Annette Kuhn, ' The camera I. Observations on documentary', *Screen*, 19/2, 1978, p. 74.
26. Ibid. p. 79.
27. Falk, 'Interview with Kim Longinotto'.
28. *Runaway* [DVD], dir. Kim Longinotto, Second Run DVD, 1998.
29. White, 'Cinema solidarity', 2006, p. 121.
30. Kuhn, 1978, p. 78.
31. Ibid. p. 79.

32. The subject's appeal to diegetic space behind the camera has been touched on in Smaill's evaluation of *Divorce Iranian Style*, when women turn and address the camera, confidentially. Longinotto testified to Mir-Hosseini's importance in this and her sharing of experiences with these women, prior to filming. See Smaill, 'The documentaries of Kim Longinotto, 2009, p. 48; and Cousins, '*Divorce Iranian Style/Runaway*'.
33. Maggie Brown, 'A lot of documentary makers look down on TV', *The Guardian*, 2015, <http://www.theguardian.com/media/2015/nov/01/kim-longinotto-television-documentary-rape> (last accessed 2 November 2015).
34. Nichols, 'The voice in documentary', p. 268.
35. Ibid. p. 269.
36. Interestingly, the process of the film involved the loss of much early footage accidentally. During this early filming, Ngassa had emerged as the key player, which enabled Longinotto and her crew to re-focus their narrative on her for the rest of the filming.
37. Brown, 'A lot of documentary makers look down on TV'.
38. Longinotto has discussed her work with Myers-Powell and Ngassa in *Sisters-in-Law* as collaborations, as a chance to promote a woman she believes deserves recognition. See Belinda Smaill, 'Interview with Kim Longinotto', *Studies in Documentary Film*, 1/2, 2007, p. 180.
39. Defined as 'an expression of real or pretended doubt' for rhetorical effect by Merriam-Webster Dictionary, it also carries the notion of an impasse which is unresolvable. <http://www.merriam-webster.com/dictionary/aporia>.
40. Jon Halliday, *Sirk on Sirk. Conversations with Jon Halliday* (London: Faber and Faber, 2011 (Kindle Edition)).
41. Ibid. 2011.
42. Quoted in Smaill, 'The documentaries of Kim Longinotto', 2009, p. 65.
43. Longinotto, quoted in Mayer, '*Gaea Girls* and *Shinjuku Boys*', p. 9.
44. That the gesture has powerful emotional resonance is reinforced by its inclusion as an illustration in the DVD booklet that accompanies the film.
45. In a similar way, an extended interview with Chigusa towards the end of *Gaea Girls* reveals the violent nature of the relationship with her father, as a context for her domineering behaviour at the training school.
46. Inderpal and Kaplan, 'Postcolonial studies and transnational feminist practices'.
47. Carolyn Pedwell and Anne Whitehead, 'Affecting feminism: questions of feeling in feminist theory', *Feminist Theory*, 13/2, 2012, p. 122.
48. Breny Mendoza, 'Transnational feminisms in question', *Feminist Theory*, 3/3, 2002, p. 302.
49. Smaill questioned Longinotto's reliance 'only on interpersonal relationships to convey cultural meaning and complexity'; Smaill, 'The documentaries of Kim Longinotto', p. 51.
50. White, 'Cinema solidarity', p. 126.
51. Smaill, 'The documentaries of Kim Longinotto, p. 65.
52. See Sumi Cho, Kimberlé Williams Crenshaw, Leslie McCall, 'Towards a Field of Intersectionality Studies: Theory, Applications and Praxis', *Signs*, 38/4, 2013, pp. 785–809.
53. This consideration – of the operation of a more uncritical empathy – is the subject of recent feminist debate in relation to the global performance of and responses to *The Vagina Monologues* and the associated event, 'One Billion Rising'. See Christine M. Cooper, 'Worrying about vaginas: feminism and Eve Ensler's *The Vagina Monologues*, *Signs*, 32/3, 2007, pp. 727–58; Geraldine Harris, 'Performing transnational feminisms? *The Vagina Monologues* and One Billion Rising' (forthcoming).

54. Mohanty, 'Under Western eyes', pp. 62–3.
55. Ibid. p. 65.
56. Longinotto can be considered as part of 'feminist transnational practices, as Grewal and Kaplan (1994) prefer to call transnational feminism' as 'forms of alliance, subversion and complicity operating in a privileged in-between space where asymmetries and inequalities between women can be acknowledged, sustained nevertheless to be critically deconstructed', Mendoza, 'Transnational feminisms in question', p. 297.
57. Trinh T. Minh-ha, *Woman, Native, Other*, p. 101.
58. Ibid. p. 101.
59. Ibid. p. 104.
60. Ibid. p. 101.
61. Quoted, in Smaill, 'The documentaries of Kim Longinotto', p. 67.
62. Clare Hemmings, 'Affective solidarity: feminist reflexivity and political transformation', *Feminist Theory*, 13/2, 2012, p. 152.
63. Ibid. p. 153.
64. Ibid. p. 148.
65. Ibid. p. 154. In a similar way, Ahmed recognises that activism may be sited at a subject's '*reading* of the relation between affect and structure, or between emotion and politics'. Sara Ahmed, *The Cultural Politics of Emotion* (Edinburgh: Edinburgh University Press, 2004), p. 174.
66. Hemmings, 'Affective solidarity: feminist reflexivity and political transformation', p. 156.
67. Of relevance, here is Mohanty's discursive reconfiguration of First/Third World into 'One-third' and 'Two-thirds' world. This recognises that patterns of power do not follow geographical lines, a concept relevant to Longinotto's disparate practice. See Mohanty, '"Under Western eyes" revisited', p. 522.
68. Smaill, 'The documentaries of Kim Longinotto', p. 44.
69. Cochrane, 'BFI Directors Q&A'.
70. It is no less crafted than, for example, the self-reflexive onscreen appearances of her friend and fellow film student Nick Broomfield, which point to the text's constructed nature.
71. For example, Kimberlé Crenshaw, 'Kimberlé Crenshaw – On Intersectionality – Keynote – WOW 2016', 14 March 2016, <https://www.youtube.com/watch?v=-DW4HLgYPlA> (last accessed 20 September 2016).

Films, Video and Radio Programmes

Cochrane K., 'BFI Directors Q&A', *Dreamcatcher* [DVD], Dogwoof Ltd., 2015.
Crenshaw, K., 'Kimberlé Crenshaw – On Intersectionality – Keynote WOW 2016', 14 March 2016 <https://www.youtube.com/watch?v=-DW4HLgYPlA> (last accessed 20 September 2016).
Longinotto, K., Sheffield Doc/Fest 2010: Kim Longinotto & Ollie Huddleston Masterclass. Sheffield Doc Fest, 2010, <https://www.youtube.com/watch?v=oEwuX9Clm0Y> (last accessed 15 January 2016).

Filmography

Pride of Place [film] (Kim Longinotto, 20th Century Vixen, 1976).
Reassemblage. From the Firelight to the Screen [film] (Trinh T. Minh-ha, 1983).
Shinjuku Boys [DVD] (Kim Longinotto/Jano Williams, Second Run DVD, 1995).

Divorce Iranian Style [DVD] (Kim Longinotto/Ziba Mir-Hosseini, Second Run DVD, 1998).
Gaea Girls [DVD] (Kim Longinotto/Jano Williams, Second Run DVD, 2000).
Runaway [DVD] (Kim Longinotto/Ziba Mir-Hosseini, 2001).
The Day I Will Never Forget [film] (Kim Longinotto, Kenya, 2002).
Hold Me Tight, Let Me Go [film] (Kim Longinotto, BBC Productions, UK, 2007).
Rough Aunties [film] (Kim Longinotto, Rise Films/Vixen Films, South Africa, 2008).
Pink Saris [film] (Kim Longinotto, Channel 4, India, 2010).
Dreamcatcher [DVD] (Kim Longinotto, Dogwoof Ltd, 2015).

6. A POLITICS OF NEARNESS: USES OF MONTAGE AND HAPTICS IN DOCUMENTING CULTURAL EXPERIENCES OF COMMUNITIES OF INDIA

Aparna Sharma

Documentary: An Act of Intervention

To document is to intervene. An intervention is not objective. It is active. It is perspectival, situated in a particular place and a particular moment in history. It is rooted in an interrogation of hegemonic views, values and rationalisations. Documentary-making about women, and by women, constitutes a means of documenting voices, experiences and histories that speak to the positions women occupy in the world; and how they navigate the conditions with which they are confronted.

As a documentary maker I have steered away from developing films that explicitly highlight women's issues and voice their concerns with a view either to create awareness of women's conditions or to seek institutional redress for them. Documentaries based on women's issues tend to be the more popular kinds of documentaries about and by women in India. Funded by agencies such as NGOs and television channels, such documentaries seek to raise awareness about women's conditions and the issues that confront them. They are principally expository, informative and investigative. Given their focus, they command limited possibilities for contemplation around film form and its politics. In my documentary practice, I am interested in investigating and exploring how documentary forms and aesthetics can be used to depict everyday life experiences and narratives, practices of living, the knowledges people embody, and how they make meaning of their existence through the labours they perform. My work often surrounds subjects who do not make any immediate claims to newsworthiness. Focusing on everyday lives, my films command the possibility to explore how documentary aesthetics can be used to study and think about categories of lived experience such as memory, resilience, aspirations, labour, visibility and voice.

My interest in aesthetics stems from the positioning of my practice in the context of academic research. As a documentary practitioner and scholar, I research and investigate issues of representation: how documentary practices articulate meanings, create understandings and uphold discourses. For this, my research focuses on both documentary content and documentary forms and aesthetics. By form and aesthetics I am referring to the approaches to documentary-making (for example, *vérité*, observational, poetic, etc.) and to the formal elements and techniques through which documentary meanings and interventions are constructed with a degree of coherence.

Premises and Provocations

My interest in aesthetics and form is not a move towards formalism abstracted from content. By turning to form and aesthetics, I am exploring how documentaries construct subjects and meanings, and how those intervene in the broader field of representational history and discourses. For it is in the field of aesthetics that the work of ideologies, political postures, creative preferences, the subjectivities of documentary actors and the dialogues between them, takes place.

In this essay, I focus on the development of my aesthetic approaches for two documentary projects, *Crossings in a Beautiful Time* (2006) and *Kamakha: Through Prayerful Eyes* (2012), the former surrounding the Gujarati diaspora of South Wales and the latter focusing on the iconic fertility worship site, the Kamakhya Temple in the Northeast Indian state of Assam.[1] In the first part of the essay, I will discuss the use of montage techniques for documenting the cultural experiences and narratives of the Gujarati community of South Wales, UK. Between 2003 and 2006 I undertook a documentary project surrounding this community as part of a practice-based, doctoral research programme at the University of Glamorgan. In this project, I studied the techniques of montage cinema as understood by Sergei Eisenstein and Dziga Vertov, and I investigated how their ideas and approaches influenced India's parallel cinemas.[2] Based on this research, which I wrote up in a dissertation, I developed a montage-based documentary film that focuses on the Gujarati community's cultural hybridity and its internal gender dynamics. My discussion of the uses of montage for my practice draws on how critical practice discourses in Indian cinema have approached montage as a discursive category through which Indian cultures are studied on terms that contest and exceed the hegemonic ideals of modern nationhood.

In the second part of the essay, I will discuss *Kamakha,* a documentary film that examines the visual cultures surrounding the Kamakhya Temple in Northeastern India. This is a region characterised by rich cultural diversity and an unequal political relationship with mainland India. This unequal political relationship has resulted in the region experiencing an acute sense of economic, social and cultural marginalisation from the Indian mainstream.[3] Since the early decades after India's independence from colonial rule (1947), the northeast region, which is composed of seven states, has been steadily militarised by the Indian State to curb numerous indigenous peoples' movements expressing different forms of political assertion. My development of documentary practice in Northeast India is invested with an awareness of how mainstream media (newsprint, television, cinema) persistently represent this region in reductive and stereotypical terms.[4] In my practice I have been interested in constructing forms of representing this region that share with the viewer the complex and sophisticated cultures and cultural practices of the people that live there, through an aesthetic approach that inaugurates a mode of viewing based on nearness to the peoples and cultures of Northeast India. To this end, I have been applying principles of haptic aesthetics – both visual and aural – in order to develop intersubjective and tactile representations of the cultures and practices my films examine.

Haptic aesthetics are a form of visuality and aurality that emphasise the textures, materiality, details and internal aesthetic unity of things. Cinematography that is haptic documents the elements of *mise en scène* from a close perspective (achieved by either placing the camera near the elements or zooming in towards them). Jacques Aumont defines haptic visuality in terms of the 'psychic distance' between the image and spectator. Aumont bases his concept on German art historian Adolf Hildebrand's 1893 theory in which two forms of vision are differentiated – the optical and the haptic. Optical visuality is a form of viewing that offers the viewer a vantage point from which they can identify what they see, and acquire mastery over it. Aumont elaborates on the difference between the optical and haptic views, stating that:

> the *optical* pole of distant vision, in which perspective plays an important part and which corresponds to those arts that prioritise appearance (Hellenistic art for e.g.); and, at the other extreme, the *haptic* (tactile) pole of close vision, in which the presence of objects is more strongly emphasised, their surface qualities more in evidence, and so on, in what becomes an increasingly stylised manner (such as in Egyptian art).[5]

As optical aesthetics are based on distance from the subject they are prone to objectify what is seen. This is indeed the basis for such regimes of viewing as the 'male gaze' through which mainstream cinemas view female subjects on screen.[6] Haptic aesthetics, on the other hand, involve cinematography and sound design that privilege nearness over distance and identification in relation to what is seen and heard. Whereas optical visuality has been understood as appealing to the intellect and reason, haptic visuality speaks to the body, the senses, and their capacities for cognition and meaning-making. Haptic visuality emphasises proximity, as if *touching* through vision.

After discussing how I devise haptic aesthetics, the essay concludes with a suggestion of how my interest in haptics extends from a critical montage-based practice.

CROSSINGS IN A BEAUTIFUL TIME

Project background

Crossings in a Beautiful Time is a short documentary that profiles the Gujarati community of Cardiff, South Wales. This is a diasporic community made up of people who are connected with the state of Gujarat in western India. Diaspora is a term that refers to any peoples who have 'undergone sustained dispersions' and the Gujarati community of Cardiff is mostly composed of members, particularly in the first generation, who migrated from Uganda and Kenya to the UK.[7] In the early decades of the twentieth century, ancestors of this community had first migrated from Gujarat to East Africa in search of work, where they joined ranks with other Indians serving as an 'indentured workforce' under the colonial regime.[8] These populations were largely concentrated in rural pockets. The expulsion of British Asians by Idi Amin in 1972 led most Gujaratis from Kenya and Uganda to London.[9] In search of jobs, many Gujaratis moved out of London to towns such as Oldham, Bolton and Cardiff. Most members of the first generation are self-employed: running corner shops, tax-consultancy and taxi services, etc. The second and third generations, born and educated in Cardiff, are bilingual and include medical, information technology, finance and legal professionals.

Much of the community's socio-cultural life is centred around the Swaminarayan Temple. The Swaminarayan is a Hindu sect that centres on the worship of Lord Krishna.[10] The Swaminarayan Temple in Cardiff serves as a seat of worship and includes a community centre where cultural activities and social gatherings are organised. It supports charitable activities and has, over the decades, become a key symbol of Hinduism in South Wales. Members of the Gujarati community live in the vicinity of the temple, and many shops, restaurants and services like South Asian film libraries have developed around this neighbourhood. The community can thus be understood as forming an 'ethnoscape', as proposed by Arjun Appadurai. According to Appadurai an ethnoscape is the 'landscape of persons who constitute the shifting world in which we live: tourists, immigrants, refugees, exiles, guest-workers and other moving groups'.[11] Approaching the Gujarati community as an ethnoscape we can appreciate the particular ways in which its members interact with their environment, spanning spaces such as the temple, their homes, places of work and leisure. This focus on the ethnoscape was a starting point to explore this community's cultural hybridity, specifically how its members express and preserve the cultures to which they belong, and make meaning of those to which they have been exposed through migration.

At the start of my film project many community members said that they would like my film to share the practices of their temple, its numerous festivals and wider cultural life as a way to assert the cultural distinctiveness of their community. Through interviews with a cross-section of community members I learned that two categories characterised their cultural experiences: tradition and modernity. The former pertained to the practices, beliefs and understandings of Gujarati culture – that which the community practices and preserves as a way of keeping its links with India, their homeland. The latter, in the community members' views, refers to all influences to which they have been exposed living in the UK. While sharing their life narratives, community members dwelled on memories of displacement and emplacement, alongside imagining a future they sought to secure for themselves. Hearing about tradition and modernity, I became interested in whether the 'traditional' and 'modern' influences experienced by the community were seen by its members as discrete categories, or did these flow seamlessly in their everyday lives?

Political commentators and anthropologists working on diasporic cultures have noted how communities such as the Gujarati diaspora, whose identity resonates with a 'prior identity' in a homeland, tend to idealise that homeland.[12] With this in view, I began to realise that the film I was developing should not unquestioningly reinforce the dominant ideological positions that I was encountering within the community. I wanted to explore whether there were any opposing views pertaining to the community's cultural life and practices, specifically, how the influences of the hostland were understood and valued. I started to explore narratives, experiences and an aesthetic mode of constructing these that widens the terms by which the community's culture can be appreciated by community insiders and outsiders. Through my practice, I was committed to reflecting the community as a heterogeneous and dynamic formation, actively deciphering and absorbing cultural influences from the home- and hostland.

Two montage constructions

Montage 1: The disparity between homeland and hostland, between tradition and modernity suggested by community members offered me an avenue

APARNA SHARMA

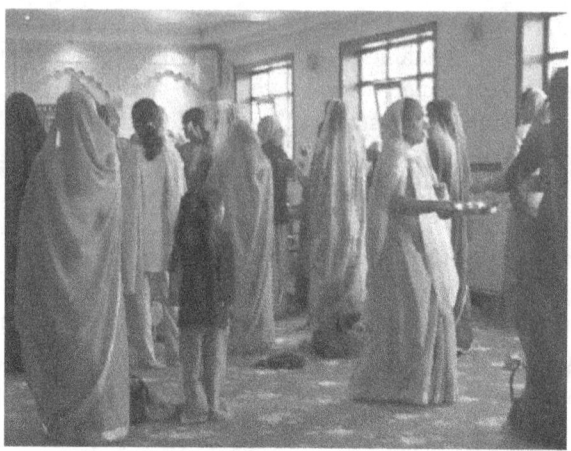

Figure 7 Gujarati women pray at the Swaminarayan Temple, Cardiff.

for considering a montage construction to depict the community as a unique cultural formation. By montage, I refer to the techniques theorised by Sergei Eisenstein in his discussion of intellectual montage. Intellectual montage as defined by Eisenstein operates at a conceptual level and provokes meaning associations; 'conflict-juxtaposition of accompanying intellectual affects'.[13] My intent in working with techniques of intellectual montage was to explore how different members from the community navigate the varied cultural influences to which they are exposed, be those from the homeland or the hostland.

In relation to the tradition–modernity theme, two montage constructions are key components of *Crossings*. The first montage surrounds a female subject who shares aspects of her everyday life in Cardiff, her memories of travel in India and her aspirations for a home there. This middle-aged subject works at a local cigar manufacturing factory where most first generation women from the community found employment on arriving in Cardiff. In an interview she had expressed how India is a revered land from where subjects such as herself derive their cultural values and traditions. The hostland, Cardiff, according to her, is a site where her family secured an economically stable life. While documenting her narrative, I followed her during the day as she worked at the cigar factory on an assembly line for making and packaging cigars. In the evenings she is seen dividing her time between domestic tasks and attendance at the daily prayer services of the temple. Following her in the cigar factory and at the temple revealed contrasts between the two spaces and the distinct ways by which women subjects navigate these spaces.

The cigar factory is thinly peopled and adopts a highly regimented layout based on the different stages of cigar manufacturing. Working in the factory, the community women appear uniformly defined in their work clothes and the functions they perform. They are dwarfed by the large machines at which they work. Their hands perform repetitive and mechanical movements. In the temple, by contrast, they conduct themselves with a greater sense of familiarity, ease and authority. They dress in varied Indian attire; they move about freely and engage in a spread of activities including praying, singing, cooking, informal conversations and reading. The montage construction depicting the female subject I was following juxtaposed images of her in the temple with those of her working in the cigar factory. This juxtaposition reflected the two contrasting spaces she navigates on a daily basis. One space, the temple, reveals her embodied sense of familiarity and ease with the environment (Figure 7), while the other, the factory, depicts her as a uniformed subject in a space where human movements are restricted and tightly choreographed, seeming minute when viewed against the large machinery.

A particular focus in this montage is on the numerous activities women perform with their hands. Cinematographically, I framed hands through very tight close-ups, to evoke the textures of the materials women work with and the rhythms of their movements. The emphasis on the hands shifted the montage's focus away from the face, fragmenting the subjects' bodies and pushing our encounter with them into a tactile register. Focusing on the activities performed by their hands, I was able to present women subjects as active at an embodied level. This tendency in documentation stirred my interest in haptic aesthetics. Through a close perspective, I was cinematographically moving away from *looking at* women subjects, towards looking from a position near to them. The tactile perspective opened possibilities for devising a filmic nearness and proximity to them. There was a freshness to this way of encountering women subjects – not as removed or distant elements within the *mise en scène*, but instead being near to them, seeing things from a perspective close to that of their bodies, without being identical to their viewpoint.

Montage 2: The second montage construction in *Crossings* focuses on a widow from the community. In an early conversation with some community women, I had been invited to share my impressions about their culture. In my response, I had queried why widows from the community always sat at the back of the temple prayer hall, separated from all other visitors. I was informed that widows, under the Swaminarayan sect, adhere to particular codes of social conduct. These codes are vast, covering an array of everyday behaviours and conduct spanning dress, food, one-to-one interactions and prayer.[14] Hearing this, I became interested in exploring a widow's perspective on the community's values. Within a few weeks, I was introduced to a widow who was willing to be interviewed for the film.

In an in-depth interview the widow shared her life narrative. She was born and brought up in Gujarat. She had been married and widowed at a young age.

In the interview, she emphasised the ostracisation she had faced as a widow in India, and which had compelled her to migrate. She went on to express how in Cardiff she was able to overcome the economic and social hardships she had encountered in India. She concluded by sharing her ways of transgressing some of the social codes that had been imposed on her as a widow. She proactively participated in the visual design of her interview and other documentation I undertook with her, suggesting locations and ideas for framing. She had requested that for the interview I be accompanied by no other crew member and that during it, I maintain constant eye contact with her.

In developing this subject's narrative for the film, I was committed to devising a visual construction that put her experiences into a wider socio-cultural context that would contain her narrative from being read as a one-off, individual account. I developed a montage sequence using her interview in which image and sound are in direct counterpoint, creating a kind of audio-visual montage. In a section of her interview, she had narrated that when she was widowed her hair was shaved and ornaments removed. She was required to relinquish all color and adornments, wearing white clothes through life. During editing, this section of the interview was combined with a visual sequence in which the widow is seen tying a coloured sari, adorning herself with gold jewellery and combing her long hair. This montage construction is based on the counterpoint between image and sound. In the audio the widow recollects a memory of the social codes that were imposed on her body, while through the actions within the images we see her violating those codes. The widow's voice communicates established social norm within her community and through that, the wider category of tradition. Her adornment of her body constitutes a transgression of social norm and through that, the problematisation of the category of tradition. While such transgression of social norm is seen among the educated and economically mobile segments of Indian society; in the case of the widow in Cardiff, this transgression has been largely possible on account of her location there. Given the structures of everyday life in Cardiff, with its possibilities for socio-economic mobility, subjects such as the widow are able to develop and enact a more individualised relationship with traditional practices.

On completing this audio-visual montage, it was felt that the widow subject's narrative could be further developed to suggest the role that migration had played in her life. For this, I developed a series of images with a group of Hindu widows in the north Indian town of Vrindavan. Vrindavan is a small town where, according to Hindu mythology, Lord Krishna spent his childhood. Today Vrindavan thrives on tourism. Apart from local residents who make up the small-scale economy of the area, Vrindavan is known for its *ashramas* or homes for destitutes, including Hindu widows who have been abandoned by their families.

I filmed at one *ashrama* that houses widows from the states of Gujarat and Bengal. Most widows here, like the widow in Cardiff, had experienced the custom of child marriage, some even having been widowed in childhood. As I approached the widows at this *ashrama* to explore whether their everyday lives coincided and/or contrasted with that of the widow in Cardiff, I was greeted with direct and sustained gazes. With some widows I developed eye contact. Some smiled. No one spoke. As I navigated this *ashrama*, the only words I gathered pertained to the religio-spiritual discourses through which the widows comprehend their lives as the workings of 'destiny'. The images I developed at this *ashrama* were of widows who were verbally silent, but whose gaze, towards the camera and through that, the audience, is laden with a sense of resilience and quiet dignity.

The images of the Vrindavan widows were juxtaposed with sections of the audio-visual montage of the Cardiff widow. There was a disparity in the landscapes occupied by the widow in Cardiff, and those in Vrindavan. This disparity extended to the socio-economic mobility of the subjects in both landscapes. The widow in Cardiff has, through migration, gained economic and social mobility. This mobility supports avenues for her to question and articulate personal re-workings of the codes of widowhood that had been imposed on her. The widows of Vrindavan command limited economic facilities and they are confined, in quite determined terms, to the religious codes that have been imposed on them. They do not adorn their bodies, their heads are shaved and they only wear white. Alternating between the widow in Cardiff and the Vrindavan widows through montage constitutes a juxtaposition between voice and silence, questioning/transgression of norms and an adherence to them. While this juxtaposition does not take away from the resilience and dignity of any widows, it opens up the Cardiff widow's narrative beyond the confines of her community, situating it within wider contexts of Hindu religious practice and diasporic subjectivity.

Montage as a Mode of Cultural Critique

The focus on gender in *Crossings* serves to push the film away from a positivist cultural mapping onto a critical portrait of a community. Introducing the Vrindavan widows in relation to the widow from Cardiff, foregrounds the disparities between homeland and hostland, problematising the category of 'tradition' and facilitating the viewer in appreciating the particular dynamics of diasporic experiences.

In this use of montage to question 'tradition' I was influenced by Indian parallel cinema masters, Ritwik Ghatak and Kumar Shahani. Ghatak, an art filmmaker from Bengal who critiqued the politics of India's partition, was deeply influenced by Sergei Eisenstein. Somewhat like Eisenstein, Ghatak worked with montage to reflect a dialectic in relation to different sections of Bengali society. Ghatak's work used the melodramatic form and montage was a means to rupture and disassemble stable categories of meanings and organisation in society. Ritwik Ghatak's student and acclaimed filmmaker, Kumar Shahani, who has himself worked with montage principles, proposes how, through a figure such as Ghatak, montage becomes more than a formal or aesthetic technique. It is a strategy for developing critical cultural discourse. Shahani states that:

> The theory that there exists a Cartesian polarity between arbitrary (aesthetic) signs and total realism necessarily led to quantitative conclusions and meaningless oppositions: the proliferation of detail against metaphysical truth (where quality cannot be seized), the fluidity of mise-en-scene as against the metre of montage, the existential tension of suspense (Hitchcock) as against the tragic release from pity and fear.[15]

Montage, through India's parallel cinema masters, can be seen as a tool to provoke a critical cultural discourse. Influenced by this, in *Crossings* montage is used to reflect how the categories of 'tradition' and 'modernity' press upon and shape diasporic cultural experience. The montages developed in this film serve in reflecting 'tradition' as not a hermetically sealed category, experienced uniformly by all diasporic subjects. Through montage, diasporic cultural experiences emerge as heterogeneous, and the category of tradition is seen both being enacted and contested from disparate subject positions.

Kamakha: Through Prayerful Eyes

Project background

Kamakha: Through Prayerful Eyes (2012, 53 mins) surrounds an ancient fertility worship site, the Kamakhya Temple, in India's Northeastern state of Assam.[16] The Kamakhya Temple is a unique place of worship as the fertility goddess to whom it is dedicated is not identified with any animate or inanimate figure. This is in striking contrast to the wider Hindu pantheon that tends to be visualised through elaborate mythic forms.[17] The temple's central shrine is a cave that contains a rock that bears a triangular impression. This impression is considered to be an abstraction of Goddess Kamakhya's *yoni* or female organ. This rock is kept covered at all times and the Goddess remains concealed from view. No filming, photography, or recording of any kind is allowed inside the shrine as a mark of respect towards the Goddess.

Goddess Kamakhya is a key fertility deity who has been historically wor-

Figure 8   A wooden model of the Kamakhya shrine, by Suban Das, 2010.

shipped by Northeast India's matrilineal Khasi and Garo peoples. It is conjectured that around the turn of the twentieth century, the site was Hinduised. Regional historians hold that this was a move by Indian nationalists to culturally amalgamate the Northeastern region into India's burgeoning nationalist project at that time.[18] Knowing this history of the site, and intrigued by the absence of an image for Goddess Kamakhya, I was drawn to exploring how people who worship this Goddess visualise her. Specifically, I wanted to investigate whether this Goddess's lack of an identifiable visual form opens up her figure for multiple forms of visual interpretation. My interest in the visual cultures surrounding the Kamakhya shrine can be situated within the context of a longstanding criticism of how Indian media visualises Northeast India generally.

Media critics are in agreement that the Indian media spanning print, television and the mammoth Hindi cinema industry contribute to the region's sense of marginalisation from mainland India as it is represented in mostly limited and negative ways. Prasun Sonwalkar uses Gramscian analysis to note that an 'us–them' binary is the key discursive framework through which the media approach the Northeastern region.[19] Reportage on the region is lacking in historical, political and cultural context, with the result that its peoples are constructed through reductive stereotypes as 'backward', 'violent', 'underdeveloped' or 'tribal' in the worst sense. Political scientist Sanjib Baruah notes that the visual regime of mainstream Indian cinema and television for viewing the Northeast region is based on what he terms a 'counter-insurgent gaze' – the gaze of those fighting insurgents in the region, that is, India's armed forces.[20] This 'counter-insurgent gaze' supports a *view* of the region and its people as being the *discordant others* of the Indian nation. I have discussed elsewhere how the 'counter-insurgent gaze' being constructed from the position of a surveillance apparatus distances and thereby disempowers, in representational terms, the Northeastern region and its peoples.[21] With this understanding, in the making of *Kamakha* I was committed to exploring how the concealed Goddess Kamakhya is visualised and given form by her devotees. In terms of representational politics, this was a move to explore and create a way of viewing that contest and advance the way in which Northeast India is represented through visual media.

While exploring whether and how Goddess Kamakhya is visualised, I was specifically interested to probe whether any competing narratives and/or visualisations, disparate from the dominant Hindu narrative related to this site, persist around the Kamakhya Temple. I encountered a number of local artists and craftspersons who live near the Kamakhya Temple and depict the Goddess through highly individualised means in media spanning poetry, music, literature and painting. They enjoy a deeper relationship with the Kamakhya shrine than that of daily visitors and devotees. Being aware of the pre-Hindu origins of the Goddess they are able to construct her in secular and more erotic terms than those related to the Hindu narrative associated with Goddess Kamakhya. Following their methods to give form to the Goddess and learning about the meanings and narratives they associate with her, opened in *Kamakha* the possibility of introducing viewers to this Goddess on terms that exceed the dominant Hindu narrative. In this sense, the film builds on the principle of montage as a mode of placing competing discourses and understandings that differ from and are *other* to the dominant, thetical national discourse, as I had developed in *Crossings*.

Varied ways of evoking a concealed Goddess

The film opens with a poem, *I'm Descending Down the Hill*, by Assam's acclaimed poet and art historian Nilmani Phookan. This poem was composed one evening at sunset when the poet, who lives near the temple, sensed that the Goddess's presence permeates the natural landscape and all its elements: rocks, soil and flora. According to Phookan the Goddess could be sensed in the ecology and elements of the Kamakhya environment.

> Evening is settling in
> On the copper coin of my face
> I'm glowing up in flames myself
> On a red lotus
> Glows a pearl
>
> I'm stone and man
> I'm the fertile soil and man . . .
>
> I'm a timeless man in the nude

> With the entire body of mine
> I perceive certain stones
> Under the water under the earth
> Lying buried ...[22]

The Goddess, concealed from view, through Phookan's words becomes coextensive with the wider Assamese environment.

A similar gesture that evokes the Goddess in elemental terms is encountered in the paintings of Kandarp Sarma. Sarma is a non-objective painter who was born and lives near the Kamakhya Temple. In *Kamakha* he shared a series of abstract compositions that are inspired by the embodied experience of visiting and *being* in the Goddess's presence. Sarma holds that since the Goddess is not represented through any single, stable form, she lends herself to multiple interpretations. Sarma informed me that for many years he has been regularly visiting the shrine to observe the act of animal sacrifice there.[23] While observing the sacrificial act, Sarma absorbs how colors and lines form as this ritual offering is performed. He asserts that as he visualises this practice, the color red explodes on to his mental canvas. Graphic lines, choreographed through the ferocious movements in the encounter of man and animal, constitute patterns that inspire the strokes of Sarma's brush on the canvas. Through Sarma's paintings I saw a mode of evoking this deity and the practice of sacrificial worship without literally depicting it.

A third artist I documented in *Kamakha* is a local carpenter, Suban Das. At Das's wood workshop, amid household and commercial furniture items, sit small wooden replicas of the Kamakhya Temple. Das uses leftover wood from his workshop to construct these replicas. The Kamakhya Temple's structure, including its unique and elaborate dome, is an identifiable image of this shrine and it circulates widely in popular visual culture related to this temple. Das's wooden sculptures are one of a kind, handmade renditions that extract and combine key, aesthetically distinctive parts of the Kamakhya shrine (Figure 8). These wooden sculptures are not an exact likeness of the shrine, but they offer a local artist's distinctive vision. By following such local artists I was able to document an extensive array of arts and crafts that make up a rich visual culture surrounding the Kamakhya Temple, one in which the dominant Hindu narrative is not the only means through which to understand Goddess Kamakhya.

Towards a Haptic Aesthetic

In the cinematography and sound design for *Kamakha* a tendency towards haptic aesthetics arose. While documenting the Kamakhya landscape, its artists and their processes, I was drawn to the textures and rhythms of everyday life and the art-making processes of the local artists. Through haptic visuality and aurality I was able to construct a viewing experience that privileges nearness to and evocation of the visual, tactile and kinetic qualities of the environments the film's subjects inhabit, which inspire and inform their creations of Goddess Kamakhya.

As haptic visuality privileges touch, texture and the materiality of things, it collapses the bounds between the viewer and the viewed. Laura Marks has noted that haptic visuality is inherently intersubjective, positioning the viewer as an active agent in the constitution of meaning from what they see. She states that:

> By interacting up close with an image, close enough that figure and ground commingle, the viewer relinquishes her own sense of separateness from the image – but to give herself up to her desire for it.[24]

Dominant forms of visuality in popular media (such as television) use the principles of optical visuality, offering the spectator a sense of command over what is viewed. Such forms of visuality risk disempowering the subject that is gazed upon because the gaze has not been instituted by them and it offers limited means of interaction between the viewed and the viewer. Optical visuality is further problematic for it provides the audience an illusion of mastery over what they see. This is certainly the case with representations of Northeast India that are based on the 'counter-insurgent gaze'.[25]

The counter-insurgent gaze through which much of Northeast India tends to be depicted in popular visual media, distances and objectifies the region and its peoples. Through haptic aesthetics, *Kamakha* offers the viewer a sense of nearness to the people and culture surrounding the Kamakhya Temple. This nearness, through image and sound, emplaces the viewer in the life-world of the Kamakhya community. The viewer is invited to experience the Kamakhya landscape and its cultural practices on terms that place the viewer and the members of the Kamakhya community in a close and intersubjective exchange. Haptic aesthetics suppress interpretation and mediation of meaning, and instead develop a form of viewing marked by a sense of immediacy, a firstness in the encounter with what is seen and heard. Haptic aesthetics can thus be understood as countering dominant and objectifying modes of viewing. Whether by way of the image or sound, haptic aesthetics call up a radical realignment of the power relations between the viewers and the viewed. *Kamakha* does not decipher or inform the viewer about the Kamakhya shrine, approaching it as an object of investigation. Instead it seeks to provoke a sensory cinematic experience based on a rearticulation of the positions from which viewers view the people and culture related to this site.

Concluding Comments

In my practice, I have collaborated with communities that have a sensitive relationship with the Indian nation. I have worked with aesthetic approaches that relate to the cultural formations and experiences of the subjects I collaborate with, and offer a realignment of the terms by which they are viewed. *Crossings in a Beautiful Time* develops a montage-based approach to documenting the culture of the Gujarati diaspora of South Wales. In this work, montage serves in disassembling this community as a homogenous or uniform body. Subjects with disparate positions and backgrounds are juxtaposed as a way to suggest how their life experiences have shaped through migration. In this film montage facilitates thinking about how cultures and cultural discourses on themes such as 'tradition' can be problematised and extended outside the narrow definitions offered by communities such as diasporas and nations.

In Indian cinema, montage has developed as a discursive category through which the neat categories of history and tradition can be interrogated and problematised. In my practice, montage has formed into a mode for thinking about competing and non-normative subject positions and experiences. I have tended to use haptic aesthetics to devise a sense of nearness and proximity towards subjects. This move towards haptics leads to a documentary practice that is less motivated towards normative techniques of interpretation and exposition, and by contrast places viewers in partial and sensory encounters with the life-worlds of the subjects they encounter. Through this my practice seeks to question and contest dominant discourses and modes of representation.

Notes

1. Aparna Sharma, *Crossings in a Beautiful Time* (28 mins). Dissertation film submitted in partial fulfillment of Doctor of Philosophy, University of Glamorgan, 2006; *Kamakha: Through Prayerful Eyes* (2012, 52 mins) Distributed by Berkeley Media LLC.
2. Parallel cinema is a term used to refer to the non-commercial and non-mainstream cinemas.
3. Sanjib Baruah, *Durable Disorder: Understanding the Politics of Northeast India*, 5th edn (New Delhi: Oxford University Press, 2012). Sanjib Baruah, *India Against Itself: Assam and the Politics of Nationality*, 6th edn (New Delhi: Oxford University Press, 2011). See also Hiren Gohain, *Assam: A Burning Question* (Guwahati: United Publishers, 1985).
4. Sanjib Baruah, 'A New Politics of Race: India and its Northeast', *IIC Quarterly*, 32/2–3, 2005, pp. 165–76. Prasun Sonwalkar, 'Banal journalism: the centrality of the 'us-them' binary in news discourse', in Stuart Allan (ed.), *Journalism: Critical Issues* (Maidenhead: Open University Press, 2005), pp. 261–73.

5. Jacques Aumont, *The Image* (London: BFI Publishing, 1997).
6. Laura Mulvey, 'Visual Pleasure and Narrative Cinema', in *Visual and Other Pleasures* (London: Palgrave Macmillan, 2009), pp. 14–27.
7. Hamid Naficy, *Accented Cinema: Exilic and Diasporic Filmmaking* (Princeton NJ: Princeton University Press, 2001), see p. 13. A small percentage of the community members have migrated directly from Gujarat to the UK.
8. Stephen Castles and Mark J. Miller, *The Age of Migration* (London: Macmillan Press, 1993), p. 49. Robin Cohen, *Global Diasporas: An Introduction* (London: University College London Press, 1997), p. 57. The Indian indentured labourers were employed contractually as construction-workers, masons, brick-layers and carpenters.
9. Even though India had acquired independence from British colonial rule in 1947, Indian subjects in British colonies such as in East Africa remained British citizens and on that basis, in the 1970s they migrated to the UK.
10. The Swaminarayan Sect was initiated by Sahajanand Swami (1837–86). The sect adheres to the Hindu religion. The teachings of Sahajanand Swami are contained in a scripture, the *Shikshapatri,* which Sahajanand Swami wrote in 1882. Sahajanand Swami shared his teachings with ascetics and followers. During his lifetime, numerous temples were built as centres for propagating his teachings.
11. Arjun Appadurai, 'Disjuncture and difference in the global cultural economy', in D. Held and A. McGrew, *The Global Transformations Reader* (London: Polity Press, 2000), p. 234.
12. Naficy, *Accented Cinema,* p. 14; Amartya Sen, *The Argumentative Indian: Essays: Writings on Indian History, Culture and Identity* (London: Penguin, 2005), p. 74.
13. Sergei M. Eisenstein, *Film Sense,* 2nd edn (New York: Meridian Books, 1957), p. 82.
14. This subject shared that widows, according to the Swaminarayan sacred text: the *Shikshaptri,* cannot interact with men in the absence of another woman within the same space. They are required to sleep on the floor and eat two meals a day. Widows cannot adorn themselves with any ornaments, their heads are shaved, and they are required to dress in either red or white attire.
15. Kumar Shahani, 'Dossier – Kumar Shahani', *Framework,* 30/31, 1986, p. 72.
16. Northeast India is made up of seven states. This region is linked to mainland India by a narrow strip of land, called 'the Chicken's Neck'.
17. Biraj Kumar Kakati, *The Mother Goddess Kamakhya* (Guwahati: Lawyer's Book Stall, 2004), p. 23.
18. Kakati; Pranay Goswami, *Festivals of Assam* (Guwahati: Anundooram Borooah Institute of Language, Art and Culture, 1995).
19. Sonwalkar, 'Banal journalism', p. 271.
20. Baruah, *Durable Disorder;* Baruah, 'A New Politics of Race: India and its Northeast'.
21. Aparna Sharma, *Documentary Films in India: Critical Aesthetics at Work* (Basingstoke: Palgrave Macmillan, 2015), pp. 126–31.
22. From *I'm Descending down the Hill,* in Phookan, N. (2008) *Selected Poems of Nilmani Phookan,* translated from Assamese by Krishnadulal Barua, Guwahati: Sahitya Akademi.
23. At the Kamakhya Temple, animal sacrifice is considered one of the few worship practices that cite the tribal linkages of this site. The Kamakhya shrine is infamous across India for the persistence of this custom that sits at odds with dominant Hindu values supporting vegetarianism.

24. Laura U. Marks, *The Skin of the Film: Intercultural Cinema, Embodiment and the Senses* (Durham, NC: Duke University Press, 2002), p. 183.
25. Sharma, *Documentary Films in India*, chapters 4, 5 and 6.

Filmography

Crossings in a Beautiful Time (Aparna Sharma, 2006).
Kamakha: Through Prayerful Eyes (Aparna Sharma, Berkeley Media LLC, 2012).

PART THREE

FEMALE AUTHORSHIP AND GLOBAL IDENTITIES

7. THE OTHER, THE SAME: TOWARDS A METAMODERN POETICS WITH HEDDY HONIGMANN

Annelies van Noortwijk

> What is it to be a woman? To be a woman is to have been born with a female sex. To be a woman is to live in a female body. It's me, my whole body is me. I am not limited to the hot spots of men's desire. I am not a sex and breasts. I am a female body. To be a women is also having a head of a woman. But a head that thinks otherwise than a man's head. Even if I find it difficult to find myself, to define myself in a society of men.
>
> Agnès Varda, *Women Reply: Our Body Our Sex*
> (*Réponse des femmes: notre corps, notre sexe*,
> France, Ciné Tamaris, cine-pamphlet, 1975)

Given that the 'female gaze' was chosen as the central theme of the IDFA (International Documentary Film festival Amsterdam) of 2014, it came as no surprise that Heddy Honigmann was invited to speak on this subject as its special guest.[1] Only one year earlier, Honigmann had received The Living Legend Award of the IDFA, an *oeuvre* prize that was presented to her by the sole previous recipient, American documentary maker Frederick Wiseman. By then, her rich body of work had already garnered numerous international awards, three of which were conferred for her life achievement: The van Praag Award from the Dutch Humanist Association (2005), the Hot Docs Outstanding Achievement Award (2008), the Golden Gate Persistence of Vision Award (2007).[2] In 2015, her status as an authority in the field of documentary resulted in a fellowship of the Royal Dutch Academy of Sciences and Arts (KNAW – Academie voor de Kunsten).[3]

Honigmann (b. 1951, Lima) is frequently denoted as a Peruvian-Dutch filmmaker, but even this is a simplification of the transcultural identity that clearly manifests itself in her work. She was born and raised in Peru as a child of Eastern European Jewish Holocaust survivors. She attended a French secondary school in Lima, studied literature for a few years and started working as a poet. After travelling around the world for some time, she studied filmmaking, specialising in documentary at the Centro Sperimentale di Cinematografia in Rome. In 1978, love led her to Amsterdam, where she has resided ever since. She directed her first documentary, *The Israel of the Bedouins* (*L'Israeli dei Beduini*, co-director Carlos Carlotti) in 1979. In the next decade she focused on avant-garde and fiction film, and her first international success was the feature *Mindshadows* (*Hersenschimmen*,1988).

However, Honigmann's real breakthrough came when she returned to documentary and her native town, Lima, in the early 1990s, where she shot *Metal and Melancholy* (*Metaal en Melancholie*, 1993), which focuses on the methods to which the middle classes had to resort during these economically trying times in order to make ends meet. The many documentaries she has since made reflect on themes as diverse as poverty, loneliness, loss, trauma, war and remembrance, but their all-encompassing theme is the power of love and art (in its broadest sense, including music, poetry, literature, dance, the visual arts, etc.) in human life. The characters in her films range from multi-employed taxi drivers in Lima (*Metal and Melancholy*), to elderly people in Rio de Janeiro (*O Amor Natural*, 1996), to musicians who, exiled from their homelands, perform in the underground of Paris (*The Underground Orchestra*, 1997) and former United Nations peacekeepers suffering from post-traumatic stress disorder (*Crazy*, 1999). Her films also include portraits of war widows living in Bosnia (*Good Husband, Dear Son*, 2001*),* Cuban exiles in New York who celebrate their Latin roots by performing and enjoying dance and music (*Dame la Mano*, 2003) and the visitors to various artists' graves in Paris's Père Lachaise cemetery (*Forever*, 2006*).* In *El Olvido* (2008) she returns to the poorest people of Lima, in *Food For Love* (*Liefde gaat door de maag*, 2009–11), a documentary volume of twelve chapters, women prepare their favourite recipe in memory of lost loved ones, and *Around the World in 50 Concerts* (*Rond de Werled in 50 concerten*, 2014) focuses on the musicians and the very international public of the Dutch Concertgebouw Orchestra. It is not difficult to see the relationship between Honigmann's engagement with the victims of war, social, political or economic injustice across the world, and her multifaceted identity. However, as I have argued elsewhere,[4] it is her innovative ethical attitude and aesthetic approach to her subject matter that accounts for the powerful impact of her documentary films. Questions of memory and self are addressed by centred and active subjects, reassessed as embodied, empowered and emotional beings, as opposed to weak, peripheral subjects that are victims of institutional forces.

In this chapter I will argue that Honigmann's work is emblematic of a tendency in contemporary culture and specifically in the arts in which a *female gaze* is becoming increasingly crucial. From the perspective of the semiotic evolution of human culture and the arts,[5] her work is part of a paradigm shift in contemporary culture from postmodernity towards a notion which I shall call *metamodernity*.[6] With this shift, a new kind of poetics emerges, a poetics in which senses of 'sameness' and 'presence' and a drive towards inter-subjective connection and dialogue are pivotal. At the same time, a (re)turn to the subject, the real and the private, is the preferred strategy to address the central topic in contemporary culture, namely (often traumatic) memory and identity. The re-evaluation of the subject as an embodied and emotional individual is fundamental to such a shift.[7] This explains why the documentary form has become for our time what literature was for the nineteenth century: the preferred form of realism. Its history may be described as a continual re-evaluation of film's potential to transmit factual information about the real world. In contemporary documentary practice, we witness a shift in focus from a modernist preoccupation with factual, objective reality towards an embracement of more diverse, subjective perspectives on reality. Central to this development, I argue, is the influence of the female gaze, resulting in a re-evaluation of the documentary subject and the blurring of boundaries between subject and filmmaker.

The Female Gaze in Metamodern Documentary

Try a Little Tenderness was the title of the masterclass Honigmann gave as special guest of the year at the IDFA 2014. In this lecture, she expanded on what the documentary film form means to her and how a sense of intimacy can be attained by the way in which films are designed, structured and elucidated, by means of the work of documentary makers she admires as well as her own. To her, it is essential to make films about people she loves and respects, which is evident in a tender gaze and a calm editing pace in her *oeuvre*. Only by giving characters sufficient screen time can they be fully appreciated.[8]

The scene from *The Underground Orchestra* to which the title of her masterclass refers is a case in point, as it is over five minutes long. In this scene, we witness an intercultural jazz trio perform Otis Redding's 'Try a Little Tenderness' in the Parisian subway. The musicians are filmed in long takes, interrupted only by shots of a young couple kissing and the smiling audience in the metro carriage. With its placid pacing, the scene seems to ask us to be patient and to fully immerse ourselves in the mood of the performance. This mood is one of tenderness; the love that these musicians put into their music is affirmed by the loving reception of the audience.

Honigmann learned her most important lessons in tenderness from Chantal Akerman's *Jeanne Dielman, 23, quai du Commerce, 1080 Bruxelles* (Chantal

Akerman, Belgium/France: Pardise Films, 1975), a film that made a deep impression on her with its long, observational shots.⁹ In addition to Akerman, she cites Agnès Varda as an important inspiration for her work. 'Agnès Varda is like my documentary mother', she said, speaking of Varda's film *The Gleaners and I* (*Les Glaneurs et la Glaneuse*; France, Ciné Tamaris, 2000). According to Honigmann, the films of Chantal Akerman have that tasteful feminine gaze that she defines as a method of filming that offers the viewer more opportunity for free contemplation and reflection, rather than forcing the viewer into a specific interpretative frame. This feminine way of looking is not exclusive to women, according to Honigmann, which is why she prefers the term 'feminine gaze' over 'female gaze'. She believes that there are plenty of female documentary filmmakers who are incapable of it, just as there are men, like Chris Marker and Jean Rouch, who seem to have mastered it. Nor does this mean that the feminine gaze cannot be ruthless at times, as a scene depicting the horrible practice of female circumcision from the documentary *The Day I Will Never Forget* (England, Women make Movies, 2002) by Kim Longinotto clearly demonstrates. But, as Honigmann explains, 'it has been filmed in a way that made me feel like I was present in the room with the girl. There was love, closeness, and the absence of moral clichés; even though a victim later, using Kim's camera, expresses her hope that her sister will never have to go through the same experience.'[10]

That a feminine or female gaze is not (or no longer) exclusive to women seems to be a notion Honigmann shares with Agnès Varda, who articulates it, for example, in Marie Mandy's *Filming Desire: A Journey Through Women's Cinema* (*Filmer le Desir: voyage à travers le cinéma des femmes*; Belgium/France, The Factory, Saga film, Arte France, RTBF, 2000).[11] This does not mean Varda believes that the male gaze has vanished from contemporary cinema, as she observes many male filmmakers still tend to represent women as objects of lust.[12] Varda's claim is backed up by an extensive body of evidence. A recent study of the most popular blockbusters of the ten largest film industries of the world by the Geena Davis Institute on Gender and Media showed regrettably little change in the ways male and female characters are depicted since Laura Mulvey analysed the 'male gaze' in 1975.[13] Sexualisation and objectification remain the standard for female characters. Girls and women, always young and slender, are shown twice as often as men in revealing outfits or fully nude. Furthermore, less than a third of all characters with dialogue are women, and women are even more under-represented in public functions than in reality.[14] Furthermore, not only does Hollywood in 2016 continue to be dominated by *white* filmmakers and actors (a fact that was underlined by the commotion surrounding the most recent Oscar nominations) but by white *male* filmmakers and actors. At the same time there continues to be a conspicuous lack of older female actors in big productions.

In *Filming Desire*, Marie Mandy engages in conversations with a wide selection of female filmmakers about the ways they have found to depict the female body and themes such as lust, desire and sexuality. In this context Varda rightly emphasises the famous statements of her short cine-manifesto *Women Reply* (*Réponse des femmes*; France, Ciné Tamaris, 1975),[15] which is again as relevant to a feminist consciousness as it has ever been; that being a woman means you have the body of a woman and think like a woman, which leads to the awareness that it is you who is watching, rather than you being watched, and this remains a fact in spite of the difficulties to find and define oneself in a society of men.[16] This way of thinking shows great similarity with what Teresa de Lauretis problematised and conceptualised in *The Technologies of Gender*[17] as the 'subject of feminism', a topic I will elaborate on further in the next paragraph.

Finding and defining a personal, and thus subjective, perspective is exactly what Honigmann has always done and continues to do in her films: watching, observing, seeking relationships with people who are in a certain situation, engaging them in conversation, giving them a voice, and representing them in a respectful manner. Her gaze is not only tender; it is female or feminine. The two terms are currently often used interchangeably to indicate everything in filmmaking that runs counter to the dominant male gaze of Hollywood, although *female gaze* seems to have become the preferred term. I therefore propose to adopt this term, and to investigate how it is understood in the current discourse, taking it that a female gaze is not by definition gender determined. As a counterbalance to the male gaze, the female gaze developed into more than a simple 'turning of the tables' that allows women to look at men in the same eroticised way the male gaze looks at women. Already, women filmmakers of the second wave of feminism in the 1970s sought their own unique way of looking, which is not an easy task in a patriarchal society, where women struggle to define themselves, as *Réponse des femmes* shows so elegantly and clearly.[18] This also explains why women, when they took up the camera in the 1970s, started observing not only men but, not so surprisingly, specifically women. As Varda already stated: the first feminist act is to look back, which means turning women into fully developed characters who do not exist for men, but for themselves. This means they are not reduced to their body or sexuality. The female body is no longer depicted in a voyeuristic fashion; it is depicted as a whole, rather than a physical object 'cut up' to its most erotic parts.

The female gaze also implies giving a voice to women, giving them the opportunity to speak and think for themselves and from themselves. As Anneke Smelik stated at IDFA 2014, the female gaze creates a point of view in which women (but also men and children) can be fully appreciated, are given a voice, a gaze and an equal part in the action. The female gaze manifests a curiosity that transcends the level of skin-deep attraction and embraces the character in its entirety. Smelik agrees that filmmakers working with the female gaze do not necessarily have to be female, nor does the perspective of the film have to be parallel to that of its maker,[19] although this, of course, raises the question to what extent we can speak for another without unjustly appropriating a perspective we can never fully know.

The construction of an alternative gaze to the male gaze conducted to a turn to the inside, to the question of how it feels to be a woman, which values are part of that and which strategies a women uses to engage with others. The development of the female gaze thus triggered the development of other visual regimes which, like the female gaze itself, drew their inspiration from existing and developing forms of non-mainstream, non-Hollywood film and culture. The revolutionary climate of the 1960s and 1970s played a big part in these developments; feminist cinema, socialist cinema and third cinema -with a film like *The Hour of the Furnaces* (*La Hora de los Hornos*; Fernando Solanas and Octavio Getino, Argentina, Pallero and Solanas, 1968) as its most outspoken example) can each trace their roots to this period. A critical reflection on the Hollywood perspective thus led to an awareness of the fact that certain voices and perspectives, of a wide range of alternative interpretative communities dealing with issues of gender, sexuality, ethnicity, disability, exile and migration are systematically under-represented in popular cinema (and mainstream culture as a whole). This resulted in the development of alternate gazes in both documentary and art cinema. Combined, these and other art forms will hopefully present an ever more powerful alternative to dominant forms of mainstream culture, an alternative way of looking at the world that is now more needed than ever.

Thus, the female gaze is a crucial factor in a shift in contemporary culture that moves away from postmodernity to what is often referred to as post-postmodernity (or post-postmodernism) but for which I propose to use the term 'metamodernity', using meta- not in its strict original sense of 'after' or 'beyond' but rather in its epistemological sense of 'about'. The term *metamodernity* implies a return to a modern attitude from a postmodern awareness. Under the dictum of postmodernity, we became aware of the fact that 'truth' is always value-based and embedded in a discourse of power. The rise of digital technology further contributed to the dissemination of the idea of reality as a multidimensional construct, of which truth is one dimension only. While this realisation seemingly opened up our culture to diverse views and voices, in reality those with power, whose voices traditionally needed no legitimisation to be heard (such as those of white, upper class men), the male gaze continued to dominate mainstream culture. Consequently, these powerful voices managed also to relativise the significance of real issues raised by other, less powerful voices.

Postmodern relativism only increased the urgency and need for those who did not see themselves represented in the dominant discourse, such as women, to develop different, alternative visual regimes and voices. This explains the need for a renewed, modern but multidimensional interest in the representation of reality. Furthermore, I argue that the transition from a postmodern to a metamodern culture, which we are now experiencing, is characterised by self-analysis, that is, by an immanent criticism of the hegemony of the analytical, operational perspective. This metamodern culture furthermore acknowledges that other forms of cognition besides analysis, such as bodily perception, emotion and creativity, have equal value and function.[20] Interestingly, this development has turned documentary film from a somewhat marginal practice into a vital field for innovation; the power of documentary film lies precisely in its emotional impact and its radical potential to attend to alternative perspectives on reality.[21]

As an eternal outsider, 'otherness' almost seems to be Heddy Honigmann's natural habitat; as an Eastern European in Peru and a Peruvian in Europe, as a woman and a member of the second generation of Jewish Holocaust survivors, she formulated such an alternative perspective. In her work, she found ways to both embrace and transcend this 'otherness' by engaging authentically with people in very diverse situations, yet finding 'sameness' in the things that make us all human and the ways we all need each other. Honingmann thus embraces a metamodern visual regime in her films.

Tenderness and Art as Care for the Self

Many first filmmakers of second wave feminism in the 1970s adopted the documentary film form as their preferred mode of representation for its ability to put 'real women' on screen, creating feelings of primary presence, and thus altering traditional representations of women. Though most of these documentaries reflect cinematic methods developed in the US from the early 1960s onwards, they also departed from it in a fundamental way by structuring it around an autobiographical discourse of its female protagonist; the personal became political. This was at odds – of course – with direct cinema's positivist perspective that situated the filmmaker as an observer who registers the action without in any way interfering what is observed.[22] With the development of feminist thinking, women filmmakers moved away from documentary, precisely because of its realism, and turned to the formulation of a feminist deconstructive counter-cinema. Feminine subjectivity, however, remained an important organising principle in feminist cinematic attempts to not only subvert dominant matters and forms of expression but eventually construct real alternatives.[23] Considering the cinematic apparatus with Teresa de Lauretis as a *technology of gender*,[24] these feminist de- and re-constructions showed that women can indeed be subjects of speech and desire and, as de Lauretis already demonstrated in *Alice Doesn't: Feminism, Semiotics, Cinema*,[25] transform the representation of women otherwise. To conceptualise the tensions between actual experience (women) and idealised representation (Woman), and in particular the consciousness of these tensions, de Lauretis introduced the notion of the 'subject of feminism'.[26]

Significantly, Honigmann, after finishing her training in documentary filmmaking, turned in the 1980s to making fiction film from a deconstructive, female perspective, resulting in films that are not only remarkable for their feminism, but equally so for their social activism. Illustrative for this period is the film she co-directed with Noshka van der Lely, *The White Umbrella* (*De Witte Parapluie*, 1983), which explores and questions the boundaries of female cinema. This film shows the attempts of two women, both equally unhappy in their lives and jobs, to change their lives. Moreover, both characters come to the same conclusion that their resistance against international political and military developments has failed to affect any real change.[27]

Making *Metal and Melancholy*, which Honigmann personally considers her real debut film, felt to her as a liberation: 'It gave me back my youth, gave me wings, freedom. I began to improvise again, to follow my intuition and to approach things spontaneously.'[28] Honigmann, who had left Peru with her family in the early 1970s, when the military regime had taken power, could, for the first time in almost twenty years, use the language of her native country again, enabling her to speak and move more freely than she had done in a long time. At the same time she also liberated herself from taking explicit political perspectives, as she came to realise that poetry and humour are far more effective authorial 'tools'.[29] This does not mean that the political is downplayed in her work from this moment on, but it is addressed in a direct and often ironic way that diverges greatly from what was still the dominant form of social-political documentary agenda in observational or direct cinema documentaries. In doing so, Honigmann effectively broke with the dogmas she had developed as a politically engaged, left-wing and feminist filmmaker, without abandoning her ideals regarding 'liberty', 'equality' and 'fraternity', and 'sisterhood' of course. This new approach resulted in the *oeuvre* she has developed over the past 25 years, and for which she is internationally admired. Typical of the reception of her work is film critic John Anderson's commentary on the Golden Gate Persistence of Vision lifetime achievement award she received in 2007:

> Heddy Honigmann is good for you. And her films are appetizing antidepressants. [...] Among the real artists of nonfiction, Heddy is as responsible as anyone for raising the standards of doc-making worldwide. She flexes the form to meet her purposes, but never sacrifices style or integrity.

> She champions the dispossessed without sermonizing, and she injects just enough of herself in her films to give us a sense of the woman behind the movie without ever eclipsing the subject or the substance, the sense of space or the sense of place.[30]

By way of example, Anderson discusses how this is achieved in *Crazy*:

> her film about U.N. soldiers who reminisce about hellish global conflicts and the music they listened to in order to stay sane. The film is a tightrope walk across an open wound – the lingering camera, the obvious pain and the vortex of memory create more tension than a week's worth of action thrillers – but neither the subjects nor their inquisitor ever lose their dignity. Or our attention.[31]

Honigmann's documentaries can be characterised, as I have argued elsewhere,[32] as cinematic contemplations on 'ars vitae', on how to survive and even create a meaningful and enjoyable existence, in spite of the (often extremely difficult) circumstances. From this perspective her *oeuvre* can be interpreted as a Foucauldian discourse of resistance – an ethics of the self – which is situated in the interstices of power relations, at the level of individuals' daily practices.[33] Like Foucault, Honigmann's approach revolves around a way of life rather than a search for truth. In dialogue with the people in her films a 'care of the self' is achieved through the practice of 'technologies (or techniques) of the self' which, in Honigmann's poetics, are articulated around the self's practices of love, passion, compassion, creativity and, last but not least, art. She guides, but is also being guided by her characters in a mutual attempt to accomplish a transformation of the self by one's own knowledge and practice. By allowing the audience to experience, as Anderson put it, 'inside the hearts of the subjects',[34] we are invited to reflect upon and participate in their struggle, but without being forced to adopt a specific framework of reflection. The open form of these films and the fact that Honigmann stays in the background and never takes an explicit stance on the subject matter or forces her ego onto the viewers, is of significant importance to her application of a metamodern gaze. As an audience member, you feel how Honigmann loves all the people she shows in her documentaries equally; whether they are male or female, young or old, all are represented in the same respectful fashion.[35] A beautiful and apposite example is found in the documentary *O Amor Natural* (1996), shot in Rio de Janeiro, in which Honigmann asks her elderly subjects (often very old) to read from the erotic poetry of the Brazilian poet Carlos Drummond de Andrade (1902–87), and captures the ruminations and meditations about the sexual part of love that are triggered by poems like 'Love – being an essential word' ('Amor – Porque É Palavra Essencial') with the opening lines : 'Love

Figure 9 *O Amor Natural* (Heddy Honigmann, 1996). Courtesy Pieter van Huystee Film & TV.

– being an essential word – / begin this song, envelop it all / Love guide my verse, and as it guides / wed soul, desire, member and vulva.' The text brings back memories to a seventy-four-year-old woman of the intense sex life she shared with her husband. Bursting with laughter, she remembers all the strange places where they used to make love. While many of the characters, like this lady, have fond memories of their sexual histories, an eighty-four-year-old lady regrets never having been able to enjoy sex and her own body, due to a very strict Catholic education that left her completely uninformed and only taught her it was her duty to fulfill her husband's desires. She did, however, as she finally confides in Honigmann, occasionally have very strong sexual fantasies in which she imagined being taken by a man with force, admitting that she is a 'violent person', and therefore 'all this gentle stroking and fussing is not for me'. While she makes this passionate and emotional confession, the camera occasionally pans to her grandson, who listens to her story with a somewhat embarrassed smile. The shots are of a long duration and include frequent close-ups of the face and arms of this woman; allowing a viewer who is sensitive to this tender and attentive gaze to see that she is very old, but beautiful and full of life (Figure 9).

The aging body is thus shown as it is, no longer smooth and sleek, but wrinkled; a shape altered by age is not hidden away but shown as a regular feature of real people, who are beautiful in a very different way than the eternally young and slender models that dominate mainstream culture.

Sexuality is thus conveyed from a female, taboo breaking, gaze. The elderly, who are normally invisible, desexualised and marginalised in our society are turned into authoritative voices (Figure 10). As an eighty-one-year-old woman, after reading a poem of 'a water ballet on a deep-pile carpet' and speaking

Figure 10　*O Amor Natural* (Heddy Honigmann, 1996). Courtesy Pieter van Huystee Film & TV.

of female orgasm remarks: 'We are old, but not dead.' Honigmann demonstrates that both elderly men and women can be subjects of speech and desire and transforms the representation of the elderly, and in particular that of (elderly) women. The tensions between actual experience (women and men) and idealised representation (Woman and Man), and the consciousness of these tensions, or the 'subject of feminism', is at the heart of *O Amor Natural*. The audience is invited to learn of the characters' memories and reflections on love and sex, to see and respect them as their own older and wiser selves, all of which is beautifully conveyed by alternating or intercutting the scenes of the elderly people every now and then with shots of young people on the beaches of Rio. Our sexual life is, Honigmann articulates in this way, a major constituent of the self's creation of a meaningful and enjoyable existence.[36]

In the documentary *Forever* (2006), a film which I consider to be the foundation, and in a sense the pinnacle of her poetics, she explores the power of art for human life in all its facets. At the same time, the film reveals Honigmann's authorship in which rhythm, tonality, melody and composition play such a crucial role. It is a practical form of research that shows how music and visual art can be reunited and transformed through the filmic medium where they are merged through movement.

The film's contemplation of art is a self-reflexive one, as it uses the medium of documentary film to explore representation through the visual arts, music and sound, in search of the essence of art itself. By focusing on Paris's famous Père Lachaise cemetery and its visitors, the notion of how art intermingles with life, love and death is shown at its most intense and moving. Marcel Proust's monumental cycle *À la recherche du temps perdu* (*In Search of Lost Time*)[37] serves as both model and method for Honigmann's approach, as shown in my text 'Ars longa, vita brevis; the importance of art in human life, a Proustian interpretation of Honigmann's *Forever*'.[38] She does so by both reflecting upon and putting into practice Proust's notion of *involuntary memory*, which implies that sensory experiences can bring back 'forgotten' memories and make us experience eternity. She also makes a masterly use of the *scene of empathy*, the filmic variation of Proust's *petite phrase* which reveals that only through repetition can the experience of art be fully comprehended or fully 'felt'. With the *scene of empathy*, as described by Carl Plantinga,[39] we refer to shots of long duration of the human face. The viewing of the human face moves us beyond linguistic communication and elicits a bodily response in the viewer, as we respond to the sight of another human face with *affective mimicry* or *facial feedback* resulting in emotional contagion. A natural reaction of *facial feedback* (and from an evolutionary perspective a very important reaction in order to survive) is to empathise with the other, which consists in the capacity to know, feel and respond congruently to what the other is feeling. However, the credibility of scenes of empathy is in fact extremely precarious; there is very little distance between empathy and sensationalism or exploitation.[40] Shots of extremely long duration on the human face, in medium close-up, close-up and extreme close-up, are widely used in *Forever*.

This is especially the case with its main character, a Japanese girl, Yoshino Kimura, who visits Chopin's grave to pay tribute to both the composer and her deceased father by leaving a red rose. She is a pianist herself and has come to Paris to study, what she calls 'the heart of Chopin's music', explaining that Chopin was her father's favourite composer. While the camera slowly zooms into her face she tells us how seven years ago, her father suddenly died at the age of only forty-seven due to overwork. Now, every time she plays Chopin, she pays tribute to him. Just when the viewer starts getting an uneasy feeling, pictures of the girl and her father from her childhood are intercut while in the voice-over she says, 'I hope he (*sic*) pleased about that'. The camera returns to her face for another twenty seconds, followed by a shot in greyish shades of a single white-grey rose between gravel and tombs in Père Lachaise. Through Chopin's music, we understand, she not only honours her father, but is also reunited with him in what Proust called an *instant of eternity*, trying to deal with the dual emotions of love and loss through the beauty of Chopin's art. In this scene at the beginning of the film, the girl is only seen in close-up, and not yet in extreme close-up. The different scenes with the girl, who we see at first rehearsing, and then finally performing, Chopin's nocturne no. 8 in D-flat major op. 27 no. 2, gradually become more intimate. After the various climaxes, distance is created again. The viewer thus gets the impression of a person who, in spite of opening herself up for us, always holds on to her dignity and autonomy. This effect is reinforced by the lack of any mediating voice-over and the limited presence of the filmmaker in the film. Honigmann generally only appears off screen in her films when prompting her characters with a minimal amount of questions that are neither leading nor suggestive.[41] In this way, in *Forever*, audiences are enabled to experience both feelings of primary presence and their transcendence, in the form of feelings of eternity.

We live in a time of conflicts. On the one hand, traditionally privileged (white, heterosexual) male forces are doing everything in their power to re-establish dominance by fuelling the dormant public fears of 'otherness', using these fears to suppress minority voices, deprive citizens of their rights and legitimise military invasions. Yet even as this reactionary movement is baring its fangs, an alternative world view emerges to challenge it. A metamodern, humanistic world view, based on a rejection of the reductive, Cartesian, male model of the rational subject in favour of a more complex, embodied, female model of the subject in transition is emerging, a model that embraces diversity, blurring traditionally rigid concepts of personal and national identity. Following years of abstract, operational thinking, the recent shift in focus towards embodiment in fields such as cognitive neuroscience places us in the midst of an emotional revolution. The study of emotions and moral behaviour has once again become a central topic of research and reflection. This emotional revolution is not only, as Antonio Damasio argues, a result of spectacular new insights into the working of the human brain and consciousness,[42] but can also be seen as a *female turn* in human consciousness. In art, we see it reflected as a renewed interest in the real, the body, subjectivity, empathy and emotion. Honigmann's *oeuvre* is emblematic of this turn, as its tender, female gaze reflects empathically on questions of emotion, trauma and the healing power of love and the arts, transcending the boundaries between self and other.

Notes

1. Departing from the central question, 'does a 'female gaze' exist within the documentary genre?', IDFA 2014 investigated not only the position of female directors in the documentary industry but the representation of women in documentary, and in more general terms how to define the term 'female gaze'. A retrospective of Honigmanns documentaries was also part of the programme, as well as different masterclasses with female directors and specialists in the field.
2. A complete list of the awards Honigmann obtained for her work is published on her homepage, last modified 2015, <http://www.heddy-honigmann.nl/hhonigmann/doc/awards/awards.php> (last accessed 29 February 2016).
3. In 2016 she received another life achievement award; the prestigious Dutch 'Prins Bernard Cultuurfonds Prijs', conferred to a person or organisation for exceptional contribution in the field of culture in the Netherlands.
4. Annelies van Noortwijk, 'Heddy Honigmann's contemplations on ars vitae and the metamodern turn', in Jinhee Choi and Mattias Frey (eds), *Cine-Ethics: Ethical Dimensions of Film Theory, Practice and Spectatorship* (London and New York: Routledge, 2013), pp. 111–23.

5. For an explanation of the semiotic evolution of culture I refer to neuroscientists and cognitivists that take a special interest in the arts, such as Merlin Donald, *Origins of the Modern Mind: Three Stages in the Evolution of Human Cognition* (Cambridge, MA: Harvard University Press, 1991); Antonio Damasio, *Self Comes to Mind: Constructing the Conscious Brain* (London: William Heinemann, 2010); and Barend van Heusden, 'Theorizing and historicizing art' (Lecture series, Groningen: University of Groningen, 2010–11), author's notes; Barend van Heusden, 'Semiotic cognition and the logic of culture', in Stephen J. Cowley (ed.), *Distributed Language* (Amsterdam: Benjamins, 2011); and, Barend van Heusden, 'Arts education after the end of art, towards a new framework for art arts education', in Barend van Heusden and Pascal Gielen (eds), *Arts Education Beyond Art, Teaching Art in Time of Change* (Amsterdam: Valiz, Antenea, 2015), pp. 153–66.
6. Annelies van Noortwijk, 'Ars longa, vita brevis; the importance of art in human life, a Proustian interpretation of Honigmann's forever', in *Wide Screen Journal*, 4/1, 2012.
7. More terms sprawl in the last decade to speak of the current paradigm shift such as 'transmodernism', 'hypermodernism', 'digimodernism', the age of 'performatism' or 'the consensual age'. See Zygmunt Bauman, *Postmodern Ethics* (Oxford/Cambridge, MA: Blackwell Publishers, 1993); and, Mikhail N. Epstein, 'Manifestos of Russian postmodernism, literary manifestos', in Mikhail N. Epstein, Alexander A. Genis and Slobodanka Millicent Vladiv-Glover (eds), *Russian Postmodernism, New Perspectives on Post-Soviet Culture* (New York: Berghahn Books, 1999), pp. 457–60. Epstein already characterised late postmodernity in a similar way. However, scholarship on the changes we are currently experiencing is still in its infancy (and the debates surrounding them are still quite confusing), see also Noortwijk, 'Ars vitae'.
8. 'Try a little tenderness', masterclass by Heddy Honigmann, IDFA 2014, 21 November 2014 (author's notes).
9. Janna Reinsma, 'De top 10 van Heddy Honigmann', in *De Filmkrant*, December 2014, <http://www.filmkrant.nl/TS_december_2014/11375> (last accessed 8 February 2016).
10. Karin Wolfs, 'Vrouwen zijn wel/niet niche', in *De Filmkrant*, December 2014, <http://www.filmkrant.nl/TS_december_2014/11387> (last accessed 29 February 2016).
11. At IDFA 2014, *Filming Desire: A Journey through Women's Cinema* (*Filmer le Desir, Voyage à travers le cinema des femmes*, 2000), by Marie Mandy, functioned as a starting point to the question of how to define the 'female gaze'. In this documentary, Mandy interviews woman filmmakers from all over the world (among them Agnès Varda, Sally Potter, Deepa Mehta, Léa Pool, Safi Faye and Jane Campion) about the ways they have portrayed the female body and themes such as lust, desire and sexuality.
12. Mandy, *Filming Desire*.
13. Laura Mulvey, 'Visual pleasure and narrative cinema', *Screen*, 16/3, 1975, pp. 6–18.
14. Stacey L. Smith, Marc Choueiti and Katherin Pieper; Geena Davis Institute on Gender in Media, Los Angles, University of Southern Califiorna, *Gender Bias Without borders. An Investigation of Female Characters in Popular Films Across 11 Countries*, <http://seejane.org/wp-content/uploads/gender-bias-without-borders-full-report.pdf> (last accessed 16 February 2016).
15. *Réponse des femmes: Notre corps, notre sexe* aka *Women Reply: our body our sex*, (Agnès Varda, Ciné-Pamphlet, France, 1975), <https://vimeo.com/46991746> (last

accessed 16 February 2016). This short film was emitted in the context of the television programme 'F comme femme' from the French channel Antenne 2, around the question 'What does it mean to be a woman?'.
16. The fact that the materiality of the body is commonly recognised in feminist theory as a determining factor in the formation of gender identity implies no denial of the historical and social dimensions of gender construction, or, as (even) Judith Butler formulates it: 'The concept of gender as construction does not mean that gender does not exist'. See 'Judith Butler: Why Bodies Matter', conference and debate, organised to celebrate the 25th anniversary of her influential study *Gender Trouble: Feminism and the Subversion of Identity* (New York and London: Routledge, 2011 [1990]). The conference was organised by the Teatro Maria Matos, Lisbon, June 2, 2015 (author's notes). See <http://www.houseonfire.eu/why-bodies-matter/> (last accessed 19 September 2016).
17. Teresa de Lauretis, *Technologies of Gender, Essays on Theory, Film and Fiction* (Basingstoke and London: Macmillan Press, 1987).
18. Varda, *Réponse des femmes*.
19. Anneke Smelik in 'De vrouwelijke blik', interview with Dana Linsen, broadcast by the Dutch documentary channel NPO DOC, <http://www.2doc.nl/speel.WO_VPRO_699389.html> (last accessed 2 February 2016).
20. Heusden and Gielen, *Arts Education Beyond Art*.
21. Noortwijk, 'Ars longa, vita brevis'; 'Heddy Honigmann's contemplations on ars vitae'.
22. Annette Kuhn, *Women's Pictures: Feminism and Cinema* (London and Boston: Routledge, 1982), pp. 147–55.
23. Ibid. 156–77.
24. de Lauretis 1987, p. 13.
25. Teresa de Lauretis, *Alice Doesn't: Feminism, Semiotics, Cinema* (Bloomington, IN: Indiana University Press, 1984).
26. Patricia White, 'Thinking feminist', in Teresa de Lauretis (ed.), *Figures of Resistance, Essays in Feminist Theory* (Urbana, IL: University of Illinois Press, 2007).
27. Homepage, Nederlands Film Fonds (NFF), <https://www.filmfestival.nl/publiek/films/de-witte-paraplu> (last accessed 7 February 2016).
28. Kiki Amsberg and Aafke Steenhuis, *Een Branding van Beelden* (Amsterdam: Contact, 1996).
29. Ibid. p. 312.
30. John Anderson 'Heddy Honigmann is good for you', <http://www.heddy-honigmann.nl/heddy/award.php> (accessed 16 February 2016).
31. Ibid.
32. Noortwijk, 'Ars longa, vita brevis'; 'Heddy Honigmann's contemplations on ars vitae'.
33. After studying the archaeology of discourse and constructing a genealogy of power in the first phases of his work, where he prioritised the power of politics and knowledge, Foucault shifted his focus to questions of ethics in his later work, prioritising the power of the individual; see Michel Foucault, *The History of Sexuality, Volume II: The Use of Pleasure* (New York: Random House, 1985); Michel Foucault, *The History of Sexuality, Volume III: The Care of the Self* (New York: Pantheon, 1986); and Michel Foucault, *The Hermeneutics of the Subject: Lectures at the Collège de France,1981-1982* (New York: Picador, 2004). The more robust account of subjectivity and resistance he thus formulated was, I believe, not only a return to his early ethics as articulated in Michel Foucault, *Folie et Déraison: Histoire de la folie à l'âge classique*, 1961 aka *Madness and Civilization*, (New

York: Routledge; 2006), but also inspired by the frequently marginalized contributions of feminist thinking as it developed from the 1970s onwards with its central notion that 'the personal is political'. In turn, Foucault offered many attractive (though seldom entirely unproblematic) features for contemporary feminist theory and politics, particularly in his later work.
34. Anderson, 'Heddy Honigmann is good for you'.
35. Noortwijk, 'Ars longa, vita brevis'; 'Heddy Honigmann's contemplations on ars vitae'.
36. Ibid.
37. Marcel Proust, *À la recherche du temps perdu* (Paris: Gallimard, 1999 [1913–27]).
38. Noortwijk, 'Ars longa, vita brevis'; 'Heddy Honigmann's contemplations on ars vitae'.
39. Carl Plantinga, 'The scene of empathy and the human face on film', in Carl Plantinga and Greg M. Smith (eds), *Passionate Views, Film, Cognition and Emotion* (Baltimore, MD: Johns Hopkins University Press, 1999), pp. 239–55.
40. Noortwijk, 'Ars longa, vita brevis'; 'Heddy Honigmann's contemplations on ars vitae'.
41. Ibid.
42. Damasio, *Self Comes to Mind*.

Filmography

Chantal Akerman, *Jeanne Dielman, 23 Quai du Commerce, 1080 Bruxelles* (1975) [DVD] (USA, The Criterion Collection/Janus Films).

Heddy Honigmann, *Mindshadows* (*Hersenschimmem*, 1988). Available on *Heddy Honigmann in Focus*, DVD Box with 13 films, Hilversum: Beeld en Geluid, 2011.

Heddy Honigmann, *Metal and Melancholy* (*Metaal en Melancholie*, 1991). On *Heddy Honigmann in Focus*, DVD Box with 13 films, Hilversum: Beeld en Geluid, 2011.

Heddy Honigmann, *The Underground Orchestra* (1997). On *Heddy Honigmann in Focus*, DVD Box with 13 films, Hilversum: Beeld en Geluid, 2011.

Heddy Honigmann, *Crazy* (1999). On *Heddy Honigmann in Focus*, DVD Box with 13 films, Hilversum: Beeld en Geluid, 2011.

Heddy Honigmann, *Good Husband, Dear Son* (*Goede man, Lieve zoon*, 2001), On *Heddy Honigmann in Focus*, DVD Box with 13 films, Hilversum: Beeld en Geluid, 2011.

Heddy Honigmann, *Dame la Mano* (2003). On *Heddy Honigmann in Focus*, DVD Box with 13 films, Hilversum: Beeld en Geluid, 2011.

Heddy Honigmann, *Forever* (2006). On *Heddy Honigmann in Focus*, DVD Box with 13 films, Hilversum: Beeld en Geluid, 2011.

Heddy Honigmann, *El Olvido* (*Oblivion*, 2008) . On *Heddy Honigmann in Focus*, DVD Box with 13 films, Hilversum: Beeld en Geluid, 2011.

Heddy Honigmann, *Food For Love* (*Liefde gaat door de maag*, 2009–11), documentary volume of twelve chapters. Available on homepage Dutch public broadcasting house NPO.nl, <http://www.npo.nl/liefde-gaat-door-de-maag/POMS_S_HUMAN_105583> (last accessed 29 September 2016).

Heddy Honigmann, *Around the World in 50 Concerts* (*Rond de Wereld in 50 concerten*, 2014). Available on homepage Dutch broadcasting house NPO, <http://www.npo.nl/2doc/03-07-2015/AT_2035238> (last accessed 29 September 2016).

Heddy Honigmann and Carlo Carlotti, *The Israel of the Bedouins* (*L'Israeli dei Beduini*, 1979) [film] (Rome: Istituto Luce SPA, 1979).

Heddy Honigmann, *Noshka van der Lely, The white umbrella* (*De witte parapluie*, 1983) [film] (Nederland: Rolf Orhel, 1983).

Kim Longinotto, *The Day I Will Never Forget* (*Dan koji nikada neću zaboraviti* 2002) [DVD] (New York: Women make movies, 2003).

Marie Mandy, *Filmer le Desir: voyage à travers le cinéma des femmes (Filming Desire: A Journey Through Women's Cinema*, 2001). Available on Dailymotion, <http://www.dailymotion.com/video/xkp8q4_filmer-le-desir_lifestyle> (last accessed 2 February 2016).

Agnès Varda, *Les Glaneurs et la Glaneuse* (*The Gleaners and I*, 2000) [DVD] (France: Artificial Eye, *The Agnès Varda Collection*, vol. 1).

8. THE MEMORIES OF *BELLEVILLE BABY*: AUTOFICTION AS EVIDENCE

Boel Ulfsdotter

Given the expanded actuality of the documentary image on film and via new media platforms since the 1990s, first person accounts are now considered a household item on a par with its earlier forerunners in the North American avant-garde and European art film.[1] The unwavering establishment of film forms such as the essay film, the video diary, the personal web page, advocating unorthodoxy regarding central documentary notions such as narrative structures, technical formats and subject matter, has permanently derailed the documentary format's longstanding tradition of objectivity, as well as a journalistic dissemination of information, as dictated by direct cinema.[2] This changed attitude towards authorship is especially pertinent in relation to Swedish documentary film production because of its longstanding and intimate dependency on Swedish public service television as its major producer and distributor. This ideological change has led to the emergence of Swedish private production and distribution companies in this area, among which Story AB (Story Ltd) is the most prolific and successful. Story AB also lists the largest group of female directors among its collaborators and this chapter focuses on the remits of female authorship and the documentary image as represented in Mia Engberg's essay film *Belleville Baby* (dir. Mia Engberg, Sweden, 2013).

Formally trained at Les Ateliers Varan in Paris in the early 1990s, Engberg's first film in the tradition of *cinéma-vérité* was *Les Enfants du Square* (dir. Mia Engberg, France, 1994). Made while she was still a film student, the film reflects all the characteristics of the observational mode of documentary filmmaking she had just learned, such as long, unedited takes accompanied by the original soundtrack instead of a traditional voice-over guiding the spectator to the goings on around the square in the Parisian suburb of Belleville where she lived. The next pivotal step on her way towards a cinema in the first person, as well as the conceptualisation of *Belleville Baby*, were *The Dirty Diaries: 12 Shorts of Feminist Porn* (dir. Mia Engberg, Sweden, 2009), in which a number of Swedish directors had been asked to make a film on the subject of female pleasure. These shorts clearly fit within the formal paradigm of the essay film in that they are both strongly individual and metalinguistic, from the point of view that the structure of the whole series allows twelve authorial voices to come to the fore. All films furthermore reflect on female sexuality and the notion of female pornography is inscribed in a feminist ideology; they all reveal a strongly articulated subjective, personal point of view; and share an obvious intention to communicate on this matter with the spectator.[3] Given Engberg's further thoughts on the reflexive and open-ended structure of the first person documentary format, the fact that the narratives in the *Dirty Diaries* series were tightly structured around a particular topic is also an important element, as is the influence of its resulting multivocal, and subsequently formally diverse structure.

Leaving to one side the dichotomy between Grierson's call for films displaying 'a creative treatment of actuality' and the truth claim in documentary film, as previously discussed by Nichols[4] and Winston,[5] this chapter revolves around the clearly experimental character of Engberg's *Belleville Baby* in relation to the traditional first person autobiographical documentary, and the possibilities of pushing the limits of its known characteristics even further. Based on Bill Nichols's ideas around the 'voice' of the documentary, I shall be doing this by exploring the epistemological uncertainty in tandem with Engberg's authorial presence that primarily emerges through the gaps created between the film's narrative, its visual form and indexicality in time and space.[6] These components of the film do not make up its entire 'voice' of course, but all three ultimately spring from her own practice as the film's director, as well as its principal cinematographer, scriptwriter and editor.

NARRATIVE

Once the idea to revisit in filmic form her memories of the love story with 'Vincent' in Paris in the 1990s had settled in Mia Engberg's mind, the question of how it should be represented had to be addressed. Engberg writes in her notes: 'To write a fictional scenario [about our love story] never entered my mind. The mere thought of having professional actors perform scenes from my life was not only unbearable, but made me laugh. Traditional fiction has never interested me . . . I wanted to reconstruct Time, Memory, and Loss. How does one do that?'[7]

In order to realise this idea, Mia Engberg initiated a transcendental process with the aim of visualising the invisible reflection of Time, Memory and Loss. According to Erik Knudsen, such a notion of a filmic representation of lived events is driven by the experimental rather than by meaning and illustration. He mentions Jean Rouch, the French director and co-founder of Les Ateliers Varan, as an advocate for a documentary structure in which immaterial elements of the spiritual, mental and physical have equal bearing on the film's epistemological form.[8] It therefore seems to me that Erik Knudsen's suggested tripartite structure of the artistic process at work in such documentary films is interesting in relation to the epistemological ambivalence that is allowed to riddle *Belleville Baby*.

The first step in this model concerns the existence of reality as experience in order to begin the process. 'What is relevant is that the filmmaker is prompted by something and feels it necessary to express that something and that they see the means to do so in events and imagery going on around them.' In this process, Knudsen writes that 'dreams, imagination and intuition can and should be as much a part of documentary' as fact-based observations and authenticity.[9] The second step of the artistic process involves the creation of a cinematic narrative based on a transcendental form of reality, which engages with participatory feelings such as sorrow, longing and joy that allow us to open up the narrative to a greater whole. Such a narrative is not characterised by a series of cause and effect driven events, but rather motivated by different emotions. Traditional ingredients of the classical narrative, such as a well-defined protagonist and a clear movement of the narrative arc, are reduced, with the benefit of creating a certain erratic and fragmented epistemology which is allowed to dominate the film's overall narrative structure.[10] According to Knudsen, the third step is based on the artist answering his/her inner call for creation: to transpose the lived experience into a tangible filmic form which is not primarily based on intellectual reflection or a didactic mission to enlighten the audience through facts and figures.[11]

In the case of Mia Engberg, she has recorded and published her notes of the filmic process surrounding the production of *Belleville Baby* and it seems clear that the filmic process at play during the production of her film, in tandem with a certain amount of unconventional intellectual reflection and inspiration from other art forms, allowed her to once again push the boundaries and challenge the very foundation of traditional documentary film practice. In *Belleville Baby*, she thus created a number of disjointed narrative texts by consciously muddling and investigating the expected relationship between memory and fact, image and sound, as well as time and space regarding her love story with 'Vincent', leaving the spectator wavering.

In *family secrets* Annette Kuhn distinguishes between memory work and memory texts.[12] Memory work, she writes, 'undercuts assumptions about the transparency or the authenticity of what is remembered, treating it not as "truth" but as evidence of a particular sort: material for interpretation, to be interrogated, mined for its meanings and possibilities'.[13] The memory text created on the basis of the memory work is 'typically a montage of vignettes, anecdotes, fragments, "snapshots", flashes'.[14] In *Belleville Baby* the montage informing the narrative is based on a plurality of voices in conversation, created mainly by Engberg (as 'Mia') and 'Vincent', through a number of edited telephone conversations, as well as in the form of individual monologues in voice-over. While the narrative topic was initiated by Vincent, who unexpectedly called Engberg up after ten years of silence, the realisation of its contents is based on Engberg's recollection, in notebook form, of their telephone conversations, and thus utterly epistemologically doubtful. The factual reliability is further diminished by the fact that Vincent's reason for calling was that he wanted them to talk about their memories of their love affair in Paris in the early 1990s, during her tutelage at Ateliers Varan, to which we must add that they talked in French, while she made her notes in Swedish. The scripted telephone conversations were consequently set up and translated back into French at a much later date.

Engberg inverts the classical myth of Orpheus in Hades and has herself come looking for her former boyfriend in her own memory bank, as the framework for the film's narrative, and thus sets herself up as the film's enunciator. Although it was allegedly Vince who stirred her into reminiscence, it is Engberg who primarily communicates her memories of, and thoughts around, her love affair with Vincent, to the spectator. Speaking with Michael Renov, it would thus seem that 'experiences, impressions, or memory traces are altered after the fact as a function of new experiences and are thus rendered capable of reinvestment, producing new, even unexpected, effects of meaning'.[15] An interesting result of these fictive alterations is that the narrative ends up being heavily disrupted, without beginning or end, and no dramatic arch. Instead, we are prompted into action by an old-fashioned telephone signal, or Engberg's didactic voice introducing the enunciator by saying 'A memory', whereupon she reiterates that particular memory. Some of these memories have only indirect bearing on Vincent's and her love affair, or their personal backgrounds, such as the so called Rey-Maupin affair, which took place in Paris at the time of Vincent's and Engberg's relationship.[16] Florence Rey and Audry Maupin were well brought up and ambitious youngsters taking part in higher education programmes until radicalisation led them to drop out and join politically extreme groups. Vince's disenfranchised background and poor education possibilities within the segregated French school system, and Engberg's political commitment to radical socialism, allowed them to understand Rey-Maupin's wish for a radical change in society. Like Rey-Maupin, Engberg and Vince also lived rough in a small attic room in the Parisian suburb of Belleville, with

Vince making money selling narcotics and slowly becoming a proper member of a Parisian mafia group. As a token of further kinship, and mind-map in navigating around the act of remembrance, Engberg brings up her paternal grandmother's secret love affair with a married man during the Second World War. Reading her Nan's diaries, Engberg comes to understand the deep affection between the two, and yet they decided to part and were never to meet again. Instead, her Nan went on with her life, married Engberg's grandfather and had his children, just like she herself carried on with her life, relationships and bringing up her children, after the love affair with Vincent had come to an end. This reiteration of her own sad love story along with other women's similar experiences indicates Engberg's open leaning towards autofiction when working out the narrative of *Belleville Baby*, and the pivotal inspiration she allegedly found in the creative treatment inspiring the works by both Sophie Calle and Marguerite Duras.[17] By autofictionally repositioning herself and her love story through others' similar experiences, Engberg arrives at a broader first person narrative, well aware that such an unstable subject positioning further lessens the documentary actuality of her film from a factual perspective. On the other hand, she strengthens her authorial presence in the work through her total fictionalisation of Vincent as a character enacted through a professional voice actor, reading from her manuscript.

From a practical point of view, autofiction functions 'as repetition, as the rewriting, in "real" life, of past experiences, which will then be transposed to the written page'.[18] Anette Kuhn identifies this type of memory work as making 'secondary revisions of the source material of memory' and extends a warning that 'the relationship between actual events and our memories of them is not mimetic [in that] memory never provides access to or represents the past "as it was".[19] . . . [T]he past is always mediated – rewritten, revised – through memory . . . and the activity of remembering is far from neutral.'[20] Kuhn's argument is endorsed by Trinh T. Minh-ha's by now well-known notion of 'speaking nearby', which is a 'speaking that reflects on itself and can come very close to a subject without, however, seizing or claiming it.' . . . 'The challenge is to materialise it in all aspects of the film: verbally, musically, visually.'[21] I argue that Engberg has practised this poetic approach to the full in *Belleville Baby*, thus openly challenging the documentary idea of its referentiality and transparency by instilling a considerable degree of uncertainty in the spectator, when it becomes clear that 'Mia' and 'Vince' do not share the same memories at some points. The authenticity of the memories we are revisiting is thus suddenly brought into question, while at the same time the depersonalised and highly ambiguous structure of the film's first person narrative rather encourages the viewer to consider *Belleville Baby* as a mockumentary. Mia Engberg herself refers to *Belleville Baby* as an 'autodocumentary', thus underlining the role of the self in the film, as well as its documentary quality. For an outsider, the highly unstable subject positioning of the film's first person, as well as its enunciator, instead brings to the fore its hybrid, fragmented and multivocal character.

The film essay's deliberate generic inbetween-ness at the crossroads of documentary, art film and avant-garde practices has been pointed out as one of its main characteristics and is used in a yet more radical and experimental way by Engberg in *Belleville Baby* because of its close vicinity to Trinh's idea of a poetic approach to memories, discussed above. The unorthodox practices typical for this format involve every aspect of film production, from the filmmakers' approach to technical formats, to subject matter, to aesthetic values, to narrative structures, and practices of production and distribution.[22] Let us just say that *Belleville Baby* ticks all the boxes.

Visual Form

The documentary actuality of *Belleville Baby* is further undercut by the film's aesthetic values, in that there is no alignment between the (admittedly fragmented) narrative and its visual form. The integration of visuals thus acts merely as a way of further 'multiplying [the] possibilities of representation', adding further to the ambiguity and doubt of the retold event.[23]

First, Engberg's voice-over is often accompanied by the blackness of empty film frames. This is the case when she recites the myth about Eurydice's attempt to bring Orpheus back from Hades at recurrent intervals throughout the film. On other occasions, 'Mia' and 'Vince' reminisce around a particular event, but although they agree on how it played out, there is no imagery to illustrate their conversation. A rational reason for this omission is the fact that Engberg decided against re-enactment early on in the filmic process, as already mentioned.

Second, the lack of alignment between the memories appearing in the conversation between 'Mia' and 'Vince', is also considerable, and naturally limits the possibility of any visual representation. Instead, Engberg creates a visual reconciliation of their differing recollections by implementing Trinh's poetic approach of 'talking nearby', because of the impossibility of remembering correctly. Their ensuing winter in Stockholm in the mid-1990s, may serve as an example, since these differing memories are accompanied by excerpt footage of children playing in the snow, and floating ice floes under one of the city bridges, which I take to have been shot by Mia for her very first film in the 1980s.

A third obstacle to factuality, is the fact that most of the visual material is blurred and/or lacking all trace of intellectual content (Figure 11). The bulk of this footage was shot in 2012 by the real 'Vince' with his mobile telephone, and it represents his point of view of Paris as a longtime member of the French

Figure 11 *Belleville Baby* (2013). Photo: Mia Engberg.

criminal (under)world.[24] These images have little or nothing to do with the contents of the telephone conversations between 'Mia' and 'Vince', nor their relationship, since he really does not want to, and cannot, talk about his criminal activities. The empty corridors in industry buildings, interiors from parking spaces or rooftops could rather be seen as a visual metaphor for the audience's – and Mia's – lack of knowledge of the social interaction and human relationships governing Vince's working life.

Intermingled with these empty images, we see sequences of documentary footage shot by Mia Engberg at the time of their romance. A sequence of Vince shaving in their miniscule bathroom is especially favoured and repeated several times in the film. His magnificently toned torso and advanced tattoos are being idolised from behind right, as if Engberg were shooting a commercial for some shaving foam or other. From an epistemological point of view, the repetition of this cherished sequence of the Vince she once knew must be understood as an act of love towards him on her part, in 2012. These are the only occasions we get to see his face in the film, and they are not accompanied by any sound.

A large quantity of the footage has an overtly experimental character, which denies the expected, factual quality of the traditional documentary format. It is shot in ways that result in lack of focus, insufficient lighting or other types of inferior technical quality. The discernable imagery has only a vague connection to the remediated narrative, as when 'Mia's' voice-over relates to Vince's unhappy childhood in Marseilles and shows a couple of establishing shots from the town's immigrant quarter to the sound of seagulls and quietly mumbling voices from the street. There, all of a sudden, the collagist character of *Belleville Baby*'s premise allows Engberg to create a very tangible mood, reminding me of those we find in art films like *In the Mood for Love* (dir. Wong Kar-wai, Hong Kong, 2001) or *India Song* (dir. Marguerite Duras, France, 1974), films that are also based on memories which have been created through 'secondary revisions of the source material'.[25]

Indexicality in Time and Space

The fragmented character of *Belleville Baby*'s sujet has a decisive effect on the spectator's ability to place the film's fabula in time and space. Because of its demanding sujet, the perseverance needed to actively deconstruct the film's fabula in relation to its indexicality is instilled in the viewer only after a second or third screening. To no avail, it seems, because there simply is no linearity or chronology to be found in the film's fabula. No search, or journey, with a clear beginning, middle and end, working as a framework, like those we find in the traditional direct cinema format. In my view, Engberg abandoned that avenue of representation already when she decided that she did not want to make a regular re-enacted docudrama. Instead, Engberg decided to structure her narrative around a reiteration of her telephone conversations with Vincent, from memory. Fully aware that such a working method is unavoidably riddled by inaccuracy, she writes in the production notes: 'Given that I did not record the telephone conversations I cannot know if [the dialogue in *Belleville Baby*] is identical with what was actually said. Probably not. It took days, sometimes weeks, before I copied down the conversations in my diary.'[26]

Consequently, the indexicality of time and space in *Belleville Baby* is thoroughly disrupted and fragmented. There is an identifiable diachronical timeline at play in the film, in that 'Mia' and 'Vince' are talking about their past realtionship in a number of telephone calls in the present. These conversations and 'Mia's' self-asserted 'memories' in monologue form, guide us through the film, but are not presented in a clearly chronological order, either with regard to their individual content (which memory is reiterated), or their placement within the film's fabula (Figure 12). The indexicality of time in *Belleville Baby* thus confirms Annette Kuhn's suggestion that in memory texts, 'time tends not to be fully continuous or sequential. Literally, formally, or simply in terms of atmosphere created, the tenses of the memory text rarely fix events to specific moments of time or temporal sequences.'[27]

As already discussed, the indexicality of the film's space is equally veiled, instilling a fair amount of doubt in the spectator. Instead of establishing a confidential communicative structure vis-à-vis the spectator as required of a proper essay film, Engberg consciously destabilises the indexical information as to the factual circumstances alleged in the film.[28] Are these fragmented images reflecting an actual event? Is *Belleville Baby* a mockumentary, after all?

Figure 12   *Belleville Baby* (2013). Photo: Mia Engberg.

Is all this just a fictive love story, after all? The observant spectator is actually reassured of its reality, although the conclusive indexical signifiers may emerge only at the second or third screening of the film. Identifying them allows the spectator to actually place the batches of footage relevant to 'Mia's' and 'Vince's' reminisced fragments of common memories, in either the past (mid-1990s), or the present (2012–13).

Conversely, the inserted details referring to the Rey-Maupin affair, or Mia's Nan's secret romance, are reiterated in full accordance with a traditional historical documentary. The indexical demands are fulfilled through ample photographs of the main characters, their letters, newspaper items, and filmed footage. The clarity of these representations thus give the spectator little or no reason to distrust the information in *Belleville Baby*, despite the fact that these narrative threads also explore acts of memory.

Discussion

Having thus established *Belleville Baby*'s generic inbetween-ness and ambiguity to the full, it would seem that Mia Engberg's grounded reputation as a daring and uncompromising director cum producer of deeply subjective documentary films has reached a new limit. Given that Les Ateliers Varan is a film school promoting the interactive mode of *cinéma-vérité* as the main method for documentary film production, it also promotes auteurism as one of its foremost tools, in line with the practice of its founder, Jean Rouch's. Engberg has clearly embraced the idea of a strong authorial figure (Engberg and her memories) as a constant reference in *Belleville Baby*. Laura Rascaroli's demand for an explicit enunciator who comes forward to present his/her own personal viewpoint in the first person film is, however, problematised by Engberg by the inclusion of both 'Mia' and 'Vince' in the central fabula, regardless of the fact that she has used filmed footage produced by both in the film, in order to ultimately meet with the requirements of the enunciator's own reality.[29] Instead, having their sometimes diverging memories create exactly that plurality of voices which renders the essay film indeterminable, epistemologically uncertain and reflexive allows Engberg to destabilise the entire film form.[30]

Engberg's 2009 *Dirty Diaries* series, in which a number of selected female filmmakers had been asked to produce a short film on the subject of female pleasure as an expression of feminist pornography, is based on exactly that same plurality of voices. The project as such was otherwise clearly positioned within a framework championing the reflective, introspective and authorial modes characteristic for the traditional essay film, augmented by the condition that their own mobile cameras were to be their only means of production.[31]

As for *Belleville Baby*, Engberg found artistic inspiration in the already mentioned French conceptual artist Sophie Calle's work 'Prenez soin de vous' (2007), in which Calle used an unexpected letter of goodbye from a lover as a point of departure for her narrative. Calle initiated the transition of the document into her artistic practice by asking 100 women from all corners of society to decode the letter, and either video-recorded the women's oral presentations of their interpretations, or asked them to write it down. Given the women's differing biographies as to education and present occupation, they interpreted the letter very differently. What impressed Engberg from a methodological point of view was that through this creative treatment, Calle's work no longer had a personal frame of reference to it, but exerted a plurality of voices which so utterly redefined and reconceptualised the material that it became symbolic, and thus of common interest. With that, the general feelings of loss and chagrin immersed in a separation, in combination with Calle's 'artistic treatment' of the representation of these feelings, became the work's central theme, instead of the factual reality that went before it.

This construction of Sophie Calle's work is strongly reflected in Engberg's idea of writing down – from memory – the telephone conversations that she and Vincent had over a period of nine months. These recaptured but completely unauthentic dialogues now form the narrative lead of the fabula of *Belleville Baby*. The notion of oral *evidence* in the film is again diminished by the already mentioned language shifts, and re-enacted telephone conversations using a male voice actor, allegedly belonging to her former boyfriend, as far as her enunciation towards the audience is concerned. Engberg's narrative strategy in the film thus involves several conscious distancing effects which have an immediate bearing on the sound and voice representation in *Belleville Baby*, rendering redundant the original telephone conversations between her and the former boyfriend, despite the fact that they constituted her only authentic source of evidence. The extent of her effort to reconceptualise their love story for her own artistic purposes becomes clear through this rejection of firsthand information for the possibility of fictionalising it.

Engberg has characterised her overall approach to the *Belleville Baby* project as being autofictional, and has labeled the film as an 'autodocumentary'. In her production notes she writes that it is Marguerite Duras and her film *Les Mains Négatives* (1978) which inspired her to appropriate this literary notion as a working method for the project.[32] In her role as the film's director, Engberg is inspired by Duras's ability to *exactly* identify the focal point and mood of the story she wants to tell in *Les Mains Négatives* and then finding a *precise but abstract* way of visualising Time – Memory – Loss, through this process.[33] All efforts to aspire a narrative based on traditional dramaturgy have been left out, including the cinematographical strategies that can be expected. A key method to obtain this abstraction is Engberg's use of *métissage* or blending, as once introduced by Duras.[34] A striking example of this technique is reflected in the occasionally inserted almost painterly images of a panoramic view of Paris, or the images from the Parisian Undergrouynd, emptied of information for the benefit of an aesthetic effect. By thus blurring and merging genres, texts and identities, Engberg eschews our hopes for an illustrated recapitulation of her love story, by introducing us to feelings of Time – Memory – Loss through an experimental application of *métissage*.

Conclusion

Although Engberg does not mention the film, I suggest that the *mise en scène* and mood created in Marguerite Duras's film *India Song* is perhaps closest to the overall narrative dissolve and visual abstraction at the heart of *Belleville Baby*. The fictive telephone conversations in both films are accompanied by seemingly random images from documentary and staged footage, presented without any valid time references or narrative, and without any immediate attempt at identification with the onlooker. The abstract, visual discourse, and above all its refusal to introduce readable images and dramatised enactment of particular events, which characterises both films therefore add a crucial obscurity to the creative dimension of the presented love stories. Engberg's final challenge to the onlooker occurs when she allows the filmed footage to *seemingly* illustrate events similar to those which she and the male voice simultaneously revisit together over the phone, without being finally affirmative.

It is therefore my conjecture that one of the main objectives informing *Belleville Baby* is to openly challenge the spectator's voyeuristic gaze in the tradition of Laura Mulvey's address of the visual pleasure derived from watching classical Hollywood film.[35] The to-be-looked-at-ness and voyeuristic spectacle expected to emerge from the screening of a reiteration of a love story is undoubtedly deeply instilled in all cinema audiences around the world, regardless of the film's format. Engberg's creative treatment of both fabula and sujet in *Belleville Baby*, however, denies the audience its expected voyeuristic satisfaction, which, in my view, suggests that the work should be seen as an example of counter-discourse in documentary cinema. This suggestion seems to be epistemologically confirmed by the film's scarce proximity to reality in relation to both its visible evidence and narrative exposition. Therefore, in *Belleville Baby*, Engberg uses her authorial voice to display her preference for a creative treatment above adhering to the traditional demand on documentary cinema, and especially direct cinema, to reflect absolute reality. When considering Engberg's effort to make a film about Time, Memory and Loss in relation to the general epistemological tradition informing documentary cinema, it could be argued that her articulation of reality through the film's form and style clearly indicate the difficulty of representing the materiality of these sensations.

Michael Renov has suggested that 'autobiographical work can breed a kind of healthy skepticism regarding all documentary truth claims'.[36] On another occasion he has claimed that filmic self-inscription has to do with 'larger relations between autobiographical practices and the documentary project, resulting in the *very idea* of autobiography reinventing the *very idea* of documentary.[37] I now suggest that filmmakers like Mia Engberg take Renov's thesis one step further by working in a clearly counter-discursive auto-fictional and autobiographical manner which denies the supremacy of all material evidence in relation to traditional documentary practice.

From a formal point of view, *Belleville Baby* is the most remarkable result of such a transition, in that it describes a transcendental, non-sensible, process with the objective of visualising/evoking the normally invisible manifestations of Time, Memory and Loss. The premise for *Belleville Baby* is thus not primarily intellectual, but intuitive, and the challenge for the filmmaker lies in the necessary negation of traditional documentary working methods without turning the project into a work of art. Mia Engberg does nothing to hide the fictive side of her documentary production, or the imprint of her authorship on it. The boyfriend's voice rejects traditional documentary realism through the written dialogue, while at the same time representing a vocal 'evidence', and thus confirming the main character's 'real' memories of her relationship with him. *Belleville Baby* subsequently diverges heavily from the traditional indexical and epistemological demands we make on a documentary film, by being in full compliance with John Grierson's idea of a 'creative treatment of actuality'.

Another conjecture regarding *Belleville Baby* and its implicit challenge to the traditional first person autobiographical documentary is that Engberg has indeed managed to push the limits of this format in two major instances. First, there is Laura Rascaroli's statement that essay films generally 'set up a particular communicative structure' vis-à-vis the spectator,[38] which Engberg has unpicked by consciously confronting the film medium's dependency on inherent voyeurism through her unwavering resistance to all illustrative imagery in *Belleville Baby*. I furthermore suggest that Engberg problematises Rascaroli's premise regarding 'the identification of the general rhetorical structures by which essayistic films express their subjective viewpoint',[39] by blatantly exploring the avenues toward a pointed epistemological uncertainty that primarily emerge through the gaps created between the film's narrative, its visual form and indexicality in time and space. By rejecting the general rhetorical structure informing the first person documentary, which is to say its traditional narrative arc form which suggests a journey from obscurity to enlightenment, Engberg expresses her preference for a narrative structure which is circular in *Belleville Baby*. She clearly demonstrates this preference through her reinterpretation of the myth about Orpheus in Hades, and her own, failed attempt to bring Vincent back into the light, by coming to the conclusion that the memories of him could not be brought back with complete and real accuracy. A fact, which brought about the opportunity for a creative treament of reality. The formula of such a circular narrative would thus read normality-disparity-normality, suggesting the ruffling of lived memories ('Vince's' first telephone call), a failed attempt to make them come alive (the following telephone conversations and 'Mia's' wish to meet him again in France), after which they resume the character of 're-lived' memories (the narrative suggested in *Belleville Baby*). Engberg thus manages to extrapolate the epistemological gaps and visual moods which are conveyed through such an experience, indicating the random and fragmented character of *her own* memories, as well as *her own* feelings of loss, longing and time's passing. Whether or not *Belleville Baby* should be seen as an instance of counter-cinema, or merely an expanded form of the first person documentary through *métissage*, every inch of it, is the result of Engberg's female authorship.

Notes

1. See for exampel Michael Renov, 'First person films: some thesis on self-inscription', in Thomas Austin and Wilma de Jong (eds), *Rethinking Documentary: New Perspectives, New Practices* (Maidenhead: Open University Press, 2010), pp. 29–50; Michael Renov, *The Subject of Documentary* (London and Minneapolis, MN: University of Minnesota Press, 2004); Laura Rascaroli, *The Personal Camera: Subjectivite Cinema and the Essay Film* (London and New York: Wallflower Press, 2009); Alisa Lebow, *The Cinema of Me: The Self and Subjectivity in First Person Documentary* (London and New York: Wallflower Press, 2012).
2. See Renov, *The Subject of Documentary*, and Rascaroli, *The Personal Camera*.
3. Rascaroli, *The Personal Camera*, p. 3.

4. Bill Nichols, *Representing Reality: Issues and Concepts in Documentary* (Bloomington and Indianapolis, IN: Indiana Unviersity Press, 1991).
5. Brian Winston, *Claiming the Real:The Documantary Film Revisited* (London: BFI Publishing, 1995), ch. 3.
6. Bill Nichols, 'The voice of documentary', *Film Quarterly*, 36/3, 1983, pp. 17–30.
7. Mia Engberg, *Belleville Baby: Anteckningar från en filmisk process* (Göteborg: Filmkonst 135/Story AB, 2013), p. 35. Translation by Boel Ulfsdotter.
8. Erik Knudsen, 'Transcendental realism in documentary', in Thomas Austin and Wilma de Jong (eds), *Rethinking Documentary: New Perspectives, New Practices* (Maidenhead: Open University Press, 2010), pp. 108–20, 108–9.
9. Ibid. pp. 111–12.
10. Ibid. pp. 113–17.
11. Ibid. pp. 118–19.
12. Annette Kuhn, *Family Secrets: Facts of Memory and Imagination* (London and New York: Verso, 2002).
13. Ibid. p. 157.
14. Ibid. p. 162.
15. Renov, *The Subject of Documentary*, p. 114.
16. <https://en.wikipedia.org/wiki/Rey-Maupin_affair>.
17. Engberg, *Belleville Baby*, pp. 43–4, 87–95.
18. Elise Hugueny-Léger, 'Broadcasting the self: autofiction, television and representations of authorship in contemporary French literature', *Life Writing*, 14/1, 2016, pp. 5–18.
19. Kuhn, *Family Secrets*, p. 5.
20. Ibid. 157.
21. Trinh T. Minh-ha, *Cinema Interval* (London and New York: Routledge, 1999), p. 218.
22. Rascaroli, *The Personal Camera*, p. 2.
23. Hugueny-Léger, 'Broadcasting the self', p. 2.
24. Engberg, *Belleville Baby*, pp. 103–4.
25. Kuhn, *Family Secrets*, p. 5.
26. Engberg, *Belleville Baby*, p. 87. Translation by Boel Ulfsdotter.
27. Kuhn, *Family Secrets*, p. 162.
28. Rascaroli, *The Personal Camera*, p. 3.
29. Ibid. p. 3.
30. Renov, *The Subject of Documentary*, p. 70.
31. Rascaroli, *The Personal Camera*, p. 15.
32. Engberg, *Belleville Baby*, pp. 88–90.
33. Ibid. pp. 92–3.
34. Shirley Jordan, 'Autofiction in the feminine', *French Studies: A Quarterly Review*, 67/1, 2013, pp. 76–84, 81.
35. Laura Mulvey, 'Visual pleasure and narrative cinema', *Screen*, 16/3, 1975, pp. 6–18.
36. Renov, 'First person films', p. 41.
37. Ibid. pp. 40–2.
38. Rascaroli, *The Personal Camera*, p. 3.
39. Ibid., p. 3.

Filmography

Belleville Baby (Mia Engberg, Sweden, 2013).
The Dirty Diaries: 12 Shorts of Feminist Porn (Mia Engberg, Sweden, 2009).
Les Enfants du Square (Mia Engberg, France, 1994).
Les Mains Négatives (Marguerite Duras, France, 1978).
In the Mood for Love (Wong Kar-wai, Hong Kong, 2001).
India Song (Marguerite Duras, France, 1974).

9. TO::FOR::BY::ABOUT::WITH::FROM:: TOWARDS SOLID WOMEN: ON (NOT) BEING ADDRESSED BY TRACEY MOFFATT'S *MOODEITJ YORGAS*

Sophie Mayer

> I've always looked up to the idea of communications 'cos I worked at the A.B.C. [Australian Broadcasting Corporation] for three and a half years and appreciate the power that a control of communications gives you . . . the spoken word [has] more communication value for Aborigines than the written word, in this context. But then of course the written word is preserved. I still think the most effective means of communication is . . . we call it the 'noongar grapevine'. It's quicker than news. More effective, too. It uses a sort of communication that can only be understood by Aborigines and it's highly functional.
>
> Gloria Brennan.[1]

Gloria Brennan was a Wongi speaker of Pindiini (Nyanganyatjara) descent; claiming Weebo as her doogurr (birthplace), she was a linguist and anthropologist deeply concerned with speech and story.[2] Reflecting on the contemporary cultural use of the Nyungar phrase 'murdidj yorgas', which translates as 'strong/clever women', feminist anthropologist Pat Baines cites Brennan as a shining example, noting that Tracey Moffatt's film *Moodeitj Yorgas* (*Solid Women*, 1988) was 'a tribute to Wongi academic Gloria Brennan, who in her middle years had died of cancer'. In its celebration of Brennan's legacy as a community organiser, linguist and anthropologist, the film confirms that 'the notion of strong and talented women is part of Nyungar cultural representations'.[3] As Baines notes, Nyungar/noongar is a post-settlement nomenclature adopted by a collective of distinctive communities in the southwest of Western Australia, from just north of Gingin and Moora, eastwards to just beyond Merridin but west of Southern Cross, and southwards includes Hyden and the Stirlings to the south coast. The western boundary is provided by the Indian Ocean . . . The term 'Nyungar' means 'man', a fact that cannot go unnoticed in a discussion about southwest women.[4]

Looking at the work done by Nyungar grandmothers on land claims, Baines is keen to establish both the traditional and contemporary continued usage of murdidj/moordeitj yorgas as referring to respect for women's law within Nyungar communities, a respect that settler writers had argued was absent.

Noongar lawyer Hannah McGlade notes that the film emerged from a similar urgency towards redefining the mainstream narrative:

> The production was conceived by a small group of Perth-based Aboriginal women, including myself, who made the decision to actively promote Noongar women as moorditj yorgas, not because we are 'cultural revisionists' but because it is what we know to be true of our knowledge of history and culture.[5]

Where Baines is contesting historical accounts of Nyungar women as subservient to men, McGlade is challenging a claim by settler academic Joan Kimm that Aboriginal women who deny the existence of what she terms 'sacred rape' are in denial about their own cultures. Judy Atkinson has comprehensively dismantled Kimm's argument, showing her lack of evidence and highly subjective research, and demonstrating the insidious and negative effect that settler media's positive reception for Kimm's 2004 book *A Fatal Conjunction* had for Aboriginal women's services.[6]

The stakes for the *Moodeitj Yorgas* project were therefore high: contesting historical erasure, contemporary misrepresentation by settler culture, and – as McGlade argues – ways in which settler patriarchy had been internalised within Aboriginal communities to devalue women's law. Both Baines, on the page, and Moffatt, in the film, develop a positive strategy for contestation: representing a community of living Nyungar moodeitj yorgas articulating the impact of colonisation and strategies of resistance, in solidarity with the example of their ancestors. Baines notes that 'Nyungar elders emphasise that they have "survived." They underline in their testimonies to a non-Indigenous world just how extraordinary this is, for they have survived against the odds.'[7] Moffatt's film is both a document of this survival, and a strategy therein, placing its speakers on record at a moment when Aboriginal feminism was coming into prominence, and when Moffatt's own work was achieving international attention with the release of *Nice Colored Girls* (1987). The work of this essay is to further the film's survivance; for Anishinaabe poet and theorist Gerald Vizenor, who appropriated the term from colonial legal jargon, 'Survivance is an active sense of presence, the continuance of native stories, not a mere reaction, or a survivable name. Native survivance stories are renunciations of dominance, tragedy and victimry.'[8] Just as Baines insists on the continuance of murdidj yorgas as a self-naming practice among Nyungar women, so the aim of my essay it to amplify Moffatt's attention to Noongar moodeitj yorgas by reading it through its immediate contemporary and communitarian context: that is, in relation to, and in respect of, the larger Aboriginal women's community it implies, not least in its dedication to Gloria Brennan.

Writing in 2001, Baines is building on two decades of attention to and through 'women's business' to which Brennan was central, to borrow the title of the 1986 report of the Aboriginal Women's Task Force edited by two Aboriginal women, Phyllis Daylight and Mary Johnstone.[9] Moffatt's documentary was part of a wave of activism, research and documentation of the mid-1980s that appears to have been prompted by the run-up to the bicentenary of the First Fleet's landing on 26 January 1788, (re)named Invasion Day by Aboriginal communities. Moffatt protested at a bicentennial re-enactment of the fleet's launch that took place in Plymouth, UK, in 1987, according to a news article that the artist loaned for reproduction in Catherine Summerhayes's catalogue raisonné. Moffatt, who was in the UK with a touring Arnhem Land dance troupe, was escorted away by police after she 'blackflagged' the ship; that is, brought a black, red and yellow Australian Aboriginal flag to the site. 'Why should we celebrate an invasion of backward Englishmen into our traditional lands?', she told reporters.[10]

Speaking to Eurowestern interviewers and critics, Moffatt frequently dodges labels such as 'Aboriginal artist' or 'political artist', for example telling American art critic Sebastian Smee in 2001, 'I was always very – I am still, kind of – political. But I wanted to make my own images, and not work on political documents.'[11] The conjunction of her action in Plymouth – taking her protest to the source of colonisation – and her involvement with *Moodeitj Yorgas* argues that what she is avoiding are the reductive strategies of a colonial culture still obsessed with classifying 'specimens'. Fellow feminist performance artist of colour Coco Fusco notes that, when she interviewed Moffatt, there was a resistance not marked in their off-the-record conversations, a refusal to be pinned to labels or meanings. Fusco writes that she 'realized that [Moffatt] was leaving gaps not so much to pass herself off as an aesthete but to encourage a metaphorical reading of her work by an audience that still treated artists of colour as unimaginative reporters of abject social realities'.[12]

Moffatt's work is both political and Aboriginal within, and addressed to, its own Nyungar communitarian context, in which those adjectives are seen as part of a complex holistic practice, not pigeonholes that shelve her work away from the status of 'high art'. This is particularly true in the mid to late 1980s, as an active feminist community took shape, sparked by a conference co-organised by Brennan and fellow Aboriginal anthropologist Marcia Langton, which resulted in the resonantly titled anthology *We Are Bosses Ourselves*.[13] Both Brennan and Langton contributed to *Women's Business* as researchers, and Langton would later play the daughter Jedda, a deconstructive reference to Charles Chauvel's film *Jedda* (1955), in Moffatt's film *Night Cries: A Rural Tragedy* (1989). Like Brennan, she was interested in the potential of Aboriginal-produced media, authoring the report *'Well I Heard it on the Radio and Saw it on the Television': An Essay for the Australian Film Commission on the Politics and Aesthetics of Filmmaking by and about Aboriginal People and Things*, which included a cover photograph from Moffatt's *beDevil* (1993) and a case study of *Night Cries*, as well as of Arrernte filmmaker Rachel Perkins' autoethnographic documentary (as producer) *Jardiwarnpa – A Warlpiri Fire Ceremony* (1993).[14]

The connections between Brennan, Langton, Moffatt and the network of activists, researchers and community women who contributed to the publications suggests the formation of a 'noongar grapevine' specifically contoured to sharing and foregrounding 'women's business', and both Brennan and Langton argue that audiovisual media plays a significant, and significantly indigenised, role therein. 'The enormous output of visual art, film, video, music and performing arts currently produced by Aboriginal people is a modern development of the great value they have traditionally placed on the visual and oral arts', argues Langton, noting that 'much of it remains uncommodified and subject to traditional Aboriginal social rules', a negotiation she particularly explores with regard to Perkins's and Ned Lander's *Jardiwarnpa*.[15] In *Women's Business*, Langton is quoted as saying that 'Song, dance, body, rock and sand painting, special languages and the oral explanation of the myths encoded in these essentially religious art forms have been the media of the Law to the present day'; her subsequent study suggests that new audiovisual media continue this encoding.[16]

Langton's reading of Aboriginal-authored film and video as a continuation of ceremony, and thus resistant to commodification and general distribution, is particularly significant when reading Moffatt's *Moodeitj Yorgas*. In contradistinction to her film, video and photographic work, which has been widely exhibited in Eurowestern art spaces and analysed within postmodern, postcolonial and feminist theoretical frameworks, *Moodeitj Yorgas* has been excluded from such exhibition and discussion – or, at least, withheld. The film was commissioned by the Women's Advisory Coucil rather than originated by Moffatt, and made with an entirely female crew; as such I would argue belongs collectively to the participants and producers.[17] Its address was to Western Australians, as it was launched on 24 February 1989 with a screening hosted by Elsie Kay Hallahan, the minister assisting the Minister for Women's Interests, Western Australia, and screenings in schools and community centres then followed.[18]

Yet, unlike Moffatt's HIV/AIDS prevention public service announcement 'Spread the Word' (1987), made the year previously for Redfern Aboriginal Health Service, *Moodeitj Yorgas* does not have a localised address, nor an instrumentalised or instructive documentary approach. 'The interest we've had from overseas has been enormous', Moffatt told Diana Callendar in 1989.[19] The film was picked up in 1990 for UK distribution on Umatic video by one of two feminist distributors, Circles or Cinema of Women, who merged the following year as Cinenova.[20] As Summerhayes, one of the few Moffatt scholars to write about the film, argues, the film can be paired with *Nice Colored Girls* as being a multi-layered, transhistorical representation and re-imagination of Aboriginal women that combines narration, performance, historical documents and argument. Summerhayes aligns both films with Bill Nichols's 'poetic mode' and 'performative mode' of documentary.[21]

This is borne out by the colour stills from *Moodeitj Yorgas* reproduced over eight double-page spreads, including a headshot of each of Moffatt's speakers, generally showing their name as a subtitle. The headshots are mixed in with several from each of the chroma key sections Summerhayes designates as poetic/performative, wherein female figures in silhouette dance and/or gesture in front of backdrops painted by artist Sue (Susan) Wyatt.[22] As Fusco notes, 'You have a consistently tough array of women in your work. Your women are not femme . . . They're not delicate, they're not frail, they're not . . .'; Moffatt responds, 'Passive.'[23] In fact, the range of female embodiment seen in this film is very broad, but even the performative hyper-femininity of teenage ballroom dancer Tanya Corbett is revealed as moodeitj: solid, strong, capable.

The film does not prioritise Eurowestern forms of femininity (as Fusco observes), nor does it attend to conventional Eurowestern female masculinities, even as it foregrounds professionalism and attainment. Baines argues that 'Academic performance has certainly marked some younger women as murdidj ("solid" is also used as a designation for capable)', that is, insofar as their studies in settler institutions increase their capabilities for their own communities.[24] This is certainly how Moffatt represents her speakers such as Helen Corbett, executive officer of the Aboriginal Legal Service in Perth, and Professor Pat Dudgeon, a Bardi woman dedicated to developing indigenous psychotherapy. Dudgeon comments in the film that she sees

> the Aboriginal way forward this century as being two-pronged: one, that we should be encouraged to take on white skills and some white ways, on our own terms; and another way is to give respect to our cultural ways of doing things.

Speakers such as Denise Groves, project officer at the Department of Aboriginal Affairs, Perth (also an adviser on the film), and Joan Winch of the Aboriginal Medical Service, Perth, also reflect this stance of negotiating with settler culture 'on our own terms'.

Given the 'noongar grapevine', we can also read Dudgeon's remarks as commentary *on* the film, and the filmmaker's approach, from *within* the film. Like the work of Trinh T. Minh-ha, Moffatt's work bridges settler and indigenous culture, or rather, indigenises useful aspects of settler culture, both technological and formal, on her own terms, and this strategy is both supported by Dudgeon, and aligned with her own practice as a community worker. Filmmaking, in Moffatt's hands, is both a 'white skill' and 'our cultural way of doing things'. Trinh notes that this synthesis particularly emerges from a sense of practice that refutes the Eurowestern ideal of the individual artist, expressed not least in the concept of the cinematic auteur. Arguing that experimental form is as, if not more, valid as part of the radical struggle, because it disrupts even the hierarchy of subject/object or artist/audience, Trinh writes that:

> A writing for the people, by the people, and from the people is, literally, a multipolar reflecting reflection that remains free from the conditions of subjectivity and objectivity and yet reveals them both ... In this unwonted spectacle made of reality and fiction, where redoubled images form and reform, neither I nor you come first. No primary core of irradiation can be caught hold of, no hierarchical first, second, or third exists except as mere illusion. All is empty when one is plural.[25]

Although dominated by talking heads, *Moodeitj Yorgas* is not only 'made of reality and fiction', but does not observe the Eurowestern hierarchical distinction between them, integrating traditional storytelling and oral history among the factual reports.

The film is also a palimpsest of 'redoubled images' that 'form and reform' the community that is speaking and being spoken to, for and with. As well as the living speakers appearing as talking heads – and, with a cut in each interview, as moving, gesturing, lively bodies – and the ancestor stories related in silhouette (and the dedication to Brennan), there are also hundreds of photographs of Nyungar women from a number of archival sources, as well as photographs taken for the film credited to McGlade, Lorrae Coffin and Carolyn Lewis. These photographs are sometimes flat, parallel to the frame, and sometimes tilted, as if in a photograph frame set up at an angle to the screen. All of them appear against an image of the night sky. The first time the image of the starry sky is seen, it is a map of Australia that flies in. The names of different Nyungar mobs – Baada, Aranda, Wadjari, Njangamarda – fly out of the southwestern corner of the map, tellingly almost too fast to read. The conjunction of pre-colonial community names and the vast diversity of images of Aboriginal women 'redouble[s]' the presence of the community on screen, both geographically and temporally, summoning ancestors.

It also stretches the film's reach into the astronomical zone, as the starry sky is not a site of a space-age future, but of a connection to the deep past and the Dreamtime. Baines notes that, unusually, while

> the whole earth is regarded as a mother and emphasises the considerable significance of women . . . it does not go together with a masculising of the sky. Many of the stories about the star beings have ceased to be told in the southwest.[26]

Moffatt suggests through her use of the image that they may still be remembered, if not shared with settler scholars such as Baines. 'What is therefore at stake in Moffatt's work is that site where the corporeal body (the body immersed in the material life) intersects with ethereal relations, or the unseen energies in the life of the spirit', for Cathie Payne.[27] It is in the seemingly conventional act of including archival photographs in her documentary, as much as in the richly imaginative, gorgeously vivid and extremely powerful poetic/performative silhouette sequences, that Moffatt connects to these 'unseen energies'.

As the photographs appear in this first iteration, Lucy Cox's song 'Who Dat' plays. Cox was a popular performer who recorded an album, *Kimberley Legend*, but otherwise her only presence in the (Eurowestern) documentary record is as composer for Moffatt's film.[28] Cox's story is indicative of *Moodeitj Yorgas*' work as an expanding community of solid women, but also of the ways in which Moffatt is following Dudgeon's advice of grasping and indigenising some white ways, preserving Cox's performance and status as an artist. It is particularly pertinent given that her song asks 'Who dat?', which at first seems to address the people seen in the photograph, asking who they are if they have passed out of memory and/or if their cultures and languages have been erased. The second line of the chorus, however, asks 'Who's a-calling my name?', as if the people in the photographs were speaking, asking their successors who was calling them back to earth.

Cox's question makes us aware of our position as documentary viewers, and forecloses the conventional, and asymmetric, demand for access to knowledge about people, places and histories implied by that position. It is also a marker of the very different viewing position that may be taken by Aboriginal viewers of the film. Australian Screen's webpage for *Moodeitj Yorgas* foregrounds the signal reminder that the film 'may contain names, images or voices of deceased Aboriginal or Torres Strait Islander people'.[29] Such respect for the manifestations of ancestors is qualitatively different from Roland Barthes's assertion of the photograph as always already a site of mourning, or of Jacques Derrida's notion of archive fever, both of which have been applied extensively to film. Cox's insistent querying of 'Who dat?' acts as a reminder to afford respect, not melancholia, when viewing the photographs, to listen to the summoning being exchanged and be present to honour it.

One of the moodeitj yorgas shown in the film, Sally Morgan, tells a story that speaks to this distinction in her hugely successful book *My Place*, and also to the work that the film is doing with traditional song, dance and story in the chroma keyed sections. Morgan dedicates her book to her family, whose narrative she has altered by asking questions about her grandmother's once-suppressed Aboriginality, stating: 'How deprived we would have been if we had been willing to let things stay as they were. We would have survived, but not as a whole people. We would never have known our place.'[30] The inversion by which she alters 'known our place' from a classist and racist pejorative, an insistence on immobile social categories, into a fulsome embrace of Aboriginal identity, is palpable in Moffatt's film work as well, particularly in its negotiation of individual authorship and communal ceremony. Morgan's seemingly autobiographical book takes a shift that seems surprising to a Eurowestern reader, changing halfway through to a verbatim record of her Nan's life story.

Among her fascinating and complex history, Talahue tells her granddaughter a story that is very evocative of the form of Moffatt's documentary:

> Now this is something I've told no-one. You mightn't believe me. 'Member when we first moved there [to Morgan's childhood home]? Couple of nights, you came out on the back verandah and found Gladdie [Talahue's daughter and Morgan's mother] and me sittin' there, 'member we made you go away? You was always in the wrong place at the wrong time. Well, we was listenin' to music. It was the blackfellas playin' their didgeridoos and singin' and laughin' down in the swamp. Your mother could hear it. I said to her one night, 'I'm goin' down there are tell those natives off. Who do they think they are, wakin' all the white people up'. That's when Gladdie told me. She said, 'Don't go down there, Mum, there's no one there, only bush'. You see, we was hearin' the people from long ago. Our people who used to live here before the white man came. Funny, they stopped playin' after your father [who was white] died. I think now they was protectin' us. Fancy, eh? Those dear, old people. You see, the blackfella knows all 'bout spirits.[31]

As well as returning to Morgan a part of her childhood that she could not have understood while her father prohibited Talahue from admitting her Aboriginality, she also teaches Morgan the correct way to hear, see and address her ancestors, 'those dear, old people'. Her daughter was able to hear them; in bringing forth and listening closely to her story, her granddaughter has shown the potential to carry this story.

Moodeitj Yorgas similarly teaches its (whitefella) audience how to listen, not through straightforward storytelling, but by fragmenting and braiding the multiple formal aspects of the film. It opens with a female voice, unsubtitled and thus speaking to Noongar audiences from the outset, singing/speaking from offscreen, but far forward in the mix so it sounds intimately present, beneath a soft, soughing wind. The first image is a silhouette of a female body lying down, stroking her rounded belly which fills the bottom half of the frame. Subtitles appear as the voice changes to a higher-pitched voice that sounds like it has been double-tracked to register as choric. Payne notes that as 'the ear listens for such arrangements and rhythms, these subtle shifts escape, like changes in air currents across the earth', but the abstract elemental serves to draw our attention to the cultural specificities of those who descend from, and guard, the elements.[32]

The first three subtitles read: 'Long ago when | we lived in the | desert my mother'. Moffatt, who speaks English, would not be unaware of the double meaning of the third subtitle: on the surface, it tallies with Baines's recognition of the maternal land; in the context of speaking back to colonisation, what Joy Harjo and Gloria Bird call 'reinventing the enemy's language', the caesura between 'the' and 'desert' allows 'desert' to act as a verb, an accusation that settler society has deserted the holistic ecosystem as well as/by its desertion (and desertification) of Aboriginal cultures and communities.[33] I do not know whether the voice-over contains a similar play on words; I cannot know. The English subtitle is aimed at me, and from the beginning of the film I am aware of what I cannot hear, and what I am not permitted to hear.

The long ago story repeats, in fragments, throughout the film, narrating a refusal to wear European clothes. The final iteration appears just before the end credits, and the subtitles read 'we used to wear them [the clothes] | upside down | or inside out'. Once again, Moffatt instructs us on how to read her documentary form: it wears its Eurowestern clothes of cinematic technology and narrative but reverses and inverts them playfully. Each of the silhouette sequences is equally as complex in its provision of aesthetic pleasure and narrative interest balanced with a withholding of culturally specific detail that would allow a non-Noongar viewer to understand fully the relation between, for example, the three women who dance with branches in their hands, the traditional male-voiced song, and the voice-over. Baines notes that grandmothers 'swept around their own homes to create a place testifying to the alert wakefulness of their care for their successors … Some grandmothers would then move on to perform the same duties of sweeping with a branch around ancestral graves in the country cemeteries.'[34] The sweeping motions that the dancers execute may be preparing the space for each new speaker and a newly attentive audience, or may be keeping clean the ancestral space summoned by the inclusion of photographs.

Addressing the three ghost stories in Moffatt's film *beDevil* (1993) that speak to the in/ability of settlers to hear, Corinn Columpar particularly relates the film's mode of address, in its use of non-sync sound which is developed through the talking head sequences in *Moodeitj Yorgas,* to its enunciation of an auteurial Aboriginality.[35] With *Moodeitj Yorgas* her argument could be used to identify a(n auteurial Aboriginality *as* a) spectatorly Aborginality (and vice versa). Fusco's observation that Moffatt wishes 'to encourage a metaphorical reading of her work' is true also for a film that appears to stand at a tangent to her *oeuvre* due to its invocation of classical, informational documentary norms; they are, after all, being worn inside-out – to show they are worn out.

While feminist documentary studies have addressed the objectification of the female (mindless) body as the grounds of the cinematic apparatus, they have paid less attention to its intersections with what Fatima Tobing Rony calls 'fascinating cannibalism', the ways in which early cinema purveys images of 'the racialized Other known as the Primitive' for consumption.[36] Faye Ginsburg has long argued that: 'Efforts to produce indigenous media worldwide are generally small-scale, low budget and locally based; because of this, their existence is politically and economically fragile, while their significance is largely invisible outside of occasional festivals or circles of specialists.'[37] Writing about *Moodeitj Yorgas* within the context of feminist documentary, I try to mark its significance without cannibalising it. The film bears witness to its Indigenous feminism, located in women's law, story and ceremony that predates colonisation, and its artful, joyful blending of performative and informative modes. By inserting it into the discussion of what constitutes feminism and documentary, I want to advocate for more people to see and hear it, and to note that I cannot completely see or hear it, and certainly cannot fully translate it to the page.

'I do not want to retell in detail what is the proper property of Nyungar families to tell or recount', writes Baines.[38] As Morgan says in *Moodeitj Yorgas* about her new-found designation by the Australian media as Aboriginal spokeswoman, a role that discomfits her, 'I think people like to have experts.' Despite the development of poetic and performative modes, documentary (and film scholarship likewise) still rests on an ideology of expertise and authority, on hierarchies of knowledge – including the emplacement of that which is inscribed on any media over that which is performed bodily, and on (notions of) transparency and objectivity over practices of appropriate access and subjectivity. In accordance with Brennan's idea of the 'noongar grapevine' and Talahue's 'dear, old people', in *Moodeitj Yorgas,* Moffatt repositions communications as within, across, by, about, to and for Noongar women's community, not from it. Finally, the film and its address is moordeitj: belonging to itself, solid on its own ground, knowing its place.

Acknowledgements

With huge gratitude to Cinenova for continuing the work of feminist distribution, and particularly to Irene Revell, who generously made it possible for me to work on *Moodeitj Yorgas*.

Notes

1. Gloria Brennan quoted in Kevin Gilbert, 'Gloria Brennan [interview]', in *Living Black: Blacks Talk to Kevin Gilbert* (Ringwood, VIC: Allen Lane, 1977), p. 88.
2. A note on Indigenous words: these are not italicised in the essay except where original speakers/writers have italicised them. This is a standard practice in contemporary Indigenous studies. Similarly, I follow the transliterations used by individual speakers/writers rather than attempting to standardise.
3. Pat Baines, 'Seeking justice: traditions of social action among Indigenous women in the southwest of Western Australia', in Peggy Brock (ed.), *Words and Silences: Aboriginal Women, Politics and Land* (Crows Nest, NSW: Allen and Unwin, 2001), pp. 84–5.
4. Ibid. p. 59.
5. Hannah McGlade, *Our Greatest Challenge: Aboriginal Children and Human Rights* (Canberra: Aboriginal Studies Press, 2012), pp. 63–4.
6. Ibid. p. 64; Judy Atkinson, 'To do nothing is tantamount to genocide [book review]', *Indigenous Law Bulletin*, 6/20, 2006, <http://www.austlii.edu.au/au/journals/IndigLawB/2006/41.html>
7. Baines, 'Seeking justice', p. 69.
8. Gerald Vizenor, *Manifest Manners: Narratives on Postindian Survivance* (Lincoln, NE: University of Nebraska, 1999), p. vii.
9. Phyllis Daylight and Mary Johnstone, *Women's Business: Report of the Aboriginal Women's Task Force* (Canberra: Australian Government Publishing Service, 1986).
10. Quoted in J. Rowbowtham, 'Fleet replay blackflagged', article reproduced in Catherine Summerhayes, *The Moving Images of Tracey Moffatt* (Milan: Edizioni Charta, 2007), p. 331; the header identifying the publication has been cropped out of the image.
11. Sebastian Smee, '"Just don't call me an Aboriginal artist": Tracey Moffatt's roots play a big part in her spellbinding new work', *The Independent*, 16 April 2001, quoted in Summerhayes, *The Moving Images of Tracey Moffatt*, p. 19.
12. Coco Fusco, 'Bad grrl bravado: a conversation with Tracey Moffatt', *The Bodies That Were Not Ours and Other Writings* (London: Routledge, in collaboration with Iniva, 2001), p. 129.
13. Faye Gale (ed.), *We Are Bosses Ourselves: The Status and Role of Aboriginal Women Today* (Canberra: Australian Institute of Aboriginal Studies, 1983).
14. Marcia Langton, 'Well, I heard it on the radio and I saw it on the television': *An Essay for the Australian Film Commission on the Politics and Aesthetics of Filmmaking by and about Aboriginal People and Things* (Woolloomooloo, NSW: Australian Film Commission, 1993).
15. Ibid. p. 9, pp.75–80.
16. Langton, quoted in World Council for Churches, *Justice for Aboriginal Australians* (Sydney: Australian Council of Churches, 1981), p. 13, quoted in Daylight and Johnstone, *Women's Business*, p. 62.

17. D. Callendar, news story, *The West Australian*, 25 February 1989, p. 39; reproduced in Summerhayes, p. 34; the headline has been cropped out of the image.
18. Ibid.
19. Ibid.
20. <http://www.cinenova.org/filmdetail.php?&filmId=350>.
21. Bill Nichols, *Introduction to Documentary*, Bloomington, Indiana University Press, 2001), pp. 102–3 and Bill Nichols, *Blurred Boundaries* (Bloomington: Indiana University Press, 2004), pp. 95–6, both quoted in Summerhayes, *The Moving Images of Tracey Moffatt*, p. 39.
22. Summerhayes, *The Moving Image*, pp. 62–75.
23. Fusco, 'Bad grrl bravado', pp. 133–4.
24. Baines, 'Seeking justice', p. 86.
25. Trinh T. Min-ha, *Woman, Native, Other: Writing, Postcoloniality, Feminism* (Bloomington, IN: Indiana University Press, 1989), p. 22.
26. Baines, 'Seeking justice', p. 73.
27. Cathie Payne, 'Visible spaces, electronic records: John Conomos and Tracey Moffatt', *Continuum: Journal of Media & Cultural Studies*, 8/1, 1994, p. 320.
28. 'Cox, Lucy', *Recordings by Indigenous Artists (1899–1998): A Guide to Holdings in the National Film and Sound Archive of Australia* (Canberra: National Film and Sound Archive of Australia and Australian Institute of Aboriginal and Torres Strait Islander Studies, 1999), p. 36.
29. <http://aso.gov.au/titles/documentaries/moodcitj-yorgas/clip1/>.
30. Sally Morgan, *My Place* (Fremantle: Fremantle Arts Centre Press, 1987), p. 5.
31. Ibid. p. 426.
32. Payne, 'Visible spaces, electronic records', p. 322.
33. Gloria Bird and Joy Harjo (eds), *Reinventing the Enemy's Language: Contemporary Native Women's Writing of North America* (New York: W. W. Norton, 1997).
34. Baines, 'Seeking justice', p. 79.
35. Corinn Columpar, 'At the limits of visual representation: Tracey Moffatt's still and moving images', in Corinn Columpar and Sophie Mayer (eds), *There She Goes: Feminist Filmmaking and Beyond* (Detroit, MI: Wayne State University Press, 2010), pp. 152–60.
36. Fatimah Tobing Rony, *The Third Eye: Race, Cinema and Ethnographic Spectacle* (Durham, NC: Duke University Press, 1996), p. 10.
37. Faye Ginsburg, 'Indigenous media: Faustian contract or global village?', *Cultural Anthropology*, 6/1, 1991, p. 92.
38. Baines, 'Seeking justice', p. 77.

Filmography

Chauvel, C.. dir., *Jedda* (Charles Chauvel Productions, 141 mins, 1955). Colour, 35 mm.
Cox, L., perf., 'Who Dat', 1988. Soundtrack to *Moodeitj Yorgas*.
Lander, N., dir., *Jardiwarnpa – A Warlpiri Fire Ceremony* (City Pictures in association with SBS Indigenous Unit and Warlukurlangu Artists Association, 55 mins, 1993). Colour, VHS.
Moffatt, T., dir., *beDevil* (90 mins, 1993). Colour, 35mm.
Moffatt, T., dir., *Moodeitj Yorgas (Solid Women)* (24 mins, 1988). Colour, Umatic video.
Moffatt, T., dir., *Nice Colored Girls* (18 mins, 1987). Colour, 16mm.
Moffatt, T., dir., *Night Cries: A Rural Tragedy* (19 mins, 1989). Colour, 35mm.
Moffatt, T., dir., 'Spread the Word' (10 mins, 1987). Colour, VHS.

10. CONSTRUCTING AN INTIMATE SPHERE THROUGH HER OWN FEMALE BODY: NAOMI KAWASE'S DOCUMENTARY FILMS

Wakae Nakane

Japanese female director Naomi Kawase (1969–) came into critical prominence with works such as *Suzaku* (*Moe no suzaku*, 1997) and *Mogari: The Mourning Forest* (*Mogari no mori*, 2007), both of which won prizes at the Cannes Film Festival. Born and raised in Nara, Japan, she started filmmaking in earnest soon after graduating from a film college. Since then, her consistent efforts and the presentation of her works at various international film festivals have won her a global reputation as one of Japan's most prominent female film directors, particularly on the arthouse and film festival circuit.

Although Kawase's works are recognised internationally and not only in her home country, there is a paucity of academic commentary on her work. This could be connected to the general tendency in film scholarship that, whilst female involvement in both industry and independent filmmaking (especially documentary filmmaking) is growing these days, not enough attention has been paid in terms of academic inquiry.[1] Therefore, by analysing Kawase's documentary films as a pivotal practice in women's documentary filmmaking, this chapter aims to complement the insufficient research into female authorship, within the Japanese film production context.

Since the late 2000s, Kawase has largely been known for fictional works such as *Mogari* or *Sweet Bean* (*An*, 2015). She originally started her career, however, as a documentary filmmaker, and more than half of her works are documentaries. One of the most interesting aspects of her documentaries is that the majority of them reflect her own life experiences. *Embracing* (*Ni tsutsumarete*, 1992), which was released when she was twenty-four years old, centres on her own process of internal reflection on a father from whom she had been separated for a long period, and uses a journey format that culminates in a temporary reunion with him. We can also see similar autobiographical elements in films such as *Katatsumori* (1994), a portrayal of her everyday life with her foster mother, and *Kya Ka Ra Ba A* (aka *Sky, Water, Fire, Wind, Earth*, 2001), which details her reminiscing for her father, who had passed away just before she started to make this film. What she focuses on in these films, however, is not only the figure of herself, but also the relationship she has with the people surrounding her. In this sense, we can define her documentaries more precisely as films not only about herself, but also as films that show the relationships she constructs with others. Her documentary films show the construction of a community, one that could be called an 'intimate sphere', centring on the presentation of the filmmaker's own, female body.

Documentary films in which filmmakers present their lives are generally labelled as a form of 'self-documentary (or *serufu-dokyumentari*) in Japan', and have been produced in the country since the 1970s. The best internationally known *serufu-dokyumentari*, and one of the earliest examples of the form, is probably Kazuro Hara's *Extreme Private Eros: Love Song 1974* (*Kyokushiteki erosu renka*, 1974), a documentary in which Hara films Miyuki Takeda, his former lover and a feminist activist at the time. The film includes her giving birth to a child. However, in spite of the fact that it is Hara's male gaze that dominates the film's visual regime, this film must be considered primarily as a site of the performer's expression as the film advocates the politics of the women's liberation movement at the time.[2] The way Miyuki Takeda acts in *Extreme Private Eros* has much in common with Kawase's filmmaking, insofar as both women exhibit their own bodies giving birth to a child to the camera, in the hope of connecting and constructing a network of relationships among women through the documentary film format.

Still, most self-documentaries have been criticised for revolving primarily around subject matter related to the private sphere, and therefore lacking a social or political intention.[3] Kawase's films have been subject to similar accusations.[4] However, if one pays more careful attention to her documentary works, it would seem that these criticisms are not necessarily true. When it comes to the filmmaker's own body, they instead show an alternative way of constructing relationships among people, one that goes beyond the binarism between 'individual' and 'society'. Kawase here intimates that it is possible to form communities which connect to an 'intimate sphere' using a female gaze, and thus transcending the conventional framework of a 'family' traditionally based on a blood or legal relationship.

According to political scientist Junichi Saito, the 'intimate sphere' is not restricted to conventional family relationships but also applicable to every 'sustainable relationship to the extent that is mediated by concern or consideration for the lives of specific others, especially in relation to their anxiety and difficulty'.[5] In Kawase's *oeuvre*, the intimate sphere covers everything from the family-like relationship with her foster mother to the network among women who are connected to each other by sharing similar concerns for their bodies, for instance during pregnancy.

Furthermore, another important element of Kawase's documentaries is that they show bodies in the process of constructing an intimate sphere. In addition, the films represent women's bodies as entities that are constructed performatively as well as being highly material. More precisely, bodily characteristics and activities which are connected to women's corporeality, such as breasts and childbirth, are represented as a performance that blurs the boundary between documentary and fiction, and at the same time, these bodies are represented as something highly material in nature. Analysing the representations of these bodies brings to mind the concept of 'material feminism', as advocated by Stacy Alaimo and Susan Hekman. For fear of essentialism, Alaimo and Hekman argue that feminists have long avoided paying attention to materiality or corporeality, but that it is now necessary to look more closely at materiality itself in order to deconstruct the binarism of materiality and discourse.[6] Kawase's films represent an interesting example, since they clearly reflect this longstanding and highly controversial question in feminist scholarship.

In the scholarship on Kawase's work, Rie Karatsu's argument is key to this discussion, because she situates Kawase's output in the realm of women's cinema by paying specific attention to the expression of intimacy, pointing out that there is a political significance to Kawase's work in terms of its showing a woman's identity as a creative, fluid realm.[7] Her argument is important in that it digresses from scholarship that tends to view Kawase's work as apolitical. Building on Karatsu's research, this chapter focuses especially on two of Kawase's documentary films, *Tarachime* (aka *Birth/Mother*, 2006) and *Genpin* (2010), where bodily performativity and materiality are presented most vividly.

Other than Karatsu's commentary, the remaining scholarship on Kawase tends to ignore these gender-related issues, regardless of the fact that they are an essential element of her work. When occasionally a gender-related perspective is taken, the emphasis is put on the autobiographical aspect of her work only.[8] Therefore, by paying careful attention to the presentation of female bodies, I would like to clarify some of the essential characteristics of her work that have been overlooked so far. This will be done in an attempt to interrogate both the notion of the 'self-documentary' form, and to investigate several gender-related issues.

Performance as Self-representation

'For me, the subject matters of my films always expose myself.'[9] Kawase makes this remark regarding her second feature-length fiction film, *Hotaru* (2000), whose protagonist and story are based on her own life experiences of losing her family. Kawase's words clearly indicate that this motivation is persistent throughout her *oeuvre*. Whether the form is fictional or documentary, Kawase frequently connects her work to her real-life experiences. Her private life therefore is the subject of her documentaries as well as the starting point for her fictional filmmaking. What kinds of characteristics, then, can be noted regarding her self-representation in her work? The answer may be found within the blurred boundary between documentary and fiction.

When we think about self-representation in documentaries, it appears to be commonly believed that such films show the subjects as they are in a natural way, as many viewers naively take documentary to be a film form that somehow tells the 'objective truth'. However, as we shall see, many discussions on this topic have shown that documentaries do not really relate events neutrally. Rather, there are various factors that intervene in the presentation of 'reality', such as the camera angle that is chosen, the way the footage is edited, and so forth.

Such deliberation seems to constantly characterise Kawase's self-representation in her documentaries. In *Kya Ka Ra Ba A*, for example, in the sequence where Kawase visits a tattooist in order to have the same tattoo that her father had, the camera captures the clapperboard which signals the beginning of a take. The scene self-reflexively draws attention to the artifice of filmmaking, even if it is nominally a documentary. Likewise, at the end of the film, a sequence shows Kawase with a tattoo on her naked back, running across a field. Without providing a definitive answer as to whether she really obtained a tattoo or not, the sequence simply shows the slow-motion image of Kawase, with her father's photo juxtaposed before and after the shot. The effect of editing such an arrangement of images, with the use of birdsong as a sound bridge to link the shots, implies some kind of reconciliation between her and her father. Here, Kawase blurs the boundary between fiction and reality through deliberate performance, by first showing her father's tattoo on her back and then juxtaposing the image with her father's photograph. Indeed, her own remark on the nature of her filmmaking that at first glance seems contradictory, corroborates these characteristics of her work: 'The most important point in documentary for me, is its fictional aspect. I mean, how I interpret reality.'[10]

The nature of documentaries to blur the boundary between the artificial and the actual reminds us of Bill Nichols's classification of the modes of documentary. Nichols classifies documentaries into six modes and loosely ties them to the historical development of the form. According to this classification, Kawase's documentaries correspond to the 'performative mode'. Placing the performative documentary at the end of his historical chronology, Nichols connects it to the onset of identity politics, which according to him has been prevalent from the 1990s onwards. As a consequence, 'performative films give added emphasis to the subjective qualities of experience and memory that depart from factual recounting'.[11] For Nichols, therefore, performative documentary shows us incidents based on subjective experience while linking them to the presentation of identity. Furthermore, by observing that 'the free combination of the actual and the imagined is the common feature of the performative documentary',[12] Nichols points out that the boundary separating the genres is blurred.

Stella Bruzzi, however, questions Nichols's comment, arguing that since Nichols connects the meaning of 'performativity' only to issues of 'subjectivity', a full-fledged discussion on the relationship between the filmmaker's identity and the film text has not been achieved.[13] Moreover, Bruzzi emphasises the necessity to pay more careful attention to 'performativity' in the way that Judith Butler uses the concept.[14] What Bruzzi emphasises here is the necessity of regarding the nature of documentary not as something fixed but as something constructively formed. That said, the issue of subjectivity that Nichols highlights is still significant and cannot be overlooked in considering the relationship between documentary and performance. While paying attention then to the issue of subjectivity, a careful consideration of the nature of the documentary form that has emerged through the interaction of performance and reality might be necessary in order to achieve an understanding of Kawase's documentary films.

To be sure, Kawase's documentary films have a lot in common with the 'performative documentary' as described by Nichols and Bruzzi, because, as already mentioned, when Kawase presents herself in her works, she does so through her subjective perspective and use of performativity.[15] Indeed, she consistently captures incidents occurring around her from a very personal perspective. In terms of subjectivity, this could be said to be an act of constructing selfhood through sounds and images. This is evident from such stylistic aspects as the point-of-view shots and voice-over commentary that are frequently employed in her early works.

In addition to such techniques, her performative self-representation can be observed through the way she represents 'everyday life'. In thinking about the relationship between everyday activities and performance, referring to Erving Goffman's argument, Elizabeth Marquis proposes a three-tiered model. According to Goffman, performance is 'all the activity of an individual which occurs during a period marked by his [or her] continuous presence before a particular set of observers and which has some influence on the observers'.[16] Goffman takes all the activity that takes place in front of others in everyday life as performance. Building on this argument, Marquis introduces a three-tiered model, 'which takes into account everyday performative activity (tier #1), the impact of the camera (tier #2) and the influence of specific documentary film frameworks (tier #3)'.[17] With these ideas in mind, I suggest that Kawase sublimates the performance of everyday activity into her work through the performativity of the filmmaking process.

As for Kawase's intention of self-representation and its characteristics, Mayu Ueda has put forward that a consistent element of 'self-projection' can be seen in both Kawase's documentary and fiction films, and points out that there is an interaction between the filmmaking and her private life.[18] Using the word *riaru*,[19] which Kawase often uses to describe her work, Mitsuyo Wada-Marciano argues that Kawase's documentaries, especially *Tarachime*, display the illusionary aspects characteristic of 'realistic film'.[20] According to Wada-Marciano, whilst Kawase shows us her everyday 'reality' in *Tarachime*, the combination of a shot of her foster mother in an ambulance with another shot that shows her face covered with bruises, leads us to believe in the fictional narrative of the death of the foster mother, who in reality was still alive after the film was made.

Such examples clearly indicate that Kawase's work in both documentary and fiction can be situated in a realm where reality and illusion are deeply imbricate. Whilst keeping this point in mind, however, I want to pay more attention to her performative self-representation as a form of mediation that produces the link between documentary and fiction. Looking more carefully into the performativity instead of the reality of her work may lead us to a more precise understanding of Kawase's aesthetics. After all, it can be said that the reality itself emerges from the performativity. More importantly, the self-representation seen in Kawase's work is characterised not only by its performativity but also the point that it is made through the relationships she constructs with others. These relationships connect to female bodies in a crucial way and will be explored now in further detail.

'Intimacy' Mediated through Bodies and the Materiality of Bodies

In *Katatsumori*, whilst portraying her everyday life with her foster mother, Kawase – operating the camera herself – films a sequence where she gazes continuously at her foster mother through her camera. As Kawase shoots her, the foster mother flashes a bashful, little smile towards the camera. Holding the camera in one hand, Kawase extends her arm and touches her foster mother on the cheek (Figure 13).

Coupling the camera eye with her own eyes as the filmmaker, Kawase touches another person who is close to her. As the act visualised here indicates, Kawase's work consistently thematises her approach to others and the construction of her relationships with others through the formation of an 'intimate sphere' or a network of intimacy that is based on corporeality.

To think about the element of constructing an intimate sphere, Alisa Lebow's argument regarding films that are characterised by self-representational

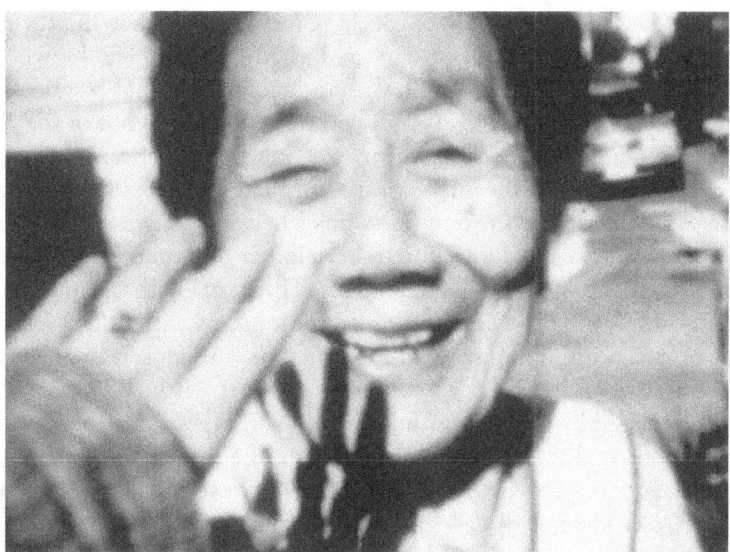

Figure 13   *Katatsumori*. © Kumie Inc.

aspects is thought-provoking. Lebow suggests that such documentary films are both 'singular' and 'plural' at the same time, for as she puts it, 'despite the fact that we believe it to express our individuality, it nonetheless also expresses our commonality, our plurality, our interrelatedness with a group, a mass, a sociality, if not a society'.[21] Far from suggesting a retreat, then, the essay film is tinged with characteristics that suggest the private self being open to others.

What, then, is the nature of these intimate relationships so essential to Kawase's documentaries? I suggest that we conceive of them along the lines of an 'intimate sphere', as conceptualised by the political scientist Junichi Saito. Developing Hannah Arendt's argument, he defines 'intimate sphere' as a 'realm of sustainable relationships which are constructed with a mediation of the self's relations with specific others', and thinking highly of its political possibility.[22] Importantly, Saito's 'intimate sphere' is not an abstract space or set of connections based on such concepts as the 'individual' or 'society', but rather it is a material, living network that is based on concrete, individual beings and actual, physical others. Moreover, as Saito claims, the 'intimate sphere' involves a procedure of 'acceptance', which is different from an ordinary network driven by a social evaluation system that tends to problematise the values inherent in the construction of a society.[23] With this in mind, we can reaffirm the political significance of the 'intimate sphere' that has conventionally been thought to be inferior to the 'public sphere' in terms of a binary opposition.

In Kawase's work, the representation of relationships with others and the performative self-representation are inseparable. As mentioned earlier, at first glance it appears that the act of approaching her foster mother and the conversations she has with her are being captured as part of daily life. However, it is in fact Kawase's explicit relationship with the camera that makes it possible for them to appear. According to Kawase, without the interference of the camera, it might be difficult to show the warm affection that is reflected through her films.[24] However, despite the interaction of intimate feelings, the process of film shooting also functions to prompt a conflict between Kawase and others. In *Embracing*, Kawase casts a question to her biological mother over the phone – 'why did you abandon me?' – which indicates her strife with the mother. Here, Kawase shows us the process of building relationships with others – including her lack of success in doing so. At the same time, this closely connects to the subject matter of 'searching for a father' in her first work, *Embracing*, which is partly motivated by her interest in filmmaking. In these sequences, Kawase's remark that 'there are two selves of me facing the camera'[25] implies that the camera eye is equal to Kawase's own eyes. Kawase has always recognised the double roles she has as a documentary filmmaker and also a social actor who is a part of the work, with her actual identity remaining suspended also within the films. It is an 'intimate sphere' she focuses on in her work, expressing the duality of being both the filmmaker of and the performer in a film.

To think about these issues, Tianqi Yu's argument on Chinese 'first-person' documentary in the 2000s is suggestive. Situating these documentaries in the context of a sociopolitical situation of decollectivisation and individualisation in China, she points out that these films show, on the one hand, reconnected family relationships and on the other hand, an attempt to challenge the problematic family relations and the conventional expectations of women in Chinese society.[26] My argument on Kawase's intimate sphere conflates with her argument in terms of its emphasis on the importance of 'communicative practice', as she regards the subjects in these documentaries as 'relational selves'. However, unlike Yu, I would also like to address the importance of another mediator of relationships, similarily based on the presence of the bodies in front of the camera, but related to relationships that go beyond conventional family relations.

Kawase's work pursues intimacy by presenting bodies – particularly female ones, including her own – in a performative manner. Often, the camera is in close proximity to the body, to an almost extreme degree, with Kawase shooting the body alongside such material objects as plants or food. These bodies seem to exist as part of the surrounding environment, as opposed to something distinct or disconnected. In addition the frequent lack of a voice-over commentary on the abstract images draws the audience's attention to the material character of the bodies, forcing us to recognise their female characteristics. This quality relates closely to the presentation of bodies that I shall discuss in the following section.

Kawase's work develops the representation of the bodies to search for an intimate sphere. By filming and highlighting such tactile acts as touching her foster mother, Kawase shows a connection with others through the visualisation of various physical sensations. It could be said that the frequent presentation of food or the act of eating, in her films, also points to her longing to connect with the world through bodily acts and sensations. The bodies shown in Kawase's cinema thus function as basis for constructing an intimate sphere by foregrounding its female attributes. Leading on from this, let me now examine these characteristics of Kawase's work through a close reading of *Tarachime* and *Genpin*.

Bodies Giving Birth: *Tarachime* and *Genpin*

'The internal organs which connect me and you taste like blood.' In *Tarachime*, after a scene where the camera captures the moment a baby is leaving its mother's womb, Kawase's voice-over commentary narrates over the image of a glistening object. This object is Kawase's own placenta. The way Kawase describes it as tasting like blood in her voice-over is a recognition of the links connecting lives, while at the same time confessing her continuous longing for relationships with others through her physical senses. In this section, I argue that a space somewhat like Saito's 'intimate sphere' is constructed through a connection between performative self-representation and femininity, as seen in Kawase's documentaries thematising childbirth, *Tarachime* and *Genpin*.

In *Tarachime*, Kawase gazes into the relationship of a foster mother with her child, through the in/experience of childbirth. What she focuses on is the gradual connection of life between Kawase and her foster mother, and then to her own child. The absence of a biological relationship between Kawase and her foster mother may at first glance appear to be something negative in contrast with Kawase's relations with her own child, who indeed is her blood relative. Her foster mother's denial of the blood relation, by saying that 'you are not from my womb' at the beginning of the film, seems to be foreshadowing their quarrel in the following sequence. In the subsequent scenes, Kawase directs her anger at her foster mother over a childhood memory where her foster mother threatens to abandon her by saying 'go wherever you want'. This causes her foster mother to finally start crying as a response to Kawase's severe questioning. In these sequences, a conflict between the two is thrown into relief as resulting from the absence of blood relations.

The relationship between Kawase and her foster mother, however, is also implied to be an alternative relationship, one which transcends an actual blood relation. Frequently in *Tarachime* the naked bodies of Kawase and her foster mother are shown. In such moments, the camera focuses on their breasts, the parts of the anatomy particular to women. This suggests an intimate sphere between the two. In the middle of the film, for instance, Kawase juxtaposes the naked body of her foster mother with her own while taking a bath. Here, going beyond the differences in experience, age, and the absence of a biological relationship, the two bodies that are represented nevertheless share a close connection.

Such a manner of juxtaposing two naked bodies is also applied in a moment where the imaginary, shared experience of childbirth is suggested. The word used for the title of the film, *tarachime*, is an old Japanese word that is derived from another word, *tarachine*, which means 'mother'. It is said that the word means women who become full-breasted and embody fertility after childbirth.[27] The juxtaposition of the image of her foster mother's wrinkled breasts, affected by age, with Kawase's own breasts, whose skin is still fresh and youthful-looking, leads to a projection of Kawase's experience of childbirth over her foster mother's body. In this sense, the foster mother too is represented as a 'mother'. This suggests a family-like relationship between the two and also represents a sharing of women's experiences. It should also be noted that such a presentation of a connection that is based on the representation of bodies is made performatively, as I have mentioned – that is, by shooting the elderly body of her foster mother, while projecting her own body and even exposing the process of her childbirth, an event normally hidden from public view, Kawase suggests an intimate and family-like relationship that she constructs with her foster mother.

The way of longing for and constructing relationships with others based on female bodies in *Tarachime* is also expressed in *Genpin*. *Genpin* focuses on Dr Tadashi Yoshimura of the Yoshimura Maternity Clinic, known for its particular policy of encouraging natural childbirth. This documentary does not feature Kawase as a performer, as *Tarachime* does. Instead, the film revolves around pregnant women and their families, all of whom agree with the ideas of Dr Yoshimura and want to prepare for childbirth in the manner encouraged by him.

Genpin shows the process whereby an intimate sphere is created through a female network based on the pregnant women's common interest in their bodies and experiences of childbirth. The clinic places emphasis not only on the act of childbirth itself but also on taking care of the mind and body in accordance with a more 'traditional' way, in keeping with Japanese custom. Therefore, the clinic makes opportunities for the pregnant women and their families to gather by promoting people-to-people exchange. Consequently the parents-to-be meet to share their common worries surrounding childbirth and as well as their interest in natural childbirth. Kawase's reason for taking an interest in this experience and the interactions of the pregnant women is that it is entirely based on and connected to the construction of an intimate sphere through the women's bodies. For instance, the film shows us a moment where women are talking about their own experiences to each other. Although they have had different experiences, they all distrust the methods of modern medicine and share a keen interest in natural childbirth. They also sometimes become emotional, with tears in their eyes while sharing past experiences. The sharing is deepened by shots of actual childbirth.

These scenes of actual childbirth show similarities with the capturing of Kawase's own experience giving birth in *Tarachime* in terms of the way they suggest it as an experience that women go through independently and through which they may even gain a sense of pleasure. In *Tarachime*, after the scene where Kawase, with a dignified expression, lies down, the film shows explicitly the process of childbirth, even going so far as to show the actual moment when the child is born. Right after the scene, Kawase holds the baby in her arms with a faint smile. Significantly, she does not show the painful aspect of childbirth. Manipulating through the editing process acts as one of the tiers of performativity contributing to the representation of childbirth here as something that goes smoothly and even produces some sort of sense of euphoria. Likewise, although the birth scenes in *Genpin* introduce an overlay of sound without particular manipulation in terms of editing, they also place emphasis on this euphoric feeling rather than on the pain of childbirth. After each childbirth scene, a woman says 'thank you' to the people surrounding her and another woman speaks of their impression of the childbirth: 'I'm feeling great.' The childbirth shown here is not a 'horrible' thing conducted inside a hospital with modern equipment, but that which yields pleasure to women through their subjective involvement in the childbirth (Figure 14).

With a mutual interest in childbirth as bodily activities, the women construct a connection, something that could be called a community. It might be true that there is not such a strong sense of unity inside this particular community, given that the women who go through childbirth here will eventually go back to their ordinary lives separately. However, as shown in the film, some women who experience childbirth revisit the clinic with their children. What is more, it is obvious from the clinic's guiding principle that it recommends people to pay attention to such aspects of personal health as diet and exercise, and that these principles cover not only the way of childbirth but also the everyday aspects of life. When they go back to their individual lives, it is likely that the women who together shared a particular way of thinking about their lives through the experiences they went through based on their bodies will also maintain a connection with one another in the future.

It should be noted here that the materiality of bodies, as discussed earlier, is clearly foregrounded in both films. First, the bodies are shown again as being integral to the surrounding environment as opposed to being detached from it. In *Genpin*, for example, the opening shot of the lush, natural landscape is followed by a shot of burning firewood and then a shot of running

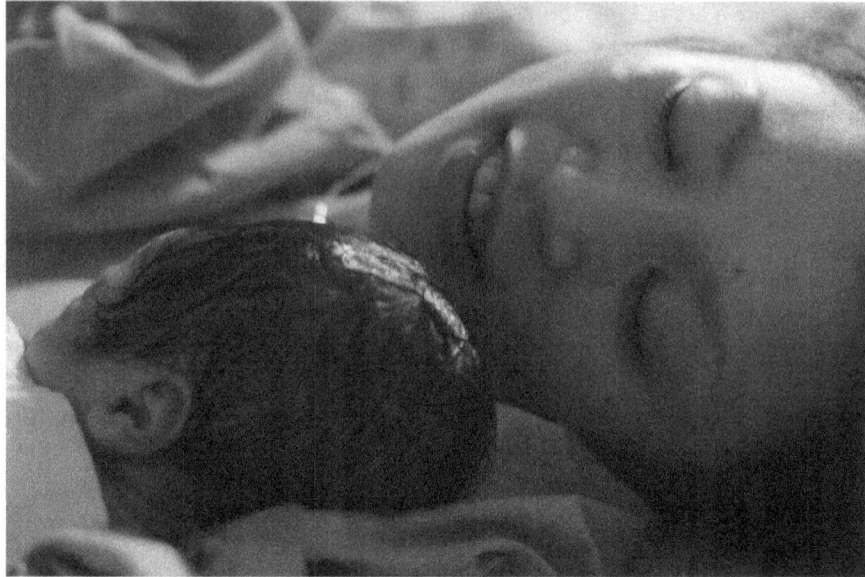

Figure 14   *Genpin*. © Kumie Inc.

water from a bamboo cylinder. It is then connected to a close-up which shows the cutting of the baby's umbilical cord, with the chirping of birds as a sound hook. Through its suggestive montage, this sequence shows the female body giving birth to a child in close connection with the natural environment that surrounds the human body and of which it is a part, alongside such man-made elements utilising nature as the firewood and the traditional water features.

The emphasis on materiality also functions as something that draws our attention to women's bodies. The extreme close-ups of the breasts of Kawase and her foster mother even manage to capture the texture of the skin because of the proximity of the camera. No explanatory comments are added to these shots, meaning the audience cannot help but pay attention to the shape and the texture of the bodies. This tendency could also be pointed out in the shot where the placenta is shown. Comments are not added to the close-up image of the glittering object when it first appears at the beginning of the documentary. Therefore, we might be unable to decide what it is for a moment. As mentioned earlier, Kawase's voice-over makes us realise that it is the placenta only when it is shown again in the middle of the film. These flows of editing make audiences pay attention to bodily characteristics of women. Similarly in *Genpin*, the bodies giving birth to children and the babies right after they come from the wombs, covered in mucus, eloquently show Kawase's emphasis on the bodies themselves. In the sequence of childbirth, the process of construction of the intimate sphere is presented through emphasis on female bodily characteristics.

Conclusion

In *Tarachime* and *Genpin*, intimate spheres that transcend conventional frameworks such as blood or legal relationships are presented through performative representation of female bodies, which are highly material. At the same time, the female bodies function as necessary mediators when constructing this intimacy. Kawase's *oeuvre* thus demonstrates the process of the construction of an intimate sphere, by showing female bodies, including Kawase's own, as something performative and material. In this sense, rather than subscribing to the conventional critical opinion which rather too easily dismisses her work as apolitical, we might wish to think anew the relationship between self-representation and gender politics in Japanese cinema at the turn of the millennium, through her unique documentaries. What this has to tell us about the time and place that produced Kawase's work will then be a matter for further speculation and debate.

Notes

1. Some alternative approaches have been taken that pay more careful attention to women's involvement in filmmaking. Such approaches aim to explore this issue in a broader sense, by going beyond the conventional conception of *auteurs*, which tend to consider films as the creations of a sole author such as the director, by paying attention instead to other elements such as performers, in the role of which women have been actively involved in filmmaking. For details, see Wakae Nakane, 'Sakusha to shite no Shutsuenjosei: Dokyumentari-eiga *Kyokushiteki Erosu: Renka 1974* to Ūman Ribu [Female Performers as Authors: Documentary Film *Extreme Private Eros: Love Song 1974* and the Women's Liberation Movement]' *JunCture*, 7, 2016, pp.138–51.
2. For details, see Nakane, 'Sakusha to shite no Shutsuenjosei'.
3. For example, whilst Abé Mark Nornes appreciates Kawase's early works to some extent, he tends to have a negative evaluation of subsequent output of 'self-documentary' by other directors, and commenting that they 'retreat from the world'; Abé Mark Nornes, 'The postwar documentary trace: groping in the dark,' *Positions: East Asia Culture Critique*, 10/1, 2002, pp. 66–8.
4. Ayako Saito, 'Yureru Onna-tachi: Ajia no Josei Eigakantoku, Sono Rekishi to Hyogen [Swaying Women: Female Directors in Asia, the History and Their Expression]', *Shakai Bungaku* [*Social Literature*], 27, 2008, pp. 111–13.
5. Junichi Saito, 'Shinmitsu-ken to Anzensei no Seiji [Intimate Sphere and Politics of Safety]', in Junichi Saito (ed.), *Shinmitsu-ken no Poritikusu* [*Politics in Intimate Sphere*] (Tokyo: Nakanishiya-shuppan, 2003), p. 213.
6. Stacy Alaimo and Susan Hekman, 'Introduction: emerging models of materiality in feminist theory' in Stacy Alaimo and Susan Hekman (eds), *Material Feminisms* (Indianapolis, IN: Indiana University Press, 2008), pp. 1–3.
7. Karatsu Rie, 'Questions for a women's cinema: fact, fiction and memory in the films of Naomi Kawase', *Visual Anthropology*, 22, 2009, pp. 167–81.

8. Academic commentary on Kawase's work so far include: Karatsu, 'Questions for a women's cinema'; Mitsuyo Wada-Marciano, *Japanese Cinema in the Digital Age* (Honolulu: University of Hawai'i Press, 2012), ch. 2; Mayu Ueda, 'Fikushon to Dokyumentari no Yūgō: *Moe no Suzaku* ni Miru Ekkyō [Fusion of Fiction and Documentary: Transgression in *Suzaku*]', *CineMagaziNet!*, no. 14, 2010; available at <http://www.cmn.hs.h.kyoto-u.ac.jp/CMN14/ueda-article-2010.html> (last accessed 10 March 2016); Mayu Ueda 'Kawase Naomi Sakuhin ni okeru Shintai to Sonzai-ninshiki toshite no Shokuchi: *Katatsumori, Tarachime, Mogari no Mori* wo Chūshin ni [Senses of Touch as an Act of Identification of Entity: Centred on *Katatsumori, Tarachime* and *Morgari*]', *CineMagaziNet!*, no. 15, 2011; available at <http://www.cmn.hs.h.kyoto-u.ac.jp/CMN15/ueda-article-2011.html> (last accessed 10 March 2016); Mayu Ueda 'Kawase Naomi ni okeru Shinshutsu Suru "Watashi" [Oozing "Me" in Kawase Naomi]', *CineMagaziNet!*, no. 16, 2012; available at <http://www.cmn.hs.h.kyoto-u.ac.jp/CMN14/ueda-article-2010-2.html> (last accessed 10 March 2016); Saito, 'Yureru Onna-tachi', pp. 101–13; Kate E. Taylor Jones, *Rising Sun, Divided Land: Japanese and South Korean Filmmakers* (London: Wallflower Press, 2013), pp. 146–71.
9. Naomi Kawase, 'Kamera no Mae to Ushiro ni Futari no "Watashi" ga Iru [There Are Two Selves of "Me" Facing the Camera]' *Kōkoku-hihyō [Advertizing Review]*, 248, 2001, p. 130.
10. Naomi Kawase, 'Kanto Intabyu Eiga-sakka Kawase Naomi: Genjitsu no Dekigoto ni Taishite Dō Kamera wo Mukeruka [The Opening Interview Filmmaker Naomi Kawase: How I Aim the Camera against Reality]' *Hōsō-bunka [Broadcast Culture]*, 16, 2007, p. 11.
11. Bill Nichols, *Introduction to Documentary* (Bloomington and Indianapolis, IN: Indiana University Press, 2001), p. 131.
12. Ibid. p. 131.
13. Stella Bruzzi, *New Documentary* (Abingdon and New York: Routledge, 2006), p.186–7.
14. Ibid.
15. Bruzzi discusses the 'performative documentary' using her own categorisation that divides the form into two possibilities: one is 'films that feature performative subjects', while the other is films 'that are inherently performative and feature the intrusive presence of the filmmaker'. Bearing this in mind, Kawase's documentaries would seem to exhibit characteristics of both categories, particularly in terms of showing herself as an authorial presence who exists also as a performer in the film text. Bruzzi, *New Documentary*, pp.187–8.
16. Erving Goffman, *The Presentation of Self in Everyday Life* (London and New York: Penguin, 1990), p. 22.
17. Elizabeth Marquis, 'Conceptualizing documentary performance', in *Studies in Documentary Film*, 7/1, 2013, pp. 45–60.
18. Ueda, 'Kawase Naomi ni okeru Shinshutsu suru "Watashi"'.
19. The word 'riaru' in Japanese is equivalent to 'reality'.
20. Wada Marciano, *Japanese Cinema in the Digital Age*, pp. 62–6.
21. Alisa Lebow, 'Introduction', in Alisa Lebow (ed.), *The Cinema of Me. The Self and Subjectivity in First Person Documentary* (London: Wallflower Press, 2012), p. 3.
22. Saito, 'Shinmitsu-ken to Anzensei no Seiji', p. 213.
23. Ibid. p. 232.
24. Naomi Kawase, 'Tenbō Intabyu: Eizō-sakka Kawase Naomi-san [Prospect Interview: Filmmaker Naomi Kawase]', *Hoken Tenbō [Insurance Prospect]*, 44, 1997, p. 56.
25. Kawase, 'Kamera no Mae to Ushiro ni Futari no "Watashi" ga Iru', p. 132.

26. Tianqi Yu, 'Toward a communicative practice: female first-person documentary in twenty-first century China', in Matthew D. Johnson, Keith B. Wagner, Tianqi Yu and Luke Vulpiani (eds), *China's iGeneration: Cinema and Moving Image Culture for the Twenty-first Century* (New York: Bloomsbury, 2014), p. 37.
27. Norio Nakada, Toshimasa Wada and Yasuo Kitahara (eds), *Kogo Daijiten* [*Dictionary of Japanese Archaism*] (Tokyo: Shōgakkan, 1985), p. 1029.

Filmography

Extreme Private Eros: Love Song 1974 (*Kyokushiteki erosu: renka 1974*/極私的エロス・恋歌 1974) (Kazuo Hara, Japan, 1974).
Embracing (*Nitsutsumarete*/につつまれて) (Naomi Kawase, Japan, 1992).
Katatsumori (*Katatsumori*/かたつもり) (Naomi Kawase, Japan, 1994).
Suzaku (*Moe no suzaku*/萌の朱雀) (Naomi Kawase, Japan, 1997).
Hotaru (*Hotaru*/火垂) (Naomi Kawase, Japan, 2000).
Kya Ka Ra Ba A (*Kya Ka Ra Ba A*/きゃからばあ) (aka *Sky, Water, Fire, Wind, Earth*, 2001).
Tarachime (*Tarachime*/垂乳女 Tarachime) (aka *Birth/Mother*, Naomi Kawase, Japan, 2006).
Mogari: The Mourning Forest (*Mogari no mori*/殯の森) (Naomi Kawase, Japan, 2007).
Genpin (*Genpin*/玄牝-げんぴん-) (Naomi Kawase, Japan, 2010).
Sweet Bean (*An*/あん) (Naomi Kawase, Japan, 2015).

11. CELEBRITY/ACTIVIST/ PHOTOGRAPHER: MIA FARROW

Catherine Summerhayes

INTRODUCTION

Mia Farrow is an acclaimed film actor who has appeared in over fifty-five films; she is a 'Hollywood' celebrity, with much of her personal life open to public perusal; she is a human rights activist, focusing on violence committed on women and children in war zones and sites of natural disaster in many countries; and she is a skilled photographer, communicating much of her activism work via video and an extensive photographic archive. *Time* magazine in 2008 named her as one of the most influential people in the world. This chapter examines her human rights-directed photographs of children, in the context of both her status as a celebrity activist and her broad *oeuvre*, and through the close study of some individual works.

Her role as a human rights activist provides this chapter with its main focus; I suggest, however, that a significant key to understanding her activist work and its social impact is to be found in aspects of her professional acting career as well as her personal 'private' life. It is useful here, then, to contextualise her activism work with her social identity in a wider context when it is relevant to examining her role as an author of the documentary image. Farrow's work with UNICEF places her as what is now known as a 'celebrity activist', alongside other well-known actors such as George Clooney, Matt Damon and Angelina Jolie.

I want, at this stage of discussion, to state that I am not introducing Farrow's private/public personal and professional life as a way into interpreting her documentary images per se, nor as the only way to interpret these images. Her works stand as texts that can be analysed and thought about in the context of several complex social environments. These include the broad contexts of world politics, geography and human rights activism as well as the interpretative frameworks associated with imaging genocide: the ethics of making images of traumatised people, especially those of children. Due to this chapter's focus on female documentary image-makers, not only on the images they create, I acknowledge the need to probe a little more into her personal and professional celebrity status than I would otherwise do when examining the work of a photographer. The identity of someone as having celebrity status makes that person vulnerable not only to adulation and admiration but also to abuse and many misconceptions about both their personal and professional lives. For better or for worse, Mia Farrow's images of children in sites of conflict and natural disaster are very much the images of an *auteur* who has had great joy in her own mothering of fourteen children; she is an *auteur* who, through her still photography, short videos and verbal testimonies, has done what she can to ease the plight of children in conflict zones by exposing the atrocities and trauma that these children experience.

The following section describes some of Farrow's life experiences that I consider relevant to understanding her position as a documentary image-maker.

Mia Farrow: Acting, Marriage and Children

Farrow was born in Los Angeles, California, on 9 February 1945. Her full name is Maria de Lourdes 'Mia' Villiers Farrow. She was one of seven children born to Hollywood actress Maureen O'Sullivan and Australian film director John Farrow. She was brought up Roman Catholic and still professes herself to be Catholic. In her own words she describes as follows some of the impact of thirteen years of convent education:

> If you're brought up a Catholic and you've had 13 years of convent education with nuns, there's no way you ever get out from under that. I've accepted that fact about myself so there are certain things – like my lost saint – that sometimes are not so lost.[1]

Having myself lived through thirteen years of such an education in the 1960s and 1970s, I am well aware of the potential feelings of guilt over whether or not one should become a 'bride of Christ' or else pursue mothering/care-giving roles in society as some kind of martyrdom-like atonement for the sins of the world. The idea of sacrifice permeated my upbringing and in her words quoted above Farrow also acknowledges these complex motivations of sacrifice and redemption that can attach themselves to many life decisions.

Farrow cites another life event as important for shaping her awareness of suffering and trauma. At nine years old, she contracted polio and was hospitalised for three weeks. She was one of many in a ward of children in iron lungs, with one child dying next to her. When it was established she would not die and would not be crippled by the disease, she went home to a house empty of her siblings, the dog having been given away and even the lawn dug up and re-seeded. She was considered contagious and except for one good friend who visited her in spite of warnings, she spent a lonely and frightened six months. Most frightening was the awareness of other people's fear of her own self as disease carrier. In the television documentary *Mia Farrow 'Intimate Portrait' About Her Life and Children*, she says the following about her experience of polio:

> I say it was constructive in the long run, because it made me aware that as we speak . . . somebody is in terrible pain and afraid, lots of somebodies. And it hadn't crossed my mind, and it never left my mind from that time on. And I have no doubt that it shaped my life and the decisions I would make in the future. I wasn't sure what to do about it, but I knew I had a responsibility.[2]

Clearly, at least in retrospect, Farrow places her memories of that time as crucial to her life plan of caring for others.

Farrow first became famous as an actor, as the youngest member of the cast, playing Allison Mackenzie in 263 episodes, between 1964 and 1966, of the very popular American television (ABC) soap opera *Peyton Place*.[3] In 1966 she also gained public attention when she married singer Frank Sinatra. In 1968 she took a leading film role as Rosemary in the film *Rosemary's Baby* (dir. Roman Polanski): 'a critical and commercial success at the time and continues to be widely regarded as a classic of the horror genre'.[4] Farrow won the Golden Globe Award for New Star of the Year for this role. She became an established actress on film and stage: appearing in over fifty films and fourteen stage productions.

In 1970 she married conductor and composer André Previn, with whom she had three biological sons. The couple also adopted two Vietnamese babies and a Korean child (five to seven years old), Soon-Yi. Previn and Farrow divorced in 1979. This year also saw the beginning of the relationship between Farrow and the director Woody Allen, who directed her in thirteen of his films. In 1985, Farrow adopted Dylan (2 weeks old) and in 1987, she gave birth to Satchel, her son with Allen.[5] In 2013, Farrow said in public that this child's father might well have been Sinatra, not Allen – thus further feeding the avid public rumour mill.[6]

The split between Farrow and Allen in 1992 took place in a media-saturated public space, full of accusations and counter-accusations between the two and riven with threatened court cases. The crucial event leading to the split was Allen's sexual relationship with Soon-Yi, Farrow's adopted daughter. Allen later married Soon-Yi. There were also allegations of sexual abuse made against Allen for interfering with seven-year-old Dylan. Allen was never formally prosecuted and denied the allegations by Farrow and Dylan, although Dylan renewed her claims in 2014. Farrow adopted five more children between 1992 and 1995. All in all, as stated earlier, Farrow has fourteen children, ten of whom are adopted. Three of these children have since died, and several had severe disabilities on adoption – including cerebral palsy.

It is clear from this brief history of her personal life that much of it has been played out in public, through mass media of the times in which it took place. Mia Farrow has been a celebrity for both professional and private reasons for a long time, ever since, it could be argued, her appearance in *Peyton Place* and her leaving this melodramatic soap opera to marry Frank Sinatra.

Graeme Turner's book *Understanding Celebrity* (2004) traces several ways in which celebrity has been discussed and defined. He cites David Giles's concept of 'fame as a "process", a consequence of the way individuals are treated by the media'.[7] In Giles's own words: 'The brutal reality of the modern age is that all famous people are treated like celebrities by the mass media, whether they be a great political figure, a worthy campaigner, an artist "touched by genius", a serial killer . . .'[8] Turner's discussion focuses on several aspects of the cultural production of celebrity, and notes a 'second "repertoire" of celebrity discourse'[9] as described by Joke Hermes in terms of melodrama:

> The repertoire of melodrama can be recognised in references to misery, drama and by its sentimentalism and sensationalism, but also by its moral undertone. Life in the repertoire of melodrama becomes grotesquely magnified. In the vale of tears that it is, celebrities play crucial and highly stereotyped roles, reminiscent of folk and oral culture.[10]

Farrow's celebrity up until 2000 mainly falls into this repertoire of melodrama. Indeed I suggest that she could also be fairly described as a 'celebrity mother' – although not necessarily of her own planning. This last attribute can be seen to play into her public support for children in places of war and natural disaster.

However, her status as a celebrity has morphed over the last two decades into another kind of celebrity – one that includes political power within its discourse. In the context of North America, Darrell M. West and John M. Orman describe a celebrity politics whereby 'Even though Americans tend not to trust politicians, they have greater respect for and confidence in celebrities who enter the world of politics'.[11] In Chapter 5 of his book *Celebrity Politics* (2013), Mark Wheeler lists a wide range of mainly film industry celebrities who campaign for particular politicians, and those who actually have become elected representatives at various levels of Government.[12] In Chapter 6, Wheeler goes on to note many examples of 'transnational celebrity activism'. He also describes the role of the United Nations in crafting a particular kind of activism based on capitalising on the fame of the celebrity in order to have her/him expose human rights issues and provide advocacy at national government levels. Wheeler concludes that 'In commercially dictated global media, the mass escalation of celebrity politics may indicate a realistic means through which to promote political engagement.'[13,14]

Farrow's status as a significant human rights activist, archivist and photographer is plainly evident in her work for UNICEF:[15]

> the United Nations Children's Fund, the driving force that helps build a world where the rights of every child are realised. It works in 190 countries and territories with a focus on improving the lives of the most disadvantaged and excluded children.[16]

Farrow accepted the role of UNICEF Goodwill Ambassador in 2000 (Figure 15); and it is this role that clearly and formally situates and recognises her as a particular kind of celebrity, whose position as a famous person means she attracts attention, to some extent, whatever she does in public. Her profile neatly fits UNICEF's brief description of how celebrity can serve activism:

> Fame has some clear benefits in certain roles with UNICEF. Celebrities attract attention, so they are in a position to focus the world's eyes on the needs of children, both in their own countries and by visiting field projects and emergency programmes abroad. They can make direct representations to those with the power to effect change. They can use their talents and fame to fundraise and advocate for children and support UNICEF's mission to ensure every child's right to health, education, equality and protection.[17]

Farrow determines that she keeps up her media presence in her role as activist by embracing the very public social media screens of Facebook and Twitter to show and maintain records of her images, thoughts, fieldtrips and other activist activities.

The term 'shining a light' on conflict and disaster situations is increasingly used among celebrity activists and commentators to describe how this kind of activism can produce positive outcomes. For example, an article on George Clooney's work in the Sudan states: 'Clooney, who endured malaria and stomach ailments during his visit, said that by shining daylight on the situation he was making it "harder to kill people."'[18] Clooney was made a United Nations 'Messenger of Peace' in 2008.[19] He describes his celebrity as a credit

CELEBRITY/ACTIVIST/PHOTOGRAPHER: MIA FARROW

Figure 15   UNICEF Goodwill Ambassador Mia Farrow holds a baby at a warehouse in the city of Gonaïves, Haiti (20 September 2008) (see note 15). Roger LeMoyne for UNICEF. © Roger leMoyne/UNICEF.

card, and his celebrity credit quotient allows him to make famous people whose crimes would otherwise remain hidden:

> If celebrity is a credit card, I'm using my credit. My job is to try and find ways of talking about issues that move us forward. I don't make policy, but I can shine a light on faulty or good policy . . . Rather than talk about who I'm dating, let's talk about saving lives.[20]

In an interview with Glen Levy in 2011 for *Time*, Farrow discloses that her original brief with UNICEF was to go on a field trip to Nigeria, thereby publicising their polio eradication programme. The interview goes on to describe her interactions with politicians and policy makers:

> *You've been speaking to the press a lot about what you've seen, but what kinds of conversations have you had with politicians?*
> Countless and all the time. You've got to be part Rottweiler and keep at it.[21]

In a 2008 article for *Time* magazine, Paul Rusesabagina described Farrow as one of the 100 most influential people in the world in terms of human rights advocacy[22] and it is with some bemusement that, when describing this chapter on Mia Farrow as an actress and photographer to people who are currently less than forty years of age, I find that some do not recognise her name as an actress. A mention of one of Farrow's early, and perhaps most famous, role in *Rosemary's Baby* (Roman Polanski, 1968), and a further mention of her deeply problematic relationship with Woody Allen, do provide a somewhat wobbly platform for the recognition of a person who has achieved so much in the sphere of human rights activism. And yet she clearly has more than enough 'celebrity credit' to do the work required of a UNICEF Goodwill Ambassador, and has created for herself a new kind of celebrity as a determined and caring human rights activist who places her own body in the same risk-ridden spaces that are occupied by those adults and children she works for through raising funds and advocacy. Farrow was presented with the Presidential Medal of Honour for her work in the Central African Republic in 2007. She has been awarded several other human rights awards, including the Lyndon Baines Johnson Moral Courage Award (2011) and the Marion Anderson Award (2011) and as noted on the UNICEF profile page, in 2008, 'Refugees International honoured both Ms. Farrow and her son, Ronan, with the 2008 McCall-Pierpaoli Humanitarian Award, given for extraordinary service to refugees and displaced people'.[23]

Whenever human rights workers and activists go into the field, they risk their own health and safety. Farrow's field trips, often repeated, for UNICEF have been to Uganda, Angola, Chad, the Central African Republic, Haiti, Sudan, Rwanda, Kenya, Gaza and Somalia. And Darfur. An extreme example of how Farrow has been prepared to take risks with her own body for the sake of her work is when she went on a hunger strike in 2009. The following excerpt from Maureen Orth's 2013 article describes the circumstances:

> In April 2009, after the International Criminal Court indicted Sudanese president Omar Hassan al-Bashir for atrocities and he ordered 40 percent of the humanitarian-aid workers out of the country in retaliation, Mia went on a hunger strike to raise awareness and put pressure on him. She had to stop after 12 days. 'My blood sugar betrayed me. The doctor said I was going to go into convulsions and then into a coma. I promised the children I wouldn't do that. I don't regret it. I did two or three Larry King shows, two or three *Good Morning America*s. My driveway was filled with satellite trucks – we couldn't have ever got that kind of press for the people of Darfur.'[24]

In 2007, Farrow wrote a letter to Sudanese President Omar Hassan al-Bashir offering to exchange herself for the safety of a significant member of the rebel Sudanese Liberation Army (SLA). Suleiman Jamous, who needed medical treatment outside that available in Darfur, had played an important role in negotiating between rival factions of the SLA. Farrow wrote in her letter:

> I am therefore offering to take Mr Jamous's place, to exchange my freedom for his in the knowledge of his importance to the civilians of Darfur and in the conviction that he will apply his energies toward creating the just and lasting peace that the Sudanese people deserve and hope for.[25]

Clearly, Mia Farrow understands her work for UNICEF as going way beyond being a 'photo opportunity' or 'sound bite' for news agencies. She is a serious player on the global stage of human rights activism. Her photographs are part of a broad range of activism.

Mia Farrow: Image-maker

Farrow has authorship in four kinds of images. The first is through images of herself with children during her field trips or of her speaking at public forms. I include these within the ambit of her authorship because she allows representation of her own self in the context of these images; she allows images of herself to be used in publicising her work with UNICEF. An example of this kind of image is included on the UNICEF webpage profiling Farrow as a Goodwill Ambassador (https://www.unicef.org/people/people_mia_farrow.html).[26] The second kind of image includes the many photographs she herself has taken of children and other people caught in conflict zones. The third includes the short videos she authors herself – appearing in them, co-directing them and/or narrating them. These include *As We Forgive*,[27] about the reconciliation project in Rwanda, which Farrow narrated; and with her son Ronan Farrow in *A Path Appears*.[28]

The fourth kind is the archive she has created as an archive of people's everyday activities – a well-intentioned form of amateur 'rescue anthropology', documenting through short videos of Darfuri culture. This long quote, from Kathleen Megan's article 'Mia Farrow documents Darfuri culture; donates work to UConn', includes Farrow's own words on how this collection of nearly forty hours of footage came about:

> When Mia Farrow first suggested that she videotape the traditions and rituals of the peoples from the Darfur region of the Sudan, refugee camp leaders were skeptical. She said they asked her: 'Will this bring us more food? Make the water cleaner? Bring us health care? Help us get home? ... What good is this?' But Farrow ... promised to stand on the edge of the refugee camp every day for a month, ready to videotape a song or dance or any other custom if anyone was interested. 'At first it seemed that no one was. And then we heard the sound of drums beating and ululating ... We heard before we saw, maybe 2,000 people approaching ... They began setting up all around us.' Farrow taped demonstrations of farming methods, dances and song, children's stories and wedding ceremonies, giving children who are growing up in the camps a chance to learn about their own heritage. 'Thank you for reminding us to remember,' Farrow recalled one camp leader telling her as the videotaping progressed.[29]

Farrow gave this collection to the University of Connecticut's Thomas J. Dodd Research Center. The Center posted a short video culled from the archive and including Farrow speaking and other information about the archive: 'Mia Farrow documents Darfur culture' (https://www.youtube.com/watch?v=AN0CNcx4LDQ). Another video about the archive appears on the UNICEF Youtube channel: 'Mia Farrow visits Darfur refugees in Chad' (https://www.youtube.com/watch?v=ih4w3zKxDuc). The university also present the Mia Farrow Collection on their website (http://sudan.uconn.edu/). The collection is available on her own website (http://www.miafarrow.org/).[30]

Farrow continues her documenting of human rights issues through her current Twitter account (https://twitter.com/miafarrow?lang=en&lang=en). She joined Twitter in 2009; previously she used Facebook as her primary tool for social media communication. Her many photo albums now can be found on Flickr: (https://www.flickr.com/photos/30238868@N08/albums). Currently there are seventeen photo albums on this site, containing overall 933 photographs at time of writing (7 December 2016).[31]

All these albums show a collection of photographs of children, both in close-up, at mid distance and in a wider frame that includes their living environment in refugee camps. The photos include images of joyful children in play (see 'South Sudan 2008 2' in which there are several photographs of Farrow herself), and of children clearly showing the trauma they have experienced. They also show Farrow interacting with children and with other activists. The albums thereby include all four kinds of images I noted at the beginning of this section – including both videos and photography but primarily still photographs.

Crisis in Darfur

I first came across Mia Farrow's activist photography in 2010. I was beginning my research into a layer in Google Earth called Crisis in Darfur; this was created by Google Earth Outreach in collaboration with the United States Holocaust Memorial Museum (USHMM) in 2007. The dreadful history of the war in the region comprises three rebellions against the Sudanese government in Khartoum. The genocide of the third rebellion began in 2001 and has been notorious for the actions of the 'devils on horseback', the *janjawiid* (or *janjaweed*) – militia mounted on camels or in trucks who burned villages and committed rape and other terrible atrocities first in Darfur and then in the border regions of Chad. Chapters 7 and 8 in Andrew S. Natsios's monograph *Sudan, South Sudan, and Darfur* provides an excellent description and discussion of the conflicts suffered by the people of Darfur. Mia Farrow appears in another and moving account of the third rebellion and activist/humanitarian efforts to provide aid and protection to Darfuri, the video *Darfur:On Our Watch ... Genocide in Darfur* (dir. Neil Docherty, 2007, 55 mins; https://www.youtube.com/watch?v=EJetVuDSusw).[32] Although Farrow has reported on and advocated for children in other sites of conflict, as noted earlier, I still consider her work on the Darfur situation to be the most substantial commitment she has made in her career as a human rights activist.

Google Earth provides a comprehensive description of the Crisis in Darfur layer – why it was created and how (https://www.google.com.au/earth/outreach/stories/darfur.html).[33] The Crisis in Darfur layer became the principal case study for my book *Google Earth: Outreach and Activism*. I focused on two particular photographs that appeared in this layer. One of them was Farrow's 'trauma kalma' shot in the Kalma refugee camp in Darfur. This photograph can now be found in Farrow's Flickr album called 'Darfur 2004–2006'; it is one of fifty-seven. Photographs shown in Crisis in Darfur are usually annotated. The photo is a close-up of a young girl carrying her baby sister on her back; both children are looking into the camera and both have a serious, almost defiant gaze. In the layer, the photo is annotated as 'GIRL WITH BABY SISTER' and 'Girl with traumatized baby sister. The baby has not made a sound since the day their parents were slaughtered and the village burned.'[34] I have already written extensively about my response to this image within *Google Earth*.[35] My response drew to some extent on my perception of Farrow as a celebrity mother.

My second case study for *Google Earth*[36] was a collection of images that appear on the Human Rights Watch (HRW) website under the heading 'Smallest Witnesses'. Webpages now present how the images came about and link to the drawings:

> In early 2005, Human Rights Watch investigators travelled to camps in Darfur and along Chad-Sudan border housing refugee men, women and children from Darfur. The purpose of the investigation was to examine the consequences of sexual violence on refugees as part of the conflict. During interviews with these refugees, Human Rights Watch investigators gave children paper and crayons to keep them occupied while they gathered testimony from the children's parents and caregivers.
>
> The first child Human Rights Watch encountered, an eight-year-old named Mohammed, had never held a crayon or pencil before. So Mohammed gave the paper to his brothers. They drew – without any instruction – pictures of Janjaweed on horseback and camel shooting civilians, Antonovs dropping bombs on civilians and houses, an army tank firing on fleeing villagers.[37]

I was interested in the difference between the images as presented by themselves on the HRW site, and photographs of the children holding their drawings. Farrow's photographs of *janjaweed* themselves also affirm her courage in placing her own body in harm's way in order to document the atrocities committed by these Sudanese government-funded militias. These militias, as well as the SLA, appear in her albums 'Chad – Darfur 2006' and 'Darfur 2004 2006'. The militia often feature in the children's drawings that are now collated in her Flickr album. She does not appear herself in the photos. The USHMM now have on its website a video called *Smallest Witnesses: The Crisis in Darfur Through Children's Eyes* that also explains the images.[38] At the time of writing *Google Earth* (2013–14) I decided that my best viewing position for these images was via a video by Human Rights Watch narrated by Dr Annie Sparrow who was in the team that gave the children the paper and crayons; Farrow's album 'Darfur' (containing images of the drawings) was not then available. My 'inner viewer' preferred to be fed the images as mediated through narration rather than searching for them via the individual web links available at the time. By arranging her photographs into albums on Flickr, Farrow has now made the viewing of the children's drawings very accessible and aesthetically pleasing, with changing frame sizes and camera framing.

The curatorship of her photographs into albums and their presentation within these albums resembles, I suggest, a gallery 'hang' in the sense that through their arrangement together – in relation to each other – the photographs are allowed to communicate their stylistic beauty. This aesthetic value can on the one hand be seen to threaten a viewer's focus on their content: the suffering of others. At the same time, it is difficult to argue that the subject of suffering should be communicated in a style that foregoes the emotional accuracy and intelligence that can be drawn from a well crafted photograph. Farrow's photographs pull the viewer into a deeply personalised space with the subject by simply, and most often, using the subject's direct gaze into Farrow's camera lens. When the eyes looking back at you from the photographic images are those of a child, however, ethical questions loom more particularly behind our interpretation of those images. These questions are relevant both to the making of the images and their viewing.

The business of creating and distributing photographs of suffering children can be morally problematic. Children are not able to give informed consent. In a refugee camp, it is often (usually?) not possible to find a responsible guardian – as in the case of the two children in the 'trauma-kalma' photograph. Put very simply, should Farrow have photographed children in refugee camps? Should she have shown the children with the drawings they made of the atrocities they witnessed? In her album that features the drawings – 'Darfur' (forty photographs), she does not name the children who gaze unrelentingly, usually very seriously into our own eyes. While the Human Rights Watch site does not appear to name the children in the current version of their website, see https://www.hrw.org/legacy/features/darfur/smallwitnesses/drawing.html.[39] For a comprehensive account of the Smallest Witnesses drawings and their context, see the Human Rights Watch pdf *Sudan Smallest Witnesses: The Crisis in Darfur Through Children'sEyes* (© Human Rights Watch 2005). Interestingly, this document notes that children whose images or stories appear in it have been given pseudonyms to protect the children's privacy. Farrow does name the camp as Djabal in several of the photographs, for example in some photographs to be found in her Flickr album 'Darfur' (https://www.flickr.com/photos/30238868@N08/albums/72157629974010955/with/7000393138/).[40] Although not stated by Farrow, it is of course quite possible that she has also given the children pseudonyms.

The ethics of photographing traumatised children has been addressed by journalism organisations and their websites such as the Journalism Center on Children and Families[41] and also to some extent addressed in scholarly writings on ethical issues of writing and image making in the digital age.[42] And

UNICEF has its own guidelines for reporting on children in distress.[43] Perhaps the most persuasive reason for viewing Farrow's photographs, however, is the empathic, compassionate connections we can make with her subjects. As noted before, Farrow creates her images by showing children close up, eyes trained on ours, the viewers', and shows them and their condition with clearly refined and respectful focus. From the access she has to these children, and her role in UNICEF, it is also clear that she has overall consent from her subjects and those who have them in their care.

When Compassion is Personal

The following quote is from Levy's interview with Farrow:

> *Your special focus is on children impacted by conflict. Does it constantly amaze you how resilient children can be?*
> You can't feel hopeless looking into the face of a child. I'm glad you mentioned hopeless and it goes with that terrible twin, helpless. I think that hopelessness and helplessness are the enemies of all progress and I think the saddest person in the world is the person who did nothing. We're not going to change the world but everybody's got to do their part.[44]

This urge for responsibility for the care of others strongly recalls Carol Gilligan's idea of an 'ethics of care' that she refines as also an 'ethic of responsibility [which] rests on an understanding that gives rise to compassion and care'.[45] There is now a growing body of work on how we connect with people in time and space in new ways since the advent of the World Wide Web. It is exciting to think that Farrow's moving photographs of children are so available to us now; and that therefore we also have access to the situations of these children who are so far away from us, and yet so close to us through our personalised computer screens. In David Morley's words: 'It is now commonplace that the networks of electronic communication in which we live are transforming our senses of locality and community.'[46] He calls for the recognition of 'new modalities of belonging that are emerging around us'.[47] As I have argued in *Google Earth*, we are now habituated to the perception that images of people on screen are closely connected to our perception of people as they exist in their actual life situations. In this sense then, Farrow's work is of great significance: she understands herself as someone who *can* and therefore *should* communicate the plights of the people she photographs. In this digital age, her images resonate within the potential of massive social media sites. Her Flickr album 'covers' note the number of views each album has had; and her photostream continues to build – providing for us access to people who live in terror at the same time as we have a glass of wine and peruse the web for our pleasure. Farrow's images can shock but also provide us with the sense that we also, with her, are witnessing the distress of these children. Much has been written devaluing 'armchair activism' – clearly UNICEF and Farrow do not agree. Advocacy begins with compassionate understanding, where compassion is understood as good will towards an other person's well-being: 'an emotion-driven imagination that draws on a person's own life experience to identify with and, to an extent, feel another's situation'.[48]

My discussion in this chapter has focused on how Farrow's photographs are motivated by a compassion for her subjects that is drawn from life experiences both before and after her inauguration as a UNICEF Goodwill Ambassador. Her compassion is embodied in her photographic work. It is also inevitably compromised by distribution and internal content – just as any published photograph of children or suffering people is compromised. Such ambivalence of innate value is magnified many times over with the advent of massive accessibility via the World Wide Web – with its archival social media websites that are so open to abuse as well as to socially constructive use. Through the filter of her work for UNICEF and through her own careful curatorship, they contribute to the 'public good'.[49] Farrow's work provides a rich field for examining how such compassion and care might be used also to contribute towards a broader discussion of the documentary image as an ethically responsible object.

Notes

1. Mia Farrow in Gill Pringle, 'Mia Farrow: "My faith helps me through hard times"'*The Independent*, UK, 2 June 2006, <http://www.independent.co.uk/arts-entertainment/films/features/mia-farrow-my-faith-helps-me-through-hard-times-480665.html#gallery> (last accessed 17 November 2016).
2. Mia Farrow in *MIA FARROW: 'AN INTIMATE PORTRAIT' ABOUT HER LIFE AND CHILDREN'*, 1998, dir. Lee Grant, *LifeTime Television*, 46 mins, <https://www.youtube.com/watch?v=fu81XtueBbc> (last accessed 28 November 2016).
3. Internet Movie Data Base (IMDb), <http://www.imdb.com/title/tt0057779/fullcredits/> (last accessed 1 December 2016).
4. Wikipedia, 'Mia Farrow', <https://en.wikipedia.org/wiki/Mia_Farrow, Updated 25 October 2016> (last accessed 17 November 2016).
5. Farrow's son Satchel is now known as Ronan Farrow and has accompanied her on some of her activist journeys. In 2013 Ronan and his mother were jointly awarded the Blue Card's Holbrooke Award. The Blue Card organisation assists Holocaust survivors.
6. Mia Farrow, interview with Maureen Orth, 'Momma Mia!', *Vanity Fair*, 23 October 2013, <http://www.vanityfair.com/style/2013/11/mia-farrow-frank-sinatra-ronan-farrow> (last accessed 1 December 2016).
7. Graeme Turner, *Understanding Celebrity* (London, Thousand Oaks and New Delhi: Sage, 2004), p. 7.
8. David Giles in Turner, *Understanding Celebrity*, p. 7.

9. Turner, *Understanding Celebrity*, p. 116.
10. Joke Hermes, 'Media figures in identity construction', in P. Alasuutari (ed.), *Rethinking the Media Audience: The New Agenda* (London: Sage, 1999), p. 80.
11. Darrell M. West and John M. Orman, *Celebrity Politics* (Upper Saddle River, NJ: Prentice Hall, 2003), p. 102.
12. Mark Wheeler, *Celebrity Politics, Image and Identity* (Cambridge: Polity Press, 2013).
13. Wheeler, *Celebrity Politics*, p. 170.
14. Wheeler's discussion could well be now extended to an appraisal of the kind of celebrity Donald Trump (President Elect of the USA at time of writing) has enjoyed and how much this might have played into his election as President of the USA in 2016. Wheeler does in fact include in his concluding chapter the seeds of such a discussion.
15. Figure 15 shows Farrow in Haiti: 'Haiti, September 2008: UNICEF Goodwill Ambassador Mia Farrow holds a baby at a warehouse in the city of Gonaives. The warehouse is sheltering people displaced by successive hurricanes and tropical storms that began on 16 August. An estimated 620,000 Haitians, including 279,000 children, are in need of humanitarian assistance. UNICEF assistance includes hygiene kits, water purification tablets, oral rehydration salts, blankets, shelters, school supplies and other essential supplies. Credit: Roger LeMoyne for UNICEF.' Date photo was taken: 20 September 2008. Source: <http://www.flickr.com/photos/unicef/5782894311/> (last accessed 9 February 2017).
16. UNICEF, <http://www.unicef.org.au/about-us> (last accessed 6 December 2016).
17. UNICEF, <https://www.unicef.org/people/people_ambassadors.html> (last accessed 2 December 2016).
18. Faith J. H. McDonnell, 'Clooney shines a light on Sudan, but terror continues', *Frontpage Magazine*, 29 March 2012, <http://www.frontpagemag.com/fpm/127127/clooney-shines-light-sudan-terror-continues-faith-j-h-mcdonnell> (last accessed 3 December 2016).
19. I have written more extensively on Clooney's activist work, including his Satellite Sentinel Project, in my monograph *Google Earth: Outreach and Activism* (New York and London: Bloomsbury, 2015), pp. 149–52.
20. George Clooney, IMDb, <http://www.imdb.com/name/nm0000123/bio> (last accessed 3 December 2016).
21. Mia Farrow and Glen Levy, 'Mia Farrow on kids and conflict in South Sudan', *Time*, 22 March 2011, <http://content.time.com/time/world/article/0,8599,2060435,00.html> (last accessed 6 December 2016).
22. Paul Rusesabagina, 'The 2008 *Time* 100 HEROES AND PIONEERS Mia Farrow', *Time*, 12 May 2008, <http://content.time.com/time/specials/2007/article/0,28804,1733748_1733756_1735264,00.html> (last accessed 1 December 2016).
23. <https://www.unicef.org/people/people_mia_farrow.html> (last accessed 6 December 2016).
24. Maureen Orth, 'Momma Mia!', *Vanity Fair*, 23 October 2013, <http://www.vanityfair.com/style/2013/11/mia-farrow-frank-sinatra-ronan-farrow> (last accessed 6 December 2016).
25. Farrow in Richard Holt, 'Mia Farrow offers freedom to save Darfur rebel', *The Telegraph*, 6 August 2007, <http://www.telegraph.co.uk/news/worldnews/1559602/Mia-Farrow-offers-freedom-to-save-Darfur-rebel.html> (last accessed 6 December 2016).
26. <https://www.unicef.org/people/people_mia_farrow.html> (last accessed 6 December 2016).

27. *As We Forgive*, dir. Laura Waters Hinson, 55 mins, 2010, see <http://asweforgivemovie.com/> (last accessed 9 December 2016).
28. *A Path Appears*, dir. Maro Chermayeff, episode 3, 2015.
29. Kathleen Megan, 'Mia Farrow documents Darfuri culture; donates work to UConn', *The Hartford Courant*, 11 October 2011, <http://articles.courant.com/2011-10-11/news/hc-farrow-archives-uconn-1012-20111011_1_mia-farrow-refugee-camp-darfuris> (last accessed 6 December 2016).
30. 'Mia Farrow documents Darfur culture', uploaded 11 October 2011; <https://www.youtube.com/watch?v=AN0CNcx4LDQ> (last accessed 6 December 2016). Another video about the archive appears on the UNICEF Youtube channel: 'Mia Farrow visits Darfur refugees in Chad', published 4 April 2012, <https://www.youtube.com/watch?v=ih4w3zKxDuc> (last accessed 6 December 2016). The University also present The Mia Farrow Collection on their website page, <http://sudan.uconn.edu/> (last accessed 6 December 2016). The collection is available on her own website, <http://www.miafarrow.org/> (last accessed 6 December 2016).
31. See Twitter, <https://twitter.com/miafarrow?lang=en&lang=en> (last accessed 6 December 2016), and Flickr, <https://www.flickr.com/photos/30238868@N08/albums> (last accessed 6 December 2016).
32. *Darfur:On Our Watch . . . Genocide in Darfur* (dir. Neil Docherty, 2007, 55 mins), <https://www.youtube.com/watch?v=EJetVuDSusw> (last accessed 7 December 2016). Mia Farrow's account of Darfur threads through the video; but see at 49 minutes on an account of her advocacy.
33. <https://www.google.com.au/earth/outreach/stories/darfur.html> (last accessed 7 December 2016).
34. Google Earth, 'Crisis in Darfur' layer, photo titled 'Girl With Baby Sister'.
35. Catherine Summerhayes, *Google Earth: Outreach and Activism*, New York, London: Bloomsbury, 2015), pp. 151–5.
36. Summerhayes, *Google Earth*, pp.155–9.
37. Human Rights Watch.org, 'Smallest Witnesses', <https://www.hrw.org/legacy/features/darfur/smallwitnesses/intro.html> (last accessed 7 December 2016).
38. <https://www.ushmm.org/confront-genocide/cases/sudan/sudan-video-gallery/smallest-witnesses> (last accessed 7 December 2016).
39. Human Rights Watch site does not appear to name the children in the current version of their website: see <https://www.hrw.org/legacy/features/darfur/smallwitnesses/drawing.html> (last accessed 9 February 2017).
40. 'Darfur', <https://www.flickr.com/photos/30238868@N08/albums/72157629974010955/with/7000393138/> (last accessed 9 February 2017). See especially 'IMG-1722' which was shot on 9 August 2007, and the image captioned 'child at Djabal refugee camp', also shot on 9 August 2007.
41. Journalism Center on Children and Families, <http://www.journalismcenter.org/> (last accessed 8 December 2016).
42. See Larry Gross, John Stuart Katz and Jay Ruby (eds), *Image Ethics in the Digital Age* (Minneapolis, MN: University of Minnesota Press, 2003, and Dennis Muller, *Journalism Ethics in the Digital Age* (Scribe, 2014).
43. See the UNICEF webpage 'Principles and guidelines for ethical reporting. children and young people under 18 years old', <https://www.unicef.org/uganda/Guidelines_for_Reporting_on_Children1.pdf> (last accessed 9 December 2016).
44. Farrow and Levy, 'Mia Farrow on kids and conflict in South Sudan'.
45. Carol Gilligan, *In a Different Voice: Psychological Theory and Women's Development* (Cambridge, MA: Harvard University Press, [1982] 1993), p. 165.

46. David Morley, 'Domesticating dislocation in a world of 'new' technology', in C. Berry, S. Kim and L. Spigel (eds), Public Worlds 17, *Electronic Elsewheres: Media Technology and the Experience of Social Space* (Minneapolis, MN: University of Minnesota Press, 2010), p. 3.
47. Ibid.
48. Summerhayes, *Google Earth*, p. 16.
49. My use of this term draws on a simple definition of a term that is now derived from economic theory: '(a) the welfare of the community as a whole, public interest; (b) a commodity held in common . . . ; (Econ.) a commodity or service provided, without profit, to all members of a society (whether by the government or privately). *Oxford English Dictionary* (Oxford University Press, 2013), http://www.oed.com, stable.

Chapter Bibliography

Alasuutari, P. (ed.), *Rethinking the Media Audience: The New Agenda* (London: Sage, 1999).
A Path Appears (Maro Chermayeff, episode 3, 2015).
As We Forgive (Laura Waters Hinson, 55 mins, 2010), <http://asweforgivemovie.com/> (last accessed 9 December 2016).
Berry, C., Kim, S. and Spigel L. (eds), *Electronic Elsewheres: Media Technology and the Experience of Social Space*, Public Worlds 17 (Minneapolis, MN: University of Minnesota Press, 2010).
Clooney, G., IMDb, <http://www.imdb.com/name/nm0000123/bio> (last accessed 3 December 2016).
Farrow, M., in *MIA FARROW: 'AN INTIMATE PORTRAIT' ABOUT HER LIFE AND CHILDREN'*, 1998, (Lee Grant, *LifeTime Television*, 46 mins), <https://www.youtube.com/watch?v=fu81XtueBbc> (last accessed 28 November 2016).
Farrow, M. in G. Pringle, 'Mia Farrow: "My faith helps me through hard times"', *The Independent*, UK, 2 June 2006, <http://www.independent.co.uk/arts-entertainment/films/features/mia-farrow-my-faith-helps-me-through-hard-times-480665.html#gallery> (last accessed 17 November 2016).
Farrow, M. in R. Holt, 'Mia Farrow offers freedom to save Darfur rebel', *The Telegraph*, 6 August 2007, <http://www.telegraph.co.uk/news/worldnews/1559602/Mia-Farrow-offers-freedom-to-save-Darfur-rebel.html> (last accessed 6 December 2016).
Farrow, M. and G. Levy, 'Mia Farrow on kids and conflict in South Sudan', *Time*, 22 March 2011, <http://content.time.com/time/world/article/0,8599,2060435,00.html> (last accessed 6 December 2016).
Farrow, M. in interview with Maureen Orth, 'Momma Mia!', *Vanity Fair*, 23 October 2013, <http://www.vanityfair.com/style/2013/11/mia-farrow-frank-sinatra-ronan-farrow> (last accessed 1 December 2016).
Gilligan, C., *In a Different Voice: Psychological Theory and Women's Development* (Cambridge, MA: Harvard University Press, [1982] 1993).
Google Earth.
Gross, L., Katz, J. S. and Ruby, J. (eds), *Image Ethics in the Digital Age*, (Minneapolis, MN: University of Minnesota Press, 2003).
Hermes, J., 'Media figures in identity construction', in P. Alasuutari (ed.), *Rethinking the Media Audience: The New Agenda* (London: Sage, 1999).
Holt, R., 'Mia Farrow offers freedom to save Darfur rebel', *The Telegraph*, 6 August 2007, <http://www.telegraph.co.uk/news/worldnews/1559602/Mia-Farrow-offers-freedom-to-save-Darfur-rebel.html> (last accessed 6 December 2016).

Human Rights Watch.org, 'Smallest witnesses', <https://www.hrw.org/legacy/features/darfur/smallwitnesses/intro.html> (last accessed 7 December 2016).
Human Rights Watch, *Sudan Smallest Witnesses: The Crisis in Darfur Through Children's Eyes* (© Human Rights Watch, 2005), <https://www.hrw.org/legacy/features/darfur/smallwitnesses/img/pdf/Smallest Witnesses 2007.pdf> (last accessed 9 February 2017).
Internet Movie Data Base (IMDb).
Journalism Center on Children and Families, <http://www.journalismcenter.org/> (last accessed 8 December 2016).
Levy, G., in 'Mia Farrow on kids and conflict in South Sudan', *Time*, 22 March 2011, <http://content.time.com/time/world/article/0,8599,2060435,00.html> (last accessed 6 December 2016).
McDonnell, F. J. H., 'Clooney shines a light on Sudan, but terror continues', *Frontpage Magazine*, 29 March 2012, <http://www.frontpagemag.com/fpm/127127/clooney-shines-light-sudan-terror-continues-faith-j-h-mcdonnell> (last accessed 3 December 2016).
Megan, K., 'Mia Farrow documents Darfuri culture; donates work to UConn', *The Hartford Courant*, 11 October 2011, <http://articles.courant.com/2011-10-11/news/hc-farrow-archives-uconn-1012-20111011_1_mia-farrow-refugee-camp-darfuris> (last accessed 6 December 2016).
Menezes, G., 'Mia Farrow visits torn community in the Central African Republic', 13 November 2013, <https://www.unicef.org/people/car_70913.html> (last accessed 8 December 2016).
MIA FARROW: 'AN INTIMATE PORTRAIT' ABOUT HER LIFE AND CHILDREN' (dir. Lee Grant, *LifeTime Television*, 46 mins, 1998), <https://www.youtube.com/watch?v=fu81XtueBbc> (last accessed 28 November 2016).
Morley, D., 'Domesticating dislocation in a world of "new" technology', in C. Berry, S. Kim and L. Spigel (eds), *Electronic Elsewheres: Media Technology and the Experience of Social Space*, Public Worlds 17 (Minneapolis, MN: University of Minnesota Press, 2010).
Muller, D., *Journalism Ethics in the Digital Age* (Scribe, 2014).
Orth, M., 'Momma Mia!', *Vanity Fair*, 23 October 2013, <http://www.vanityfair.com/style/2013/11/mia-farrow-frank-sinatra-ronan-farrow> (last accessed 1 December 2016).
Oxford English Dictionary (Oxford University Press, 2013), http://www.oed.com, stable.
Pringle, G. 'Mia Farrow: "My faith helps me through hard times"', *The Independent*, UK, 2 June 2006, <http://www.independent.co.uk/arts-entertainment/films/features/mia-farrow-my-faith-helps-me-through-hard-times-480665.html#gallery> (last accessed 17 November 2016).
Rusesabagina, P., 'The 2008 *Time 100* HEROES AND PIONEERS Mia Farrow', *Time*, 12 May 2008, <http://content.time.com/time/specials/2007/article/0,28804,1733748_1733756_1735264,00.html> (last accessed 1 December 2016).
Summerhayes, C., *Google Earth: Outreach and Activism* (New York: Bloomsbury, 2015).
Turner, G., *Understanding Celebrity* (London, Thousand Oaks and New Delhi: Sage, 2004).
UNICEF, <http://www.unicef.org.au/about-us> (last accessed 6 December 2016).
UNICEF, <https://www.unicef.org/people/people_ambassadors.html> (last accessed 2 December 2016).
UNICEF, <https://www.unicef.org/people/people_mia_farrow.html> (last accessed 6 December 2016).

West, D. M. and J. M. Orman, *Celebrity Politics* (Upper Saddle River, NJ: Prentice Hall, 2003).
Wheeler, M., *Celebrity Politics, Image and Identity* (Cambridge: Polity Press, 2013).
Wikipedia, 'Mia Farrow', <https://en.wikipedia.org/wiki/Mia_Farrow>, updated 25 October 2016 (last accessed 17 November 2016).

'BEING A WOMAN DOCUMENTARY MAKER IN TAIWAN' – AN INTERVIEW WITH SINGING CHEN AND WUNA WU

Chris Berry

Taiwan has a thriving documentary sector, with 'women making up a large part of the documentarian population'.[1] The development of the sector can be traced back to the political activism of the 1980s, for, in an era when martial law and strict censorship still prevailed, activist video was a crucial means of spreading alternative information and contesting the government-controlled media. Following the end of martial law in 1987 and the development of a liberal, multi-party democratic system, a broad range of independent documentaries engaged with the burgeoning social movements of the time began to be produced in the 1990s. As the dramatic feature film industry went into decline for various reasons, documentary became an even more important means of satisfying Taiwanese audience demand for audio-visual narratives about their own lives and society. In addition to community-based screenings, feature-length documentaries began to get theatrical releases, and the Public Television Service (PTS) channel became an important platform and source of sponsorship. More recently, a third phase of films that are more personal, and more concerned with the aesthetics of documentary has emerged.[2]

The prominent role of women in the documentary sector is part of a larger trend in Taiwanese society. Both of the main candidates in the 2016 presidential election were women, until a last minute change of candidate by the KMT Nationalist Party. However, selecting a man did not help the KMT, and Tsai Ing-wen (蔡英文) of the Democratic Progressive Party (DPP) was elected as the island's first female president. When I visited Taipei in November of 2015, I discovered a large number of women are playing prominent roles in the film industry more widely, too.³ When we consider that there are no women directors among the Taiwan New Cinema generation that includes Hou Hsiao-Hsien (侯孝賢) and Edward Yang (楊德昌), this is a remarkable shift. Among the important female players in the industry that I met in 2015 were Jennifer Jao (饒紫娟), Director of the Taipei Film Commission; and Yeh Juh-Feng (葉如芬), head of the Production Department of MandarinVision (華文創), a leading production, distribution, sales and talent management company set up in 2012 by another leading woman in the Taiwan film industry, Jessie Ho (何琇瓊).

To understand more about what it is like to be a woman in the Taiwan film industry, and specifically a woman documentary maker, I interviewed Wuna Wu (吳汰紝) and Singing Chen (陈芯宜) together in the offices of Wu's production company offices. They are two of the most prominent members of the younger generation of Taiwanese women filmmakers. Wu is associated with a shift towards personal filmmaking, such as the intense exploration of her relationship with, and effort to hang on to memories of, her deceased mother in her 2003 twenty-five- minute film *Goodbye 1999* (再會吧, 1999). She also explores the social through the personal, following the work of a modern matchmaker in *Let's Fall in Love* (尋情歷險記, 2008) at a time when she herself was wondering why she was not married, and eschews any pretence to objective observation, putting herself on camera in films such as her portrait of a family with two schizophrenic children, *Happy or Not?* (快不快樂四人行, 2003).

All these characteristics came together in *The Dream Never Sets* (日落大夢, 2010) (Figure 16), in which Wu interviews and follows her father as he tries to sell his latest invention, in the process investigating the small-scale manufacturing enterprise that has been the backbone of Taiwan's economy. Today, she is working on various projects with her own production company.

Singing Chen directs both dramatic features and documentaries. The topic of her debut dramatic feature, *Bundled* (我叫阿銘啦, 1999), the drop-outs and homeless of Taipei, could equally well have been a documentary, and indeed part of the narrative satirises the work of insensitive television journalists. Her most recent documentaries have focused on artists. She spent over ten years on *The Walkers* (行者, 2014) (Figure 17), following Lin Li-Chen (林麗珍) and her Legend Lin Dance Theater (無垢舞蹈劇場). Although 150 minutes long, the film had a successful theatrical release.

Her *Mountain Spirits* (山靈, 2014) examines the work of installation artist Wang Wen-chih (王文志), who weaves huge site-specific sculptures. If Wu's work can be said to manifest the trend to more personal filmmaking, Chen's manifests the trend towards a greater investment in cinematic aesthetics.

However, Wu and Chen share what Kuei-fen Chiu and Yingjin Zhang have claimed is an interest in new subjectivities that runs through much of current Taiwanese women's documentary cinema.⁴ Chiu and Zhang have investigated

Figure 16 *The Dream Never Sets* (Wuna Wu, 2010).

this phenomenon in more detail, and in particular with regard to women's social and interpersonal subjectivities, through some specific examples in their work. So, in this interview, I wanted to focus more on the working conditions and social environment for women filmmakers in Taiwan. What follows is extracted from a longer conversation. The discussion moves from their own backgrounds and the conditions that guided them into the wave of women entering the documentary field in Taiwan in the 1990s to a more nuanced discussion of what parts of the film industry women find it easier to work in, the particular challenges of satisfying work and personal life that Wu has encountered now she is a mother, and the obstacles that continue to make the number of women working in feature film – as Chen does – much smaller than the number making documentaries. I started out by asking them to tell me how they got involved in filmmaking.

Wu: I started making documentaries when I studied at Tainan University of the Arts in 2001, and I finished my first film in 2002. I had a lot of fun with it, and so I've been continuing until now. Before I went to Tainan, I worked for Zero Chou (周美玲)[5] as her assistant on a few documentaries. She hadn't started making features then. This was when I discovered documentaries as a way of life, which I felt to be very free and stimulating.

Chen: My college major was Mass Media, not Film. It was very focused on advertising, and I lost interest after two years. This was in 1993 or 1994. Martial Law had only recently been lifted [in 1987], and underground culture

Figure 17 Poster for *The Walkers* (Singing Chen, 2014).

was taking off. I joined something called the Taipei Post-Industrial Art Festival, and there I met Huang Mingchuan (黃明川).⁶ We worked together on a series of films about artists until I made my first dramatic feature in 1999, and I've been on my own since then. I was very lucky to be with Huang Mingchuan, because he didn't teach men and women differently. I learnt everything from him: cinematography, editing, sound and lighting. We were still shooting on 16mm then, and we had to change the rolls of film over by ourselves. But if I hadn't been with him, at that time women only got to be producer's assistants and assistant directors – they didn't get to do anything technical. I was his first female student, and only after that did other women come along. And then the arrival of small, lightweight and affordable cameras in the late 1990s made it easier for women.

CB: That technology was available everywhere, but Taiwan has especially many women directors and producers.

Wu: We often discussed that phenomenon when I was at college. There are few barriers for getting into making documentaries, and although I'm not sure when women started participating in public life in Taiwan, there certainly are plenty of them.

Chen: Taiwan's Women Make Waves film festival has been going for over twenty years already, and I'm sure it encouraged a lot of women when it was launched. Tainan University of Arts was also important. Before that, film schools had focused on fiction films, but Tainan did documentary. Furthermore, the first few classes of students were strong, and then the women graduates started making films.

CB: [Female director] Huang Yu-shan (黃玉珊) was teaching at Tainan then, right?

Wu: But I think it's not so much about gender as that being the right time for documentary. Lots of people came to Tainan with no background in documentary film but with involvement in various community building movements, and the majority of them were women. They wanted to use documentary to advance their causes.

CB: And who set up the Women Make Waves festival? Does the government support them?

Wu: I think they must get a subsidy every year. Lots of social movements sprang up after the end of Martial Law in 1987, including a very varied women's movement, some of the members of which were interested in the moving image and set up the festival, including the lawyer Yu Mei-nu (尤美女) and [Director of the Taiwan International Documentary Festival] Jane Yu (尤惠珍).

CB: So I want to get back to what's so special about Taiwan and why so many women are playing such strong roles in film. Is it social change?

Wu: Things are changing gradually, but men and women aren't equal yet. Although there are more women directors, there aren't many women in other key roles like lighting and cinematography. Women are in the areas where less technical knowledge is needed, like directing and producing, or programming film festivals – probably 80 or 90 per cent of festival curators are women.

CB: Most people think producing and directing are the most powerful roles in film. If that's where women are concentrated in the Taiwanese film industry, that's very significant.

Chen: But what's unusual about Taiwan is that we haven't developed an industry in either the documentary or fiction film fields; we're still doing independent production. It's an artisanal mode.

CB: Isn't that an advantage for women?

Wu: Yes, the documentary sector is very vigorous and lots of women are taking part, but the Ministry of Culture and the Film Bureau don't pay it much attention and so it's difficult to get resources and support, compared to feature films. It's not difficult to get into documentary filmmaking, and I think lots of women do it as part of a process of self-discovery and development. But, in my case, for example, after getting to a certain stage, I faced a new issue – family. If I had a baby, it was going to have a big impact on me. In the face of that challenge, I wouldn't want to be going so far from home, so I might need to find someone else to work with me on films. Or I might need to find a new way to earn money, like going into office work.

CB: So, that's why you've set up your own company?

Wu: Yes, with a friend.

CB: How many people are in the company?

Wu: Five.

CB: And are you directing fewer films yourself because you are a mother and have a family now?

Wu: I'm beginning to find other people to work with me now. I'm still going on location, but once I know what needs to be done, I'm handing over to someone else. I'm looking for long-term partners and training up colleagues.

CB: You both have your own production companies. Is it easy to set up your own production companies in Taiwan?

Wu: Not too difficult, and you don't need a lot of capital.

Chen: I'm trying to get a film released now, and that involves various regulatory procedures and applying for support. I want to distribute it, and I can't do that through another company, so I needed to establish my own company. I only set up my own company last year in 2014 for my documentary *The Walkers*, and before that I set up a company together with Zero Chou and a few other directors. I'm still a partner in that company. We set it up in 1999 for the *Floating Islands* (流離島) series of documentaries, where we each made a film about one of Taiwan's thirteen islands.

CB (to Wu): When did you first set up your own company?

Wu: 2008. If you want to take on a commission or apply for funding, you need to have a company. And I'd hit a bottleneck. I'd been shooting films by myself since 2001 and felt I couldn't go any further without putting together a team to work with.

CB: As well as simply having a lot of female filmmakers in Taiwan, has gender been an issue in the film world or something that has received attention?

Wu: One genre that started out at Tainan University of the Arts when I was there was self-exploratory, personal documentary, and lots of women went down that road, especially with their first films. Male directors followed later. However, we didn't think of those as women's films, but rather as about human nature.

CB: So you don't think of your own films as women's films?

Wu and Chen: Not really.

CB: Does the government encourage women to become filmmakers?

Chen: There are no special policies.

CB: Have you run into any problems at work because you are women?

Wu: I'm interested in all kinds of topics, including male topics. But as a woman, of course there are all kinds of obstacles entering a male environment. That's why I like working with [my partner] Maso (陳志漢). I can go shoot where's it's not so suitable for him, and vice versa.

Chen: With my first film, *Bundled*, I knew most of my crew through indie filmmaking, and so we got on fine. But when it came to postproduction and the sound mix, I ran into an old technician who just ignored me. I couldn't get through to him. He felt he was the teacher and I was a little girl student. So, after I finished it with him, I took it over to a new studio at Central Motion Pictures Corporation (中央電影事業股份有限公司) and redid it. Documentaries are quite simple, because you're working with a small crew, but I ran into lots of difficulties with dramatic features. I always have to spend a lot more time and energy than a man to get the older technicians to do what I want. It's better with the younger ones. I've got an interesting example. In the filmmaking world in Taiwan, it's a big taboo for a woman to sit on the camera case. But Huang Mingchuan didn't care about that, and now some younger male crew don't mind, either. But when I started out, it was absolutely forbidden. The filmmaking world is still a male world. I think smoking is a way that the crew deals with male directors. If there's something they don't see eye to eye on, they go and talk it out over a cigarette. As for women and male directors, actresses can be coquettish and that can be quite effective. But none of that's any use with me as a woman director, because I don't smoke, and actresses can't pout and flirt with me. So, I think that the crews are still working out how to deal with women directors.

Wu: I think that on set or on location, directors have got more power, but that it's difficult for women to exercise that power.

Chen: Male directors win trust easily, but women directors have to show that they are professional and have ideas before they can get people to respect them.

Wu: But this conversation is making me aware how many key players like film festival programmers and producers are women.

Chen: But women producers don't necessarily support women directors.

Wu: Whenever you read something about Taiwan's important film directors, they're all male.

Chen: There are plenty of women directors, but men and women still don't have equal conditions. Women still have to work harder to survive as fiction filmmakers. Look at [the 2011 omnibus film] *10+10*. Lots of people have wondered why I and many other women directors were not taking part. OK, so Wang Shaodi (王小棣) was involved, but she and Sylvia Chang (張艾嘉) are the older generation. But when it comes the younger directors, they're all men. I think maybe male directors are more ambitious to get things done quicker, but that's just my opinion.

Despite ending our conversation with a clear realisation of the challenges women continue to face in Taiwan's film world, and especially in making dramatic features, Wu and Chen saw no obstacles to continuing their career as documentary makers. In an era when Hollywood features dominate the Taiwan market, it is the relatively inexpensive local documentaries that are thriving. Winning local audiences by telling local stories, the most successful get both theatrical releases and television screenings.

Notes

1. Kuei-fen Chiu and Yingjin Zhang, *New Chinese-Language Documentaries: Ethics, Subject, and Place* (Abingdon: Routledge, 2015), p. 101.
2. Ibid. pp. 54–7. See also Sylvia Li-chun Lin and Tze-lan Deborah Sang (eds), *Documenting Taiwan on Film: Issues and Methods in New Documentaries* (Abingdon: Routledge, 2012).
3. I am grateful to the Taiwan Ministry of Culture for making my visit possible and assisting with arrangements. The original interview with Singing Chen and Wuna Wu was transcribed by Hsieh Chin-mei, and then translated and edited by me.
4. Chiu and Zhang, pp. 101–16.
5. Chou is one of Taiwan's most prominent filmmakers today. She launched her career in the 1990s, in the age of social movement documentaries. Her first feature, *Splendid Float* (艷光四射歌舞團, 2004), won three Golden Horse awards, and since then she has focused on dramatic features with queer themes.
6. Huang Mingchuan's *Man from Island West* (西部來的人, 1989), about a member of the Atayal Aboriginal population, is known as Taiwan's first independent dramatic feature film. As well as Singing Chen, Huang helped to train Zero Chou.

Filmography

Zero Chou, *Splendid Float* (艷光四射歌舞團, Taiwan, 2004).
Singing Chen, *Mountain Spirits* (山靈, Taiwan, 2014).
Singing Chen, *Bundled* (我叫阿銘啦, Taiwan, 1999).
Singing Chen, *The Walkers* (行者, Taiwan, 2014).
Huang Mingchuan, *Man from Island West* (西部來的人, Taiwan, 1989).
Wuna Wu, *Goodbye 1999* (再會吧, Taiwan, 1999).
Wuna Wu, *Let's Fall in Love* (尋情歷險記, Taiwan, 2008).
Wuna Wu, *Happy or Not?* (快不快樂四人行, Taiwan, 2003).
Wuna Wu, *The Dream Never Sets* (日落大夢, Taiwan, 2010).
Sylvia Chang et al. *10+10* (Taiwan, 2011) (omnibus film).

SELECT BIBLIOGRAPHY

Books

Ahmed, Sara, *The Cultural Politics of Emotion* (Edinburgh: Edinburgh University Press, 2004).
Alaimo Stacy and Susan Hekman (eds), *Material Feminisms* (Indianapolis, IN: Indiana University Press, 2008).
Alasuutari, Pertti (ed.), *Rethinking the Media Audience: The New Agenda* (London: Sage, 1999).
Aumont, Jacques, *The Image* (London: BFI Publishing, 1997).
Austin, Thomas and Wilma de Jong (eds), *Rethinking Documentary: New Perspectives, New Practices* (Maidenhead: Open University Press, 2010).
Bauman, Zygmunt, *Postmodern Ethics* (Oxford, Cambridge, MA: Blackwell Publishers, 1993).
Blee, Kathleen and France Winddance Twine (eds), *Feminism and Antiracism: International Struggles for Justice* (New York: NYU Press, 2001).
Blouin, Francis X. and William G. Rosenberg, *Processing the Past: Contesting Authority in History and the Archives* (Oxford: Oxford University Press, 2011).
Brock, Peggy (ed.), *Words and Silences: Aboriginal Women, Politics and Land* (Crows Nest, NSW: Allen and Unwin, 2001).
Bruzzi, Stella, *New Documentary: A Critical Introduction* (London: Routledge, 2000).
Cahilll, Ann J. and Jennifer L. Hansen (eds), *French Feminists: Luce Irigaray – Critical Evaluations in Cultural Theory* (New York: Routledge, 2008).
Caines, Rebecca and Ajay Heble (eds), *The Improvisation Studies Reader: Spontaneous Acts* (London: Routledge, 2015).
Carilli, Theresa and Jane Campbell (eds), *Challenging Images of Women in the Media: Reinventing Women's Lives* (Langham, MD: Lexington Press, 2012).
Chiu Kuei-fen and Yingjin Zhang, *New Chinese-Language Documentaries: Ethics, Subject, and Place* (Abingdon: Routledge, 2015).

Choi, Jinhee and Mattias Frey (eds), *Cine-Ethics; Ethical Dimensions of Film Theory, Practice and Spectatorship* (London: Routledge, 2013).
Columpar, Corinn and Sophie Mayer (eds), *There She Goes: Feminist Filmmaking and Beyond* (Detroit, MI: Wayne State University Press, 2010).
Cowley, Stephen J. (ed.), *Distributed Language* (Amsterdam: Benjamins, 2011).
de Spain, Kent, *Landscape of the Now: A Topography of Movement Improvisation* (London: Oxford University Press, 2014).
Fischlin, Daniel, Ajay Heble and George Lipsitz (eds), *The Fierce Urgency of Now* (Durham, NC: Duke University Press, 2013).
Foucault, Michel, *The History of Sexuality, Volume II: The Use of Pleasure* (New York: Random House, 1985).
Foucault, Michel, *Madness and Civilization* (New York: Routledge; 2006 [1961]).
Fusco, Coco, *The Bodies That Were Not Ours and Other Writings* (London, New York: Routledge, 2001).
Goffman, Ervin, *The Presentation of Self in Everyday Life* (London: Penguin, 1990).
Hamish, Carol, 'The personal is political', in Barbara A. Crow (ed.), *Radical Feminism: A Documentary Reader* (New York: NYU Press, 2000), p 113–17.
Heusden, Barend van and Pascal Gielen (eds), *Arts Education Beyond Art, Teaching Art In Times of Change* (Amsterdam: Valiz, Antenea, 2015).
Kuhn, Annette., *Family Secrets: Facts of Memory and Imagination* (London, New York: Verso 2002).
de Lauretis, Teresa, *Technologies of Gender: Essays on Theory, Film, and Fiction.* (Bloomington: Indiana University Press, 1987).
Lebow, Alisa, *The Cinema of Me: The Self and Subjectivity in First Person Documentary* (London, New York: Wallflower Press, 2012).
Lin, Sylvia Li-chun and Tze-lan Deborah Sang (eds), *Documenting Taiwan on Film: Issues and Methods in New Documentaries* (Abingdon: Routledge, 2012).
Marks, Laura U., *The Skin of the Film: Intercultural Cinema, Embodiment and the Senses* (Durham, NC: Duke University Press, 2002).
Moi, Toril, *What is a Woman?* (London, New York: Oxford University Press, 1999).
Naficy, Hamid, *An Accented Cinema: Exilic and Diasporic Filmmaking* (Princeton, NJ: Princeton University Press, 2001).
Nichols, Bill, *Representing Reality: Issues and Concepts in Documentary* (Bloomington, IN: Indiana University Press, 1991).
Peters, Gary, *The Philosophy of Improvisation* (Chicago, IL: University of Chicago Press, 2009).
Plantinga, Carl and and Greg M. Smith (eds), *Passionate Views, Film, Cognition and Emotion* (Baltimore, MD: Johns Hopkins University Press, 1999).
Rascaroli, Laura, *The Personal Camera: Subjectivite Cinema and the Essay Film* (London and New York: Wallflower Press, 2009).
Renov, Michael, *The Subject of Documentary* (London and Minneapolis, MN: University of Minnesota Press, 2004).
Smith, Alison, *Agnès Varda* (Manchester: Manchester University Press, 1998).
Trinh T. Minh-ha, *Woman, Native, Other: Writing, Postcoloniality, Feminism* (Bloomington, IN: Indiana University Press, 1989).
Trinh T. Minh-ha, *Cinema Interval* (London and New York: Routledge, 1999).
Turner, Graeme, *Understanding Celebrity* (London, Thousand Oaks and New Delhi: Sage, 2004).
Wada-Marciano, Mitsuyo, *Japanese Cinema in the Digital Age* (Honolulu: University of Hawai'i Press, 2012).
Wheeler, Mark, *Celebrity Politics, Image and Identity* (Cambridge: Polity Press, 2013).

Articles

Bovenschen, Silvia, 'Is there a feminine aesthetic?', *New German Critique*, 10/1977, pp. 111–37.

Chu, Sumi, Kimberlé Crenshaw and Leslie McCall, 'Towards a field of intersectionality studies: theory, applications and praxis', *Signs*, 38:4 (2013), pp. 785–809.

Citron, Michel et al., 'Women and film: a discussion of feminist aesthetics,' *New German Critique*, 13, 1978, pp. 83–107.

Hugueny-Léger, Elise, 'Broadcasting the self: autofiction, television and representation of authorship in contemporary French literature', *Life Writing*, 14/1, 2016, pp. 5–18.

Jordan, Shirley, 'Autofiction in the feminine', *French Studies: A Quarterly Review*, 67/1, 2013, pp. 76–84.

Juhasz, Alexandra, 'They said we were trying to show reality – all I want is to show my film: the politics of the realist feminist documentary,' *Screen*, 35/2, 1994, pp. 171–91.

Kuhn, Annette, ' The camera I. Observations on documentary', *Screen*, 19/2, 1978, pp. 71–84.

Lauretis, Teresa de, 'Aesthetic and feminist theory: rethinking women's cinema', *New German Critique*, 34, 1985, pp. 154–75.

McHugh, Kathleen, 'The world and the soup: historicizing media feminisms in transnational contexts', *Camera Obscura*, 24/3 72, 2009, pp. 111–51.

Marquis, Elizabeth, 'Conceptualizing documentary performance', *Studies in Documentary Film*, 7/1, 2013, pp. 45–60.

Mendoza Breny, 'Transnational feminisms in question', *Feminist Theory*, 3/3, 2002, pp. 295–314.

Mulvey, Laura, 'Visual pleasure and narrative cinema', *Screen*, 16/3, 1975, pp. 6–18.

Nichols, Bill, 'The voice of documentary', *Film Quarterly*, 36/3, 1983, pp. 17–30.

Nornes, Abé Marc, 'The postwar documentary trace: groping in the dark', *Positions: East Asia Culture Critique*, 10/1, 2002, pp. 66–68.

Pedwell, Carolyn and Anne Whitehead, 'Affecting feminism: questions of feeling in feminist theory', *Feminist Theory*, 13/2, 2012, pp. 115–29.

Raaberg, Gwen, 'Beyond fragmentation: collage as feminist strategy in the arts', *Mosaic (Winnipeg)*, 31/3, 1998, pp. 153–71.

Trinh T. Minh-ha, ' Documentary is/not a name', *October*, 52, 1990, pp. 76–98.

INDEX

Aboriginal women, 159–72
abortion, 17
activism, 16, 17, 24, 33, 90–1, 102, 134
  celebrity, 186–204
advocacy, 50, 190, 192, 199
aesthetics, 12, 13–15, 28, 30, 42, 109–23; *see also* collectivity, aesthetics
affective dissonance, 100, 101
African Americans, 31–2, 46, 77
Agamben, Giorgio, 54
agency, 80–1
aging and sexuality, 135–7
Ahmed, Sara, 100
Akerman, Chantal, 14, 129–30
Alaimo, Stacy, 173
al-Bashir, Omar Hassan, 193
Allen, Woody, 188–9
anarchism, 78
Anderson, John, 134–5
Anything You want To Be (Brandon), 27, 30
aporia, 48, 54, 64, 96–7, 102
Appadurai, Arjun, 110
archives, 33–4, 46–64, 165–6, 194–9

Armstrong, Gillian, 14, 16, 18–19
Around the World in 50 Concerts (Honigmann), 128
As We Forgive (Farrow), 194
Atkinson, Judy, 160
Aumont, Jacques, 109
auteurism, 5, 45, 79, 82, 152–3, 187
autobiography, 14–15, 75–89, 154, 172
autofiction, as repetition, 148
avant-garde theatre, 78, 79

Baines, Pat, 159–60, 163, 165, 168
Bani-Etemad, Rakhshan, 17
Baruah, Sanjib, 117
beDevil (Moffatt), 168
Bell, David M., 78
Belleville Baby (Engberg), 144–58
Betty Tells Her Story (Brandon), 27
Beyond the Family Album (Spence), 66
Bigelow, Katherine, 12
'Blood Sugar' (Daniel), 48, 50, 52, 54
bodies, female, 67, 136, 172–3, 176–83
bodily perception, 133
'Body' (Daniel), 54
Boyer, Anne, 68

217

INDEX

Brandon, Liane, 25, 26, 27, 30
Brennan, Gloria, 159, 161, 162
Bruzzi, Stella, 175
Bundled (Chen), 206, 212
Butler, Judith, 175

California Correctional Women's Facility, 49–50
Calle, Sophie, 148, 153
cameras, lightweight, 24, 84, 93, 209
Cardiff (Wales), Gujeratis, 110–16
celebrities, 187, 189–90
cell phone cameras *see* mobile cameras
Chang, Sylvia, 213
Chen, Singing, 206–13
child abuse, 13, 17
childbirth, 173, 179–85
Chiu, Kuei-fen, 206–7
Chris and Bernie (Friedman, Shaffer), 24, 27, 30
cinéma-vérité, 85, 144, 152
class, 14, 79, 101
close-ups, 113, 138, 182
Cochrane, Kira, 101
Coffin, Lorrae, 164
cognitive neuroscience, 139
Cohn, Peter, 35
collaboration, 82–3, 92; *see also* relationships
collage aesthetic, 30
collections, 33–4, 41–64; *see also* archives
collectivity, aesthetics, 24, 28, 31, 33, 34
colonisation, Australian, 161, 167
consciousness, 139
consciousness raising, 26, 32, 43
Contact Improvisation, 79
'Convictions' (Daniel), 46–7
Corbett, Helen, 163
Cox, Lucy, 165–6
Crazy (Honigmann), 128, 135
Crenshaw, Kimberlé, 99, 102
criminal justice system, US, 45–64
Crossings (Sharma), 110–16
Csikszentmihalyi, Mihalyi, 78, 82
cultural specificity, 15–16

dance/song, 78, 79, 83
  Aboriginal, 163, 165–7
Darfur Crisis, 193, 195–9
Das, Suban, 119
databases, digital, 43–64
Day I Will Never Forget, The (Longinotto), 17, 90, 130
Daylight, Phyllis, 161
de Beauvoir, Simone, 15
de Lauretis, Teresa, 131, 133–4
De Spain, Kent, 81–2
death, and illness, 66–71
difference, 14–15, 91, 98–100, 101
Direct Cinema, 92, 94
Dirty Diaries, The (Engberg), 145, 153
disappearance, 69, 95
discussion films, 24–6, 27, 35
distribution, film, 22, 26, 29, 34
Divorce Iranian Style (Longinotto), 90, 91, 92
Dream Never Sets, The (Wu), 206, 207
Dreamcatcher (Longinotto), 91, 96, 98, 99, 101
drug use, 48, 55–7, 59, 60, 64
Drummond de Andrade, Carlos, 135–6
Dudgeon, Pat, 163–4
Duras, Marguerite, 148, 151, 154

editing, 84–5, 93, 174, 181–2
Eisenstein, Sergei, 115
El Olvido (Honigmann), 128
Embracing (Kawase), 171–2, 178
emotion, 17, 90, 96, 98–100, 133, 139, 146
empathy, 99, 100, 138
Enfants du Square, Les (Engberg), 144–5
Engberg, Mia, 144–58
essay films, 144–58, 177
ethics, 197–9
Ewing, Heidi, 17
Extreme Private Eros (Hara), 172

Farrokhzad, Fourough, 11
Farrow, Mia, 186–204
female aesthetics, 12, 13–15
female gaze, 9–20, 127, 129–33, 172
female genital mutilation, 17, 90, 130

female subjectivity, 9–20, 133–4, 206–7
feminism
  and representation, 15–16
  second wave (1970s), 26, 42, 131, 133
  transnational, 90, 98–9
fiction film, deconstructive, female, 134
film essay, 144–58
Filming Desire (Mandy), 10, 130, 131
Final Project, The (Spence), 66, 67–9, 71
Fischlin, Daniel, 83, 86
Flickr, 195–7
Floating Islands, 211
Food For Love (Honigmann), 12, 18, 128
Forever (Honigmann), 128, 137–9
Foucault, Michel, 54, 135
freezeframe, 97, 101
Friedman, Bonnie, 24
Fusco, Coco, 161, 163, 168

Gadamer, Hans-Georg, 81, 82, 83, 84
Gaines, Jane, 27, 30–1
gaze, 66, 70, 97, 101, 109–10, 130, 132
  counter-insurgent, 117–18, 120
  see also female gaze
gender identity, 11, 82
Genpin (Kawase), 179, 180–3
gestures, 14, 93; *see also* dance/song
Ghatak, Ritwik, 115–16
Giles, David, 189
Gilligan, Carol, 198
Ginsburg, Faye, 168
Gleaners and I, The (Varda), 130
Goddess Kamakhya, 118–19
Good Husband, Dear Son (Honigmann), 18, 128
Google Earth, Darfur Crisis, 195–8
Grady, Rachel, 17
Granito: How to Nail a Dictator (Yates), 35–7
Grierson, John, 145, 154
Grierson Award, 91
Growing Up Female (Klein, Reichert), 26, 27, 30, 31
Guatemala, 35–6
Gujerati diaspora, 110–16
Gulabi Gang (Jain), 16

Hanisch, Carol, 43–4
Happy or Not? (Wu), 206
haptic aesthetics, 109–23
Hara, Kazuro, 172
Harlan County (Kopple), 18
health system, depersonalisation, 68, 69–70
Hegedus, Chris, 15
Hekman, Susan, 173
Hemmings, Clare, 100, 101
Henry, Beverly, 58–60, 64
hermeneutics, 81
Hermes, Joke, 189
Hernández, María Magdelena, 35, 37
Hinduism, Cardiff ethnoscape, 111
HIV/AIDS prevention, 163
Ho, Jessie, 206
Hold Me Tight, Let Me Go (Longinotto), 93, 101
Hollywood, 24, 96, 130, 154–5
Honigmann, Heddy, 12, 18, 127–43
Honkasalo, Pirjo, 12, 13
Hotaru (Kawase), 173–4
Hour of the Furnaces, The, 132
Huang Mingchuan, 209, 212
Huang Yu-shan, 209
Huddleston, Ollie, 92, 93
human rights, 190
Human Rights Watch website, 'Smallest Witnesses', 196
Humm, Maggie, 16

identity politics, 174–5
illness, and death, 66–71, 188
Images from the Corner (Zbanic), 17–18
improvisation, 75–89
independent film production, Taiwan, 210–11
India, Indians, 16, 90, 107–21
  representations of, 109, 117–18, 120
India Song (Duras), 151
Indigenous culture, 159–72
'Inside the Distance' (Daniel), 52, 62–3
International Documentary Film Festival Amsterdam (IDFA), 10, 17, 127
interviews, 30, 31, 32, 34, 50, 66–71, 81, 205–13

INDEX

intimacy, 172, 176–9
Intra-Venus (Wilke), 66, 67–8, 71
Iranian documentaries, 13, 17, 90, 92, 93–4
Irigaray, Luce, 76, 78, 79
Islamic (Sharia) law, 17
Israel of the Bedouins (Honigmann), 128
It Happens To Us (Juhasz), 32

Jain, Nishtha, 14, 15–16
Jamous, Suleiman, 193
Jao, Jennifer, 206
Japanese film production, 92, 171–85
Jardiwarnpa (Perkins), 162
jazz, 77, 78, 83
Jedda (Chauvel), 162
Johnson, Kirston, 34
Johnstone, Mary, 161
Juhasz, Alexandra, 29–30, 32
justice and punishment, US, 45–64

Kamakha (Sharma), 116–20
Karatsu, Rie, 173
Katatsumori (Kawase), 172, 176
Kawase, Naomi, 171–85
Keshavarz, Mina, 11, 18
Kimm, Joan, 160
Kinoy, Peter, 35, 36
Klein, Jim, 25–6
Kleinhans, Chuck, 24–6, 27
Knudsen, Erik, 146
Koch, Gertrud, 11
Kopple, Barbara, 11, 18
Kuhn, Annette, 93, 94, 146–7, 148, 151
Kya Ka Ra Ba A (Kawase), 174

Lakshmi and Me (Jain), 14
Land of Opportunity (Dantes, Snedeker), 35
Langton, Marcia, 162
Latif, Amber, 92, 94
Lebow, Alisa, 176–7
Leigh Foster, Susan, 82, 83–4
Let's Fall in Love (Wu), 206
Levy, Glen, 192, 198
Lewis, Carolyn, 164
Lin Li-Chen, 206

Linssen, Dana, 14
Lippard, Lucy, 14
Longinotto, Kim, 11, 15, 16, 17, 18, 90–106, 130
Lorde, Audre, 76

Mackey, Nathanial, 80
Mackinnon, Catherine, 54
Mandy, Marie, 10, 12, 13, 14–15, 130, 131
marginalisation, 44, 77
Marks, Laura, 120
Marquis, Elizabeth, 175–6
Marsalis, Wynton, 78
Marxism, 28, 29, 79
masculinity, 11, 15
materiality, 173, 176–9, 181–2
maternal care, 79–80
Mayer, Sophie, 92, 93
Mayne, Judith, 28
McGlade, Hannah, 160, 164
mediation, prison, 62–3
Megan, Kathleen, 194
memorial website, 37
memory texts, 147, 151
memory work, 146–7, 148
memory/memories
 art films based on, 151
 fragmented, 156
 and identity, 128, 129
 involuntary, 138
Mendoza, Breny, 99
Metal and Melancholy (Honigmann), 128, 134
metamodernity, 129, 132–3, 135, 139
métissage, 154
Mindshadows (Honigmann), 128
Mir-Hosseini, 94
mise en scène, 109
mobile cameras, 85, 153
Moffatt, Tracey, 159–70
Mogari (Kawase), 171
Mohanty, Chandra, 91, 99
MOMI, New Day Films, 23, 30, 33–4
montage, 31, 112–16, 118, 121, 147, 182
Moodeitj Yorgas (Moffatt), 159–70

220

Moodysson, Lukas, 11
Morgan, Sally, 166, 168
Morley, David, 198
Mountain Spirits (Chen), 206
Movement Improvisation (MI), 79
Mulvey, Laura, 28, 29, 130
Murderer or Murdered (Sheikholeslami), 13
Museum of Modern Art, New York, 23, 30, 33–4
Myers-Powell, Brenda, 90–1, 96, 97–8
myth, classical, 147, 156

narcissm, 66, 67
narrative, circular, 156
narrative cinema, 28
Natsios, Andrew S., 195
New Day Films, 22–39
New German Critique, 28
New York documentary filmmaking, 26
Newsreel Film Collective, 29
Nice Colored Girls (Moffatt), 160, 163
Nichols, Bill, 30, 31, 75, 76, 79, 81, 93, 95, 145, 163, 174–5
Night Cries: A Rural Tragedy (Moffatt), 162
Noujaim, Jehane, 15
Nyungar women, 159–60

O Amor Natural (Honigmann), 128, 135–7
objectification, 70, 120, 130, 168
observational documentaries, 92–101
Onís, Paco de, 35, 36–7
online archives, 46–64, 165–6, 193–9
optical visuality/aesthetics, 109–10, 120
Orman, John M., 189
Orth, Maureen, 193
'otherness', 11, 29, 81–2, 133, 139, 168

Path Appears, A (Farrow), 194
patriarchy, 35, 77, 160
Payne, Cathie, 165, 167
Pedwell, Carolyn, 99
performance art, 66–7, 70
performativity, 173–8, 179
Perkins, Rachel, 162

'Personal is Political' (Daniel), 42–4
'Perspective' (Daniel), 61
Peru, 133, 134
Phookan, Nilmani, 118–19
photography, activist, 194–9
phototherapy, 68, 69, 70
Picture of Health, The (Spence), 66, 68, 70–1
Pink Saris (Longinotto), 17, 18, 90, 91, 92, 94, 97, 101
'Place' (Daniel), 48
plurality, 164, 177
poetry, 118–19
point of view shots, 94, 175
police violence, 46–7
political mimesis, 27, 30–1, 32, 34, 36
pornography, female, 145, 153
postmodern relativism, 133
Potter, Sally, 29
pregnancy *see* childbirth
Previn, André, 188
prisons, US, 47–61
Probyn, Fiona, 13–14
process, 80–1, 84, 85
producers, female, 28
production crew, all-female, 92
Profession Documentarist (Abtahi et al.), 11, 13, 18
Proust, Marcel, 137–9
psychoanalytic film theory, 29
'Public Secrets' (Daniel), 46–61

racism, 44–7, 166
Rancière, Jacques, 52, 61
Rascaroli, Laura, 153, 156
realism, 24–33, 129, 154
refugee camps, children, 194–6
Reichert, Julia, 25–6
relationships, 94–6, 98, 99, 100–1, 172–3, 176–83; *see also* collaboration; female gaze
Renov, Michael, 147, 154
repetition, 138, 148
reproductive rights, 17
Rey-Maupin affair, 147–8
Rezaei, Nahid, 11
Rich, B. Ruby, 28

INDEX

Ríos Montt, Efraín, 36, 37
Rosemary's Baby (Polanski), 188
Rothschild, Amalie R., 25, 26, 30
Rouch, Jean, 146, 152
Rough Aunties (Longinotto), 90, 91, 97
Routt, William D., 84, 85
Runaway (Longinotto), 93–4, 97, 101
Rwanda, 194
Rzewski, F., 86

Saito, Junichi, 172–3, 177, 179
Salma (Longinotto), 17
Sampat Pal, 90, 94, 96, 97
Sarma, Kandarp, 119
Sawyer, Keith, 82
self-care, 70
self-documentaries, 172
selfies, 67
self-portraits, 66–71
sensationalism/exploitation, 138
sensations, bodily, 179
settler culture, 160, 164, 167
sexuality, 66, 131, 135–7, 145
Shaffer, Deborah, 24
Shahani, Kumar, 115–16
Shaodi, Wang, 213
Sheikholeslami, Mahvash, 13, 17
Sigel, Newton Thomas, 35
Silverstein, Melissa, 14
Singing Chen, 206–13
Sirk, Douglas, 96–7, 102
Sisters in Law (Longinotto), 17, 90, 92, 95–6, 99, 101
skin, 55, 56
Skylight Pictures and Labs, 35, 36–7
Smaill, Belinda, 90, 92, 99, 101
Smallest Witnesses (Farrow), 196–7
Smelik, Anneke, 131–2
Smokes and Lollies (Armstrong), 18–19
Snedeker, Rebecca, 35
social media, 67, 86, 194–5, 198
Solnit, Rebecca, 78
song, singing, 78, 79, 83, 163, 165–7
Sonwalkar, Prasun, 117
'speaking about/nearby', 99–101, 148
spectatorship, 94, 99
Spence, Jo, 66–71

Spolin, Viola, 76, 83
Startup.com (Hegedus, Noujaim), 15
stereotypes, 109, 117; *see also* difference; 'otherness'
Stewart, Susan, 33
Story AB, 144
storytelling, 92, 164, 166–7
subjectivity, 9–20, 133–4, 175, 206–7
Sudan, 190, 193, 195–8
Summerhayes, Catherine, 161, 163
survivance, 160–1
Suzaku (Kawase), 171
Swedish documentaries, 144–58
Sweet Bean (Kawase), 171

Taiwanese film industry, 205–13
Tamblyn, Jeff, 35
Tarachime (Kawase), 173, 176, 179–80, 181
Temeck, Tamar, 69
testimony, 43, 45, 50, 52
transnational feminism, 90, 95, 98–9
trauma, 128, 187, 188, 196–8
Trinh T. Minh-ha, 90, 99–100, 148, 164
Try a Little Tenderness (Honigmann), 129
Tsai Ing-wen, 205
Turner, Graeme, 189
12th & Delaware (Ewing, Grady), 17

Ueda, Mayu, 176
Underground Orchestra, The (Honigmann), 128
'Undoing Time' (Daniel), 46, 58
UNICEF, 186, 190, 192–3

Van Bogaert, Pieter, 41
Varda, Agnès, 10, 127, 130, 131
violence, gender, 13, 16, 17, 96
violence, state, 44, 46
Vizenor Gerald, 160–1
Voice, documentary, 75–89
voice-over, 18, 27, 30, 31, 93, 175
voyeurism, 154–5, 156

Wada-Marciano, Mitsuyo, 176
Walkers, The (Chen), 206, 208

Wang Wen-chih, 206
We are Half of Iran's Population (Bani-Etemad), 17
webpages, archives, 46–64, 165–6, 193–9
'Well I Heard it on the Radio' (report), 162
West, Darrell M., 189
West, Michael, 15
Western humanists, 91, 99
Wheeler, Mark, 189–90
When the Mountains Tremble (Sigel, Yates), 35–6
White, Patricia, 90, 92, 95, 99
White Umbrella, The (Honigmann, van der Lely), 134
widows, Gujerati, 113–15

Wilke, Hannah, 66–71
Women Make Movies (WMM), 24, 29
Women Make Waves festival, Taiwan, 209
Women Reply (Varda), 131
Women's Business (Langton), 162
Wu, Wuna, 206–13

Yates, Pamela, 35–7
Yeh Juh-Feng, 206
Yu, Jane, 210
Yu, Tianqi, 178
Yu Mei-nu, 210

Zbanic, Jasmila, 17–18
Zhang, Yingjing, 206–7

EU representative:
Easy Access System Europe
Mustamäe tee 50, 10621 Tallinn, Estonia
Gpsr.requests@easproject.com

www.ingramcontent.com/pod-product-compliance
Lightning Source LLC
Chambersburg PA
CBHW051056230426
43667CB00013B/2321